BURNING ISSUES OF HUMAN RIGHTS

BURNING ISSUES OF HUMAN RIGHTS

Editor
MAMTA RAJAWAT

KALPAZ PUBLICATIONS
DELHI-110052

BURNING ISSUES OF HUMAN RIGHTS

(Human Rights)

Rs. 790

ISBN: 81-7835-061-0

Published in 2001 in India by
Kalpaz Publications
C–30, Satyawati Nagar
Ashok Vihar Phase–III
Delhi–110052
E-mail: Kalpaz@hotmail.com

Laser Typesetting at: A.S. Printers
Printed at: Mehra Offset Printers, New Delhi

Preface

The concept of human rights has assumed importance globally during the past few decades and has international significance as every country is subject to international scrutiny by the world body which indicts member-states for violations, while there is increasingly widespread concern for universal respect and observance of human rights, gross violation of internationally recognised norms continue unabated in almost all parts of the world. The overall situation has been characterised by large-scale breaches of civil and political rights, as well as economic, social and cultural rights.

Today, the human rights idea is universal, accepted by virtually all states and societies regardless of historical, cultural, ideological, economic, or other differences. The universalisation of human rights is a political fact. The universal acceptance of the idea of human rights and its general content may be only formal and superficial, in some cases even hypocritical, but no government dissents from the ideology of human rights today or offers an alternative to it.

Respect of human rights makes freedom meaningful. They are part and parcel of life in society and they concern humanity. They necessarily signify human values in an absolute senses, but they have greater relevance to the real well-being of the individual if they are applied in the context of society. The whole fabric of society depends upon human rights. Without human rights the society cannot run smoothly, and there could be many chances of crimes and disturbances in the society.

The protection of human rights is a constant struggle which cannot be won unless every man and woman participate in it. In real practice the human rights is the sum of all rights necessary to ensure our rights to be human and it is the duty of all peoples and governments to create the condition headed to exercise our right to be human.

This book contains valuable and authoritative information on prons and cons of burning issues of human rights. It will be highly informative to all the concerned.

Editor

Contents

1

Introduction

Today, the human rights idea is universal, accepted by virtually all states and societies regardless of historical, cultural, ideological, economic, or other differences. It is international, the subject of international diplomacy, law, and institutions. It is philosophically respectable, even to opposed philosophical persuasions. The universalization of human rights is a political fact.

The Universal Declaration of Human Rights adopted by the General Assembly in 1948 has been accepted by virtually all of today's 150 states; even those, notably the European Communist states, which had abstained when the Declaration was approved, have now accepted it formally in the Final Act of the Conference on Security and Cooperation. Every state has adhered to at least one human rights agreement; and more than a third of the world's states have accepted the comprehensive agreements, the International Covenant on Civil and Political Rights, and the International Covenant on Economic, Social, and Cultural Rights, with more states joining every year.

The universal acceptance of the idea of human rights and its general content may be only formal and superficial, in some cases even hypocritical, but no government dissents from the ideology of human rights today or offers an alternative to it. The steady internationalization of human rights is equally impressive. Before the Second World War, how a state treated its own inhabitants was its own business, a matter of "domestic jurisdiction," not of "international concern."

Today it is the stuff of daily diplomacy among states. Numerous international organizations deal with it regularly, and it is never absent from the agenda of every organ and agency of the United Nations and of major regional organizations. There are dozens of international human rights agreements, and some of them have been adhered to by more than one hundred states. New international bodies-commissions, committees, and courts-occupy themselves with human rights daily. The contemporary philosophical respectability of human rights is itself remarkable.

The idea of limitations on government, on majorities-even on the "public good"-in favour of individual autonomy, dignity, and need, has taken root and no present political system, no contemporary political theory, rejects it. Earlier philosophical objections have subsided or have become irrelevant. Eighteenth century notions of natural rights suffered the onslaughts of legal positivism in the nineteenth and early twentieth centuries, but human rights now are attended by resurgent "neo-natural-rights" theories, and are finding a prominent place in contemporary political, ethical, and moral philosophy, now again preoccupied with "justice," "liberty," "equality," and "rights."

Today, it is human rights that claims the mantle of natural law, not-as in the past-slavery or the divine right of kings, not the inferiority of women, of particular races or of the poor. The establishment of human rights in national law and in international law has disarmed legal positivists as well. It is human rights that are positive national and international law, not the antihuman laws of Hitler or some other jurisprudence of terror.

And it is individual civil-political rights as well as economic-social and cultural rights that are the law, not unmitigated collectivism or laissez-faire. The idea of human rights is not an abstraction; it has specific content. What the world has accepted are the civil, political, economic, social, and cultural rights set forth in the Universal Declaration and the international covenants. They include rights of freedom from mistreatment and undue governmental intrusion, as well as rights to governmental support for the economic and social welfare of every human being.

Although specific, the rights are flexible enough to rise above differences among political systems; they are consistent with different degrees and forms of free enterprise as well as with socialism. Debates about conflicts or priorities between rights only confirm rather than depreciate any of the rights declared in the Declaration or protected by the covenants.

Human Rights in International Relations

Concern by some governments with the condition of individuals in other countries is not new. Centuries ago, princes and popes interceded for coreligionists and others in various countries. The nineteenth century saw a number of "humanitarian interventions" by big powers, through diplomacy and sometimes through force, to protest, end, or prevent massacres, pogroms, and other atrocities. These, however, were personal expressions of "noblesse oblige," or extraordinary reactions to egregious events; they were sharp deviations from the international political system's assumption that, in principle, how a state treated its own citizens was its own business. Surely there was no serious disposition to render the treatment of the individual human being in his own country a subject of international diplomacy and law.

Human rights did not become the concern of international politics or law until after the Second World War, but individual welfare was not wholly beyond the ken of the international system even before then. International law and human rights were linked in the history of ideas, both having antecedents in natural law and in Roman law, and common progenitors in Grotius, Vattel, and Locke. In fact, international law early included some of what we would today as human rights obligations; for example, treaty provisions in which parties undertook to tolerate heterodox religious worship and not to impose civil disabilities on religious dissenters.

Customary international law, too, has long imposed on states a responsibility not to deny justice to aliens. In the last century, nations sought to mitigate the horrors of war by developing law to forbid particularly cruel weapons, and to protect prisoners of war and civilian populations during war. Following the First World War, the dominant powers required several states to adhere to "Minority treaties," in which they assumed obligations to respect the rights of ethnic, national, linguistic, religious, or other minorities among their inhabitants.

The League of Nations Covenant provided that the mandate system established for dependent areas should be governed by the principle that "the well being and development of such peoples form a sacred trust of civilization," and imposed "conditions which will guarantee freedom of conscience and religion" and other rights. Members of the League undertook "to secure just treatment of the native inhabitants of territories under their control"; mandatory powers were required to promote the welfare and rights of the inhabitants of mandated territories. The years following the First World War also saw a major development in the law of human rights, a development that is often overlooked and commonly underestimated: the International Labour Office, now the International Labour Organisation (ILO), launched a series of conventions setting minimum standards for labour and other social conditions. This early international law of human rights, however, was limited in scope and focus, and while it had humanitarian consequences, its motivation was largely political rather than idealistic.

Christian princes had gone to war on behalf of coreligionists in other countries, and religious tolerance was a condition of peace in religiously divided, war-weary Europe; agreements for mutual tolerance made possible the establishment of the secular state and the rise of modern international law. Powerful states exporting people, goods, and capital to other countries in the age of mercantilism insisted on law that would protect the interests which these represented.

Denial of justice to an alien was an offense to the state whose nationality he bore and jeopardized its economic and political interests. (Aliens who were "stateless," who had no nationality, had no remedy for denial of justice, since no state was offended by such denials.) States insisted on an international standard of justice (rooted in natural law) for their nationals abroad even when these states did not recognize that standard for their citizens at home. Humanitarian laws regulating the conduct of war were reciprocal undertakings defending a state's soldiery and population against the enemy.

Minority treaties were required of some states, not universal norms applicable to the big and the powerful as well. The mandate provisions were seen by many as essentially hortatory, a small rhetorical price for continuing "imperialism" instead of granting the territories self-determination and self-government. The ILO conventions were capitalism's defense against the specter of spreading socialism, and states, moreover, had direct interests in the conditions of labour in countries with which they competed in a common market. Broader law came in the wake of Hitler. The international human rights movement was born in, and out of the Second World War.

The proclaimed aims of that war included the establishment of individual rights and the "Four Freedoms" for everyone in every country, and that aim also inspired the planning for the postwar world. To begin, the victors imposed human rights obligations on the vanquished in peace treaties, and included human rights violations in the Nuremberg Charter and prosecutions. Occupying powers presided at the incorporation of human rights safeguards into new constitutions and laws for West Germany, Japan, and Austria.

The UN Charter ushered in a new international concern for human rights everywhere. The Charter replaced the League of Nations' concentration on the rights of minorities in selected countries with heed to the rights of all individuals everywhere. The new commitment to "self-determination," together with universal human rights, it was apparently thought, would eliminate the minorities problem: some minorities would become independent by self-determination; the rest would find their rights protected equally with majorities by universal commitment to human rights for all. The Preamble of the UN Charter reaffirms "faith in fundamental human rights, in the dignity and worth of the human person, in the equal rights of men and women," and declares the determination of peoples "to promote social progress and better standards of life in larger freedom." The purposes of the UN include international cooperation "in promoting and encouraging respect for human rights and for fundamental freedoms for all without distinction as to race, sex, language, or religion".

Human rights are among the responsibilities for study and recommendation of the General Assembly (Article 13) and the Economic and Social Council (Article 62(2)), and a commission on human rights is expressly required (Article 68). Members pledged themselves to cooperate with the UN organization for the achievement of its human rights purposes. The various UN bodies have devoted years of arduous effort to promoting human rights. Human rights have been on every agenda of every body and have become a staple of UN activity.

A universal declaration of human rights was prepared and adopted. Even particular human rights violations have received attention, early as in the case of Russian wives of non-Russians and the treatment of Indians in South Africa, more recently in Chile and elsewhere .6 Some violations-e.g., apartheid in South Africa-are perennially on the UN agenda. Other violations in other places-the treatment of Soviet Jews, allegations of torture in Chile-were the subject of extended international debate over many years. Despite resistance, it was established that within the meaning of Article 2(7) of the Charter, UN preoccupation with human rights was not forbidden intervention.

The prevailing view was that UN consideration was not intervention, and, more importantly, that human rights are an international, not a domestic concern.

The New Law of Human Rights

The UN Charter ushered in a new international law of human rights. The new law buried the old dogma that the individual is not a "subject" of international politics and law and that a government's behaviour toward its own nationals is a matter of domestic, not international, concern. It penetrated national frontiers and the veil of sovereignty. It removed the exclusive identification of an individual with his government.

It gave the individual a part in international politics and rights in international law, independently of his government. It also gave the individual protectors other than his government, indeed protectors and remedies against his government. The international law of human rights differs from other international law in its motivations and impulses as well. Generally, international law is made, international obligations are undertaken, to serve common or reciprocal national interests; early human rights laws, too, we have seen, largely served states' political or economic purposes.

The move to a comprehensive human rights law also sought to appeal to national and transnational interests, perhaps in an effort to de-emphasize its radical nature. Human rights, it was urged, are related to international peace, for states that violate human rights at home are not trustworthy in international relations, and violations of those rights afford occasions, temptations, and pretexts for interventions or war.

The international human rights law also had a different kind of political motivation: states that had minority treaties or human rights provisions in peace treaties imposed on them resented being singled out and sought to universalise their undertakings. But whatever reasons (or rationalisations) were provided to mask it, the fact is that the new comprehensive international human rights law generally serves no patent, particular national interest. It is essentially ideological, idealistic, humanitarian; its true and deep purpose is to improve the lot of individual men and women everywhere, particularly where national institutions and nonlegal international forces are not adequate-a unique and revolutionary purpose for international law. The international law of human rights parallels and supplements national law, superseding and supplying the deficiencies of national constitutions and laws; but it does not replace, and indeed depends on, national institutions.

The constituency in every society that supports human rights law is different from the constituency that supports, say, international trade agreements, or military alliances, or peaceful settlements, or even international organization and cooperation. The pressures on a government to adhere to international human rights law are also different from those to adhere to other law, and indeed, a state's adherence to human rights conventions is far less important if in fact it behaves at home, toward its own, consistently with their terms. In other respects, too, international law and politics see human rights in the context of the international political system.

Although human rights are universal, they are the claims of an individual upon his society, not on other societies. Although the society in which one lives may be crucial to life and dignity, although a right to change one's society might well be deemed fundamental, the individual does not have an absolute right to join another society and seek his rights there. Even those who are oppressed at home do not yet have an international human right to asylum elsewhere; those who are starving at home do not have an internationally recognized human right to be taken in by the more affluent societies or to be fed by them. Like other international law, human rights law is made by treaty or convention; there is also customary human rights law made by national practice with a developing sense of legal obligation.

The declarations and resolutions of UN organs and other international bodies on human rights may have greater weight in achieving international law here than on other matters, since they purport to express the conscience of mankind on a matter of conscience. And though all law-making is a political process, humanitarian law has its own politics in both making and enforcing law.

The history of the development of the covenants is described fully by Vratislav Pechota (essay 2). It is relevant here to address the antecedents of that development. In themselves, the normative human rights provisions of the UN Charter are general and preliminary: essentially, by Articles 55 and 56, member states pledge themselves to take joint and separate action in cooperation with the United Nations to achieve respect for human rights.

Human rights are not defined or specified in the Charter, and there is no clear undertaking by every state not to commit one or another violation. The institutions, procedures, and programs for inducing national respect for rights, for monitoring the condition of human rights in different countries, and for preventing, deterring, or ending violation, are not provided. But the words of the Charter are words of legal obligation and surely the pledge of Article 56 is violated if a member state itself persists in committing gross violations of rights universally recognized as fundamental. No doubt, however, the members of the UN themselves recognized that the Charter law was insufficient. Immediately they proceeded to prepare and promulgate the Universal Declaration of Human

Rights, making specific the general Charter references to human rights and freedoms for all.

The Declaration is a remarkable juncture of political-civil and economic-social rights, with equality and freedom from discrimination a principal and recurrent theme. It declares the rights to life, liberty, and security of person, to fair criminal process, to freedom of conscience, thought, expression, association, and privacy; the right to seek and enjoy asylum, to leave one's country and return to it; rights to marriage and family, and rights of property. It declares the will of the people to be the basis of the authority of government, and provides for universal suffrage and bona fide elections. It speaks of the right to work and leisure, health care, and education. The Universal Declaration was not generally conceived as law but as "a common standard of achievement" for all to aspire to; hence its approval without dissent.

Some thought that the United Nations should rest on the Declaration and concentrate on encouraging states to raise their national norms and conform their national behaviour to its standards. Instead, governments moved to convert the Declaration into binding legal norms. The process was very, very long. In some part this was due to the ever-increasing number of states, all of which joined in the process and slowed the negotiations. In part, delay was due to the differences between a declaration and a binding covenant.

Some states that had been prepared to declare a general principle wished it carefully defined and circumscribed if it were to be clearly a legal obligation with legal consequences, for though no state was compelled to adhere to any draft covenant that might emerge, most states wanted something they might be able to adopt if it became desirable; they were reluctant, moreover, to have a covenant adopted as the international norm in whose light their behaviour would appear to be wanting.

The process was also extended because there were strong pressures on the other hand to develop and elaborate the generalities of the Declaration and give them more specific content so that they would afford greater protection. The Declaration, moreover, had not provided for its implementation, while many sessions were spent debating and elaborating means to enforce the new emerging legal undertakings. In substantial part, it took eighteen years to convert the Declaration into convention because it was necessary to accommodate, bridge, submerge, and conceal deep divisions and differences, especially between democratic-libertarian and socialist-revolutionary states—differences in fundamental conceptions about the relation of society to the individual, about his rights and duties, about priorities and preferences among them. Western states fought for, and obtained, a division into two covenants, the Covenant on Civil and Political Rights and the Covenant on Economic, Social, and Cultural Rights.

The two covenants recognize the difference in the character of rights in various subtle ways. For example, the Covenant on Civil and Political Rights is drafted in terms of the individual's rights: e.g., "Every human being has the inherent right to life"; "No one shall be held in slavery"; "All persons shall be equal before the courts and tribunals." The Covenant on Economic, Social, and Cultural Rights, on the other hand, speaks only to the states, not the individual: "The States Parties to the present Covenant recognize the right to work"; "The States Parties . . . undertake to ensure . . . the right of everyone to form trade unions"; "The States Parties . . . recognize the right of everyone to education." There was wide agreement and clear recognition that the means required to induce compliance with social-economic undertakings were different from those required for civil-political rights. But the Covenant on Economic, Social, and Cultural Rights is law, not merely exhortation and aspiration.

The rights it recognizes are as "human," universal, and fundamental as are those of the Civil and Political Rights Covenant. The obligation for a state party is "to take steps . . . to the maximum of its available resources, with a view to achieving progressively the full realization" of these rights, and fulfillment may require national planning and major programs, and international assistance. But these limitations do not derogate from the legal character of the obligations. Other delays resulted from sharp differences over the inclusion or scope of particular rights.

Most of the states were concerned, or were more concerned, with values reflecting their struggle against colonialism but not included in the Universal Declaration and not previously part of the accepted human rights ideology. They insisted that both Covenants include the right of all peoples to self-determination as well as to "economic self-determination," to "sovereignty" over their resources. Western states resisted, arguing that both are at best rights of a "people," not of any individual, and surely not-like human rights generally-rights of individual Is against their own society. They argued, too, that the content of these norms was highly uncertain and controversial.

The argument did not prevail, and identical provisions on self-determination now head both covenants. Also included in the Covenant on Civil and Political Rights were other, less controversial, rights not mentioned in the Declaration-freedom from imprisonment for debt, rights of children, and rights of minorities (Articles 11, 24, 27). That Covenant also prohibits propaganda for war and incitement to national, racial, or religious hatred (Article 20). Some rights included in the Declaration were substantially elaborated.

On the other hand, the right to enjoy private property, included in the Declaration, was finally omitted from the covenants. Much time was also spent in the attempt to bridge-, the demand of some states for effective means to enforce the covenants and the insistence of others on the "sovereignty" of states and resistance to international scrutiny and "intrusion." In sum, the international law of human rights developed by the two covenants parallels the Universal Declaration. It provides protections like those in the constitutions and laws of enlightened democratic-liberal countries as well as the promises of socialist and "welfare" constitutions.

During, and since the negotiation of these two major covenants, the UN system also promoted specialized declarations and conventions—on genocide, on the status of refugees and stateless persons, on the rights of women, and on the elimination of all forms of racial discrimination." These emphasize, extend, and supplement the protections afforded by the principal covenants. They have also made it possible to "extract" legal obligations on these particular subjects from governments not prepared to adhere to all the obligations of the general covenants. How much law various covenants and conventions have made depends, of course, on the number of adherences to them.

January 1, 1981, the Genocide Convention had 85 parties, the Convention on the Elimination of All Forms of Racial Discrimination 108, the Convention on Political Rights of Women 86, and the Convention on the Status of Refugees 81.9 Late in 1975, the Covenant on Civil and Political Rights and the Covenant on Economic, Social, and Cultural Rights obtained the adherences necessary to bring them into effect, and adherences have continued to trickle in. (As of January 1, 1981, the former had 65, the latter 66 adherences.) As to each of these conventions, some adherences are subject to reservations of greater or lesser significance. It matters, of course, whether covenants are accepted by populous nations or by those with small populations; whether the states that adhere are more or less disposed to comply with their undertakings; and whether some who have not adhered might nonetheless practice what the conventions require.

International human rights instruments do not legislate human rights; they "recognize" them and build upon that recognition." Human rights was an eighteenth century idea, rooted in notions of natural law and natural rights, and woven of several strands: original autonomy of the individual, converted in society to popular sovereignty; government by social compact of the people and subject to the continued consent of the governed; government for limited purposes only; the rights reserved for the individual even against the people's representatives in government.

The international human rights movement took these eighteenth-century ideas of individual autonomy and freedom and combined them with nineteenth- and twentieth-century ideas of socialism and the welfare state. International human rights, however, reflect no single, comprehensive theory of the relation of the individual to society (other than what is implied in the very concept of rights). That there are "fundamental human rights" was a declared article of faith, "reaffirmed" by "the peoples of the United Nations" in the UN Charter.

The Universal Declaration of Human Rights, striving for a pronouncement that would appeal to diverse political systems governing diverse peoples, built on that faith and shunned philosophical exploration. Because of that faith-and of political and ideological forces-governments accepted the concept of human rights, agreed that they were appropriate for international concern, cooperated to define them, assumed international obligations to respect them, and submitted to some international scrutiny as to their compliance with these obligations. Those who built international human rights perhaps also saw these rights as "natural," but in a contemporary sense: human rights correspond to the nature of man and of human society, to his psychology and its sociology:

— rights "derive from the inherent dignity of the human person";

— "recognition . . . of the equal and inalienable rights of all members of the human family, is the foundation of freedom, justice and peace in the world";

— respect for, and observance of, human rights will help create "conditions of stability and well-being which are necessary for peaceful and friendly relations among nations."

We are not told what theory justifies "human dignity" as the source of rights, or how the needs of human dignity are determined. We are not told what conception of justice is reflected in human rights, or how preserving human rights will promote peace in the world. International human rights are recognized as inherent, but it is not necessarily assumed that man is in principle autonomous, or that rights antecede government.

The international instruments nod to popular sovereignty, but there is no other hint of social compact or of continuing consent of the governed. Respect for retained rights is not a condition of government, or a basis of its legitimacy; violation of rights does not warrant undoing government by revolution. International human rights imply rights for the individual against society, but they are not seen as against the interests of society.

Rather, it is believed, a good society is one in which individual rights flourish, and the promotion and protection of individual rights is a public good. Any apparent conflict between the individual and society, between individual rights and a more general public good, is only temporary and superficial; in the longer, deeper view the society is better if the individual's rights are respected. Like the eighteenth century idea of rights, international human rights also, inevitably, implicate the purposes for which governments are created.

Rights against government imply limitations on government, but there is no a priori assumption that in general government is for limited purposes only. To the contrary, born after various socialisms were established and spreading, and after commitment to welfare economics and the welfare state was nearly universal, international human rights imply a conception of government as designed for many purposes and seasons.

The rights deemed to be fundamental include not only civil and political rights which government must not invade, but also rights to economic and social well-being which government must actively provide or promote. The rights declared and enumerated imply a government that is activist, intervening, that is committed to economic-social planning for the society which would redound as economic-social rights to the individual.

Human rights are rights which the individual has, or should have, in his society. If societies respected these rights adequately, there would be no need for international law and institutions to help protect them. International human rights law and institutions are designed to induce states to remedy the inadequacies of their national laws and institutions so that human rights will be respected and vindicated.

The individual must pursue his rights through his own laws and institutions. Even when these fail him, international law and institutions cannot provide those rights; they can only press the state to provide them. International human rights obligations are met when, and only when, national laws and institutions meet the minimum international standards and give effect to the minimum of human rights. International human rights agreements are international agreements like all others. They create rights and duties between states parties to the agreement; they may create also rights in third parties, whether states or individuals.

Failure to honour these undertakings brings the same consequences as for other international agreements: other parties can demand compliance and seek reparations, and may resort to any tribunal which has jurisdiction over such claims between these parties. Some agreements also provide for special remedies before particular bodies. The United Nations Charter made human rights a legitimate subject for discussion and recommendation by the Assembly and its sub-organs. Human rights may also properly come into the ken of the Security Council when it implicates peace and security, e.g., in South Africa. By discussing human rights the General Assembly does not intervene in matters "which are essentially within the domestic jurisdiction of any state" (Article

2(a)). Intervention, strictly, means dictatorial interference by force, and there have been no UN military interventions in support of human rights; discussion and recommendation are not intervention. Human rights, moreover, are a matter of international concern, not essentially within any state's domestic jurisdiction.

Enforcement measures by the Security Council are in any event exempted from Article 2(7). Article 2(7) speaks only to intervention by the UN, not by member states, but most challenges to activities by states on behalf of human rights as "intervention" are equally unfounded. Peaceful objections by states to human rights violations by other states are not interventions. Generally, human rights are no longer within a state's domestic jurisdiction. That which is governed by international law or agreement is ipso facto and by definition a matter of international concern, not a matter of any state's domestic jurisdiction.

Certainly, any state that adheres to an international human rights agreement has made the subject of that agreement a matter of international concern. It has submitted its performance to scrutiny and to appropriate, peaceful reaction by other parties, and to any special procedures or machinery provided by the agreement for its implementation.

Human Rights and International Legal Rights

The international instruments speak of human rights, but they do not purport to create them; they "recognize"' their preexistence in some other moral or legal order. They confirm the concept of human rights and give it status and value in the international system. Like other international agreements, the international human rights agreements create rights and obligations among the states parties to the agreement: every party is obligated to every other state to carry out its undertakings; every other state has the right to have the obligation carried out. But these are the legal rights of states, not the human rights of the individual. If states are the promisors and promisees, however, the authentic beneficiaries are the individual inhabitants whose "human rights" the state promises to respect.

Whether the international agreements also create international legal rights for the individual is debated. Some have strongly denied it. Others argue that as third-party beneficiaries, and the true beneficiaries, individuals have rights under international law, even when they have no direct remedy but must rely on states and international bodies to vindicate their rights. And some instruments for example the Optional Protocol to the International Covenant on Civil and Political Rights, the Convention on the Elimination of All Forms of Racial Discrimination, and the European and the American Conventions on Human Rights also provide some remedy for the individual to pursue his international legal rights by international legal remedies.

National and International Enforcement

Human rights are rights to be enjoyed by individuals in their own societies and implemented and enforced under their laws and institutions. International undertakings are designed to help assure that national societies in fact respect the human rights of their inhabitants. International instruments require states to enact legislation and otherwise ensure that the rights are respected. In some legal systems international human rights obligations may be "self-executing" and will be given effect by officials and courts without domestic legislation.

The international system also provides "enforcement machinery." Such international instrumentalities, however, do not operate directly to grant the individual his rights; they work on the state and are designed to induce the state to carry out its obligations. Even when the individual is given some kind of an international remedy, for example, the right to "communicate" to the Human Rights Committee pursuant to the Optional Protocol to the Covenant, the communication does not produce an international mandate conferring the right; it serves only to trigger an international process to induce the state to desist from violation or to provide a remedy for past violations.

Limitations on Rights

The freedom of expression, in the classic reference, does not permit one falsely to cry "fire" in a crowded theatre; the most libertarian societies do not permit slander; all countries impose some limits on freedom of movement in some circumstances to protect national security or public order. In the rights jurisprudence of the United States these permissible limitations are not expressed in the Constitution, although sometimes read into general phrases: search and seizure is forbidden only if "unreasonable," punishment only if "cruel and unusual," infringements on liberty only if they deny "due process of law." The Framers of the Covenant sought to define the permissible scope of limitations as strictly as possible, although inevitably in general phrases.

For example, the freedom of movement within a country or the right to leave it "shall not be subject to any restrictions except those which are provided by law, are necessary to protect national security, public order (order public), public health or morals, or the rights and freedoms of others, and are consistent with the other rights recognized" in the Covenant (Article 12(3)). Or, "the Press and the public may be excluded from all or part of a trial for reasons of morals, public order (ordure public) or national security in a democratic society, or when the interest of the private lives of the parties so requires, or to the extent strictly necessary in the opinion of the court in special circumstances where publicity would prejudice the interests of justice" (Article 14(l)).

One can debate the merits of these and other limitations or their particular formulations, but few would question that in principle some such limitations are inevitable and probably desirable. The limitations themselves, however, are governed by law, not by the whim of the state. Whether a particular limitation on a right is permissible under the Covenant is a question of international law, and the state's action can be scrutinized and challenged as a violation of the Covenant (see Alexander Kiss, essay 12).

Enforcing the Covenant

Like all international human rights agreements the Covenant does not eliminate the essential dependence of individual human rights on national laws and institutions. The Covenant requires states to respect the individual's rights and to "ensure" them, and the state can do that only through its own laws and institutions. Indeed, the Covenant expressly requires states to "adopt such legislative or other measures" as are necessary to give effect to rights recognized by the Covenant.

The extent of that obligation and its implications for states with different legal systems are considered by Oscar Schachter in essay 13. The Covenant's method of enforcement is described by A. H. Robertson in essay 14. There is a tendency to deprecate and depreciate it, since it is based largely on voluntary reporting, which at best tends to be self-serving and not likely to reveal violations. No doubt more intensive monitoring would be more effective. But the fact that a state has to report inevitably has some influence to induce better compliance. Further inducement will result if the Human Rights Committee develops the practice of scrutinizing these reports, asking for more information, and challenging reported claims on the basis of external evidence.

A public report by a state, moreover, will be read by other governments, and by organizations and individuals both within and outside the reporting state, and their criticism of these reports will serve to improve the state's behaviour. If states parties can be persuaded to assert their rights as parties to challenge violations, if more states accept the optional provisions under which the Human Rights Committee can receive complaints from other states (Article 41) or from private persons or organizations (under the Protocol) the remedial and deterrent influence of the Covenant will be further enhanced.

Permissible Reservations

Unlike some other international agreements, the Covenant does not expressly bar reservations generally or to particular clauses. In view of the character of the Covenant, one may assume that there was no intention to bar reservations; it is desirable to have states adhere to as much of the Covenant as possible, even if they insist on excluding some particular provision. But any state may object to a reservation by another state and may even reject a treaty relation with the reserving state as regards the Covenant as a whole. Also, there can be no reservation "incompatible with the object and purpose" of the Covenant. Major reservations that contradict the basic spirit of the Covenant would be out of order even if other parties were prepared to acquiesce in them. Surely, for a hypothetical example, South Africa could not purport to ratify the Covenant but reserve the right to maintain apartheid. Even as regards particular provisions, it would seem improper for a state to reserve a major exception permitting it to violate an important right in an important way against ail important segment of its population.

Even if most states acquiesced, a single objecting state might challenge the propriety of a reservation under the Vienna Convention and impugn the claim of the reserving state to be a party to the Convention. It has been suggested that those articles of the Covenant which are not subject to derogation in time of emergency ought not to be-perhaps a fortiori-subject to reservation generally. That argument is plausible, with some limitations.

— A state may wish to make a reservation to the nonderogation clause itself, and if the reservation is not "total," it might not be a reservation that defeats the object and purpose of the Covenant.

— Some clauses are not subject to derogation not because of their fundamental importance but because they are of a character to which public emergency is irrelevant and surely not 11 strictly required," for example imprisonment for contract debt (Article 11).

That such a clause is nonderogable, then, is no sign that it should also be not subject to reservation. Even articles that are not subject to derogation for reasons of their importance, moreover, might be treated differently for reservation purposes. The exemption from derogation is stated in terms of whole articles of the Covenant and might be deemed to exempt the entire article. But while a reservation to any of those articles as a whole may well be unacceptable as inconsistent with the object and purpose of the Covenant, a reservation to some single aspect of it might pass. Thus, for example, the right to life (Article 6) is not subject to derogation and should not be subject to reservation as a whole, But it might not be inconsistent with the object and purpose of the Covenant for a state to reserve, say, a right to impose capital punishment on persons over 17 (rather than 18) years of age. In principle, "nonderogability" should be strong but not conclusive evidence that a reservation is inconsistent with the object and purpose of the Covenant.

Human Rights Instruments

Historically, spiritually, and conceptually the Covenant-like its sibling the Covenant on Economic, Social, and Cultural Rights-is a child of the Declaration and that ancestry is not irrelevant to the Covenant's meaning. Since the Declaration has been universally accepted, it is plausible to argue that it be seen as a guide to what is in the Covenant, rather than as having been rejected and replaced by it. Thus, for one example, the presence in the Declaration of Article 17 recognizing a right to own property and not to be arbitrarily deprived of it lends support to the view that such a right is intended to be protected also by the Covenant, if only by implication from Article 5(2).23

The transformation of the Declaration into two covenants has significance for the meaning of both of them. While each Covenant rests on its own bottom, the existence of an obligation in one Covenant may suggest that it was not intended to be implied also in the other. That a provision is designated a civil-political right and included in that Covenant may also be relevant to its interpretation. Neither the covenants nor the Universal Declaration were wholly original documents. Both drew heavily on earlier national instruments-the Declaration of Independence and the Constitution of the United States, the French Declaration of the Rights of Man and of the Citizen-and they incorporated concepts from a universe of ideas that had become a common heritage.

The provision in the Universal Declaration that all human beings are born free and equal in dignity and rights, or that everyone has the right to life, liberty, and security of the person, echo the older national declarations; the accumulated meanings of their language over two hundred years cannot be irrelevant to the interpretation of that article in the Universal Declaration. Equal protection of the law, borrowed by the Universal Declaration (Article 7) and the Covenant (Article 26), brings a freight of meaning from the U.S. Constitution.

The phrase "public order," translated from ordre public, with the original French term inserted even in the English text of the Covenant, is clearly intended to incorporate the jurisprudence of that concept in French and other civil law. Even common terms like "national security" come into international documents with national meanings, and one is entitled to, indeed one must, go to national laws and practices to determine its meaning-and its limits. The Declaration and the covenants are comprehensive human rights agreements designed to be complete lexicons of rights. But even while these were developing, the UN was promoting other agreements on specific rights for some categories of persons.

The Convention on Genocide was adopted at the same time as the Declaration. Later the Convention on the Elimination of All Forms of Racial Discrimination, the Convention on Political Rights of Women, the Convention on the Status of Refugees, and others, supplemented the covenants, expanding on particular rights and providing additional implementation machinery. While in some respects the special agreements add new obligations and are binding therefore only on parties to those agreements, in other respects they may spell out obligations already implied in the Covenant and are available therefore as sources for interpretation of the Covenant. The Declaration and the covenants grew up while regional human rights agreements were also developing, in sight and knowledge of each other, dealing with the same problems, in the same universe, with some of the same participants. Inevitably, they drew on and reacted to each other, even when one rejected or avoided what another chose.

Different agreements may have different texts as well as different contexts, but common phrases suggest common meanings, and practice under, or accepted or authoritative interpretations of the European Convention and later the American Convention, are not irrelevant to interpretation of the International Covenant.

Human Rights and Political Ideology

The Universal Declaration was written by diverse authors representing different ideologies. It expresses commitment to "democracy" but is consistent with different brands of democracy and with various degrees of economic free enterprise as with different kinds of socialism—provided the parties accept commitment to individual rights and respect the particular rights enumerated, as properly construed in accordance with their spirit and purpose. The variety of governments that have adhered to the Covenant suggests that they at least thought their political economic systems were consistent with respect for the rights enumerated. And in fact no system claims that it must, or has the right to, violate any of those rights. Issues arise particularly as regards the right of every person "to take part in the conduct of public affairs, directly or through freely chosen representatives," and "to vote and to be elected at genuine periodic elections which shall be by universal and equal suffrage and shall be held by secret ballot, guaranteeing the free expression of the will of the electors." (In the Declaration, these rights follow the assertion that "the will of the people shall be the basis of the authority of government." 24) western societies tend to believe that only parliamentary multi-party democracy satisfies that requirement, not the party rule of Communist or other single party states, or military or other dictatorships ruling by decree for extended, indefinite periods.

Many such systems, however, claim that the requirements of popular sovereignty and authentic vote are satisfied by occasional plebiscites and that a vote is genuine even if the individual has no choice between candidates, since he can vote "no" to the single-party slate. In today's world, authentic parliamentary democracy is not common. The Communist states surely show no signs of modifying their system (which they claim to be more democratic than Western parliamentary systems); surely they consider their system "nonnegotiable," not anyone else's business, not a subject for discussion whether in relation to human rights or in any other context. If there is to be a universal human rights ideology, if there are to be international human rights agreements including both Communist and Western states, in the hope of protecting other civil and political rights, the West will have to acquiesce in the view that the Communist system is not intrinsically inconsistent with the Declaration and the Covenant, even while the West may hope and work for movement towards greater political freedom in Communist countries. Other idcological differences are another matter. Accepting the Communist political system in principle does not mean that one should accept Communist interpretations or applications that are inconsistent with the very idea of individual rights or with the essential scope of a particular right.

Freedom of expression, for example, can be limited for reasons of national security and public order (Article 19(b). That does not permit extravagant claims of the needs of national security. Nor does it permit identifying that specific, narrow exception, or the equally specific and narrow exception for "public order," with the "needs of Socialism" or the "revolution." That would essentially deny individual rights in the name of an overriding public good as a state perceived it. Similarly, limitations on other freedoms, for example, the right to leave or return to one's country, can be limited only as "necessary to protect national security, public order or public morals," not for other reasons of national or international policy or politics.

Problems in Interpretation

Some issues of interpretation suggest themselves to any reader of the Covenant, and were foreseeable when the Covenant was concluded. States identified others when they adhered, deeming it desirable to articulate reservations or understandings. Since the Covenant has been in effect and in operation, parties have been reflecting their understanding of various provisions when they report on their compliance to the Human Rights Committee, suggesting some readings which the Committee and other readers of the reports have questioned. Some issues have arisen under similar provisions in other documents. It is not possible to anticipate or hypothesize all issues; the principal ones are identified in this volume in the essays dealing with various rights. One set of issues that may raise particular difficulties deserves special attention: those arising out of conflicts between rights.

The Covenant does not deal with possible conflicts between rights in general. In one particular case, the Covenant in effect resolves a conflict between rights: despite the provision that the state must respect the freedom of expression (Article 19(2)), the Covenant requires every party to prohibit war propaganda or any advocacy of national, racial, or religious hatred (Article 20). Similarly, Article 19(3) expressly provides that the freedom of expression may be subject to restriction necessary "for respect of the rights or reputation of others." Those provisions do not indicate which rights or freedoms of others may be protected at the expense of the freedom of association or expression, but they might well authorize states to prefer other recognized human rights, e.g., the right of privacy or the right of an accused to a fair trial (see Article 14(l)), and curtail the freedom of expression or association as "necessary" to safeguard those other rights. In other cases, the Covenant does not consider the possibility of conflict and provides no guidance as to permissible resolution.

A state might argue that since it cannot literally carry out conflicting provisions, it is free to choose between them. But usually conflict will be between a principal right and some peripheral application of another, and it may be possible to derive from the Covenant some evidence as to the choice permitted to the state. In any event, if a state may be entitled to choose between individual human rights enshrined in the Covenant, it ought not be able to prefer other rights and interests which it might create by its own law for its own purposes. It is not possible to anticipate all the issues that may arise under the Covenant. But good faith in applying the Covenant in the spirit in which it was conceived, and for the purpose for which it was created, should resolve most issues.

The important and controlling considerations are: that the Covenant is a bill of rights for the individual even against his own society, even when it acts in what it sees as the public good; that derogations from and limitations upon rights are exceptional and to be sparingly and strictly invoked. Especially because the individual is at the mercy of his government and it is the government that decides in the first instance what his rights are, it is of supreme importance that all recognize that a government's interpretation or application is not final but is subject to scrutiny by other states parties, by the Human Rights Committee and other international bodies.

Historical Background

This book views the human rights as an on going attempt to define human dignity and worth and to create human rights' culture in future for society. The basic principles of a human rights' culture will survive only if people continue to see a point in it doing so. It needs to be constantly defended. We have a right to this. It is not just what we want or need. It is your right. There is a responsibility to be met. The concept of human rights tells a detailed story of the attempts made to define basic dignity and worth of the human beings and his or her most fundamental entitlement.

The denial of human rights and fundamental freedoms not only is an individual and personal tragedy but also creates conditions of social and political unrest sowing the seeds of violence and conflict within and between Societies and Nations. Just to avoid these problems various international agencies including League of Nations, U.N.O., laid stress for the protection of human rights permanently, although the idea of human rights predates the United Nations. It can be easily appreciated that human rights and fundamental freedoms allow us to develop fully and use our human qualities, our intelligence, our talents and our conscience and to satisfy our spiritual and other needs. They are based on mankind's increasing demand for a life in which the inherent dignity and worth of each human being will receive respect and protection. In the language of United Nations Center for human rights—"human rights could be generally defined and those rights which are inherent in our nature and without which we cannot live as human beings". Shree D.D. Basu has considered about human rights in detail.

According to him, "the expression human rights had its on in international law relating to the development of the status of an individual in the international legal system, which was originally confined to the relation between sovereign states, who were regarded as the only person in international law. For all practical purposes, the genesis of human rights is not older than Second World War though the concept of individual having certain inalienable rights as against state had its origin in the dim post. Thus the concept of human rights, embodying the minimum rights of an individual versus his own State is as old as political philosophy."

Hence, D.D. Basu defined human rights "are those minimum rights which every individual must have against state or other public authority by virtue of his being a member of human family, irrespective of any other consideration". He has also said that the concept of human rights is as old as the ancient doctrine of natural rights founded on natural law, the expression human is of recent origin. It is only natural rights which eventually led to the formation of human rights. Ex-chief Justice R.S. Pathak' has described about human rights in these words: "The human rights movement represents the historical journey travelled by man ever since the beginning of an institutionalized political and social order. It was a response to that order, when the importance of the development and expression of individual personality began to acquire material significance in relation to the community.

In the repeated interaction between the individual and the State, the urge to recognize a charter of basic individual rights has expressed itself in a continuous struggle which has seen the reaffirmation and evolution of the rights of the individual against the power of established authority. The concept of human rights, in its expanding comprehension, has now travelled to encompass what are called "third-generation" or "solidarity" rights. At the very beginning stands the rights of self-determination, a fight regarded as belonging to peoples rather than individuals, and which India, with its emphasis on national integrity, has rightly identified as a right applicable only to peoples under foreign domination.

Then, there is the right to sovereignty over the natural wealth and resources of the country and the right to the peoples of developing countries. Both rights are found in identical language in both covenants, and therefore may be regarded as civil and political rights as well as economic, cultural and social rights. The third-generation rights extend to the right to international peace, the right to a satisfactory environment favourable to development, and the rights of ethnic, religious and linguistic minorities. It can no longer be doubted that the concept of human rights, at one time indulgently looked upon as the impracticable dream of natural law philosophers, has became in the course of these four decades an international reality. But problems remain in the application, implementation and protection of human rights.

A not inconsiderable degree of intellectual confusion prevails among political scientists and international lawyers in adequately formulating the more fundamental problems, and in performing the necessarily intellectual tasks relating to establishing and maintaining appropriate constitutive processes and public order policies. The principal difficulty lies in the non-availability of an adequate substantive definition of human rights.

The definition provided by Richard Wasserstrom reflecting the common general understanding of the concept, that "one ought to be able to claim as entitlements (that is, as human rights) those minimal things without which it is impossible to develop one's capabilities and to live life as a human being "fails as an insufficient and simplistic definition. In that context, referring to the doubt raised on whether economic, social and cultural rights can be classified as human rights, some commentators cite concerns" about definition imprecision, unenforceability, unmanageability of the concept as a whole, and the difficulty of achieving the full justiciability of the rights in question".

Similar problems arise in relation to the "third-generation" rights. Described as the rights of "problem", their claim to be considered as human rights are doubted because, as Paul Sieghart points' out, they "cannot belong to any identifiable individuals". Little effort has been made to create a comprehensive map of the totality of human rights, and there has been no appreciable discussion of the detailed content of particular rights.

The importance of precise definition cannot be underestimated. For, as Bilden observes, "what we think human rights really are will inevitably influence not only our judgment as to which types of claims to recognize as human rights, but also our expectations and programs for implementation and compliance with these standards". Sometimes human rights are conceived in terms of natural law absolutes and buttressed by trans-empirical justifications, both theological and metaphysical. At other times, human rights are defined in terms of the demands made by individuals or groups at particular times within their particular communities.

Human rights may also often be confined to the particular rights which the ruling system of law in the state will protect. Human rights may, further, be defined solely by reference to a larger regional or global community context. The problem often arises because of difference in approach and perspective, for instance whether the concept of human rights is related to the Natural Law approach, the Historical approach, the Positivist approach or the Marxist approach. In the Third World, the perspective applied to the concept and reality of human rights varies with prevailing local philosophy, culture, ideology and historical tradition.

Understandably in the case of former colonies the emphasis will lie as much on civil and political rights and the "third-generation" rights, with a somewhat decisive inclination in favour of community interest, where in the context of community interest, where social and economic progress and development are regarded as of primary importance. Credit must go to those commentators who have attempted to reconcile development with respect for human rights, especially when it cannot be doubted today that the enjoyment of human rights bears an essential connection with economic development, each being necessary to the other.

Following the proposal suggested by the International Commission of Jurists, Sieghart treats of development as conceivable in two directions, the right vested in the state (that is, the "people"). The individual right to development is the right to participate in, and benefit from, the process of development intended by the state for all members of the community so that each individual may enjoy all his human rights, whether civil, political, economic, social or cultural. And a state which can demonstrate that it has fashioned such an environment for its citizens will be legitimately entitled to claim a right to development on the international plane, calling upon other states to assist it in the realization of its internal ethos. To find their place in the catalogue of human rights. Sieghart says,

"The new 'third generation' rights must accord with formulations whereby they can be clearly seen to vest in to be exercisable by them and to impose precise correlative duties on States".

The human rights movement has progressed to a point where in its fundamental conception it treats of members of the human race as members of a global community and, therefore, broadly entitled to a common pattern of human rights. The pervasive presence of human rights in almost all the dimensions of daily fife in most societies provides a cementing influence in the realization of the world recognizing the need in the current political climate for examining issues on a global basis, the internationalization of human rights values can be excepted to proceed apace.

The process may move slowly, but the beginning of the trend is unmistakable. We have growing evidence already of reference by domestic courts to international human rights norms when construing municipal legislation. Eminent Judge V.M. Tarkunde has attributed about the human rights as follows:

> The term human rights, in its normal usage, comprises the rights of the individual in all spheres of social life. They are exercisable by the individual against those who possess political and economic power and also against harmful social customs as untouchability in India, racialism in South Africa and inequality of women in all parts of the world. The recognition of rights in individuals also marks the recognition of certain social obligations on them. Since individual freedom can be experienced only in a moral society, the rights and duties of the individual are necessarily interconnected. Freedom and morality are the two essential components of a healthy Society.

The question of primacy between society and the individual is a perennial problem of social philosophy. If the question is considered chronologically against the backdrop of biological evolution, it is similar in the conundrum; which came first, the hen or the egg. Human beings have always been gregarious. It is well established by now that the origin of the new species was through a chance mutation in the composition of a genetic cell.

This may indicate that a new species is born with the birth of an individual having a different gene than its parents. It is at the same time obvious that the further development of a new species might have taken place through a series of sexual combinations which caused further genetic alterations. Thus the origin of a new species appears to be both an individual and a social phenomenon.

The science of biological evolution does not help in establishing the primacy of society over the individual or vice versa. There is, however, a reason, logical rather than chronological, Which justifies primacy of the individual over society. This is that the individual is a biological being, possessed of consciousness and pain, progress and regress. Society is not a biological being and it is not possessed of a consciousness of its own. It cannot as an entity have any mental experience. Its happiness and its progress can be measured only in terms of the happiness and progress of the individuals, which compose it. It is in this sense that primacy belongs to the individual. The fact that the human individual is alone possessed of consciousness and not any combination of individuals such as a society, a nation or a class, justifies the humanist principle that man (the human individual whether male or female) is the "measure of things".

The question of the comparative worth of social institutions, such as democracy versus dictatorship in politics or capitalism versus state ownership in the economic sphere, can only be decided by assessing its impact on the individuals who constitute a society or a nation.

Dr. Upendra Baxi has described human rights as follows:

> "For the first time in recent history, we move from conceptions of tights as resources for individuals against state power to a conception of human rights as species rights as well. And it is natural to this conception that the rights

> stand addressed not just to states but to international organizations as well, whose major world-historical role,, all said and done, is to enunciate new human futures through a reconstruction of human person whose loyalties are global or planetary. Transcendence of state sovereignty where it matters for mapping new trajectories for alternate human futures, can only be achieved by retooling the notion of human person, the bearer not just of the benefits but also the burden of human rights and fundamental freedoms. It is for this reason that the preamble lays such powerful stress on the centrality of the human person.

The urge for the protection of human rights emanated out of the gross violations preceding and during the two world wars of the century. The protection of human rights, one of the war aims of the allies in the Second World War, was translated into reality with the formation of the United Nations. It was realized that only international protection and promotion of human rights can achieve international peace and progress.

Thus, in the Atlantic Charter of 14 August, 1941, subscribed to and endorsed by 47 nations, the president of the United Kingdom expressed the hope, "to see established a peace which will afford to all nations, the means of dwelling in safety within their own boundaries and which will afford assurance that all the men in all the lands may live out their lives in freedom from fear and want".

Rose M.D.S.A. Research Officer, Human Rights' office, Commonwealth Secretariat, London, explained "Human Rights as a parallel growth of public awareness world-wide of the meaning and significance of concept of human rights." A sharpening global consciousness against inhumanity, which has in turn led to increased recognition by governments both of their internal accountability to the people they govern, and also of the need for international legitimization to confirm and supplement their political legitimacy at home.

The key test of the entire human rights' regime is not the existence of such mechanism, but their effectiveness. In particular, what really matters is the degree to which they harmonies with and are reflected in the domestic laws, regulations or administrative provisions and practices, which impact daily on the lives of millions of people, particularly those who may be regarded as the vulnerable, the weak, the oppressed or the exploited. Boven has also expressed the same kind of expressions.

The American jurist, Wesley Hohfeld, while addressing the students of Yale Law School on 'human rights' hinted that 'human rights as tailed in international politics, consisted of utopian stock-in-trade. He emphasized the different meanings of 'Right' and opined that it was doubtful whether the human rights, as declared in the charter of 10 December, 1948, were 'Rights' at all. Having said this at a time when the concept of human rights was conspicuously displayed on the fast-food counter of politics.

Human rights' in the current political and international vocabulary is a child of the theory of natural rights'. 'Human Rights' is nothing but 'natural rights' in a modern rhetorical garb.

Leonid F. Evmenov described about human rights as follows:

> "Human rights should not only be declared but be codified in legislation. Not only codified in legislation but realized according to the norms of national legislation and international human

> rights acts-that is the only objective condition under which humanism of any social shade can be revealed, from Mahatma Gandhi's ahinsa a to Lenin's philanthropy."

That is why to arrive at a choiceless option it is necessary to achieve not only comprehensive nuclear disarmament, the wise unambitious solving of the nuclear energetic problems, or the protection of dying nature, the cradle of humankind and its civilization, but effective human and peoples' rights' protection. Mikhail Gorbachev put it very well: the modern world today needs global strategies of life and environment protection. It should be added that Modern-world stands in need of human and peoples' rights protection. It is impossible to solve the one problem without confronting and solving the other.

Indeed, now-a-days it is impossible to attain nuclear disarmament and reasonable exploitation of nuclear energy, to set up a comprehensive system of international security and global strategy of life protection without working out the theoretical aspects of the problem, without sizing up the ways of its practical realization, and codifying by law and constitution the right to life as one of the fundamental human and people' rights.

Many western scholars do not consider this right to be a human right, alleging that taken in broad philosophic terms and interpreting it as a right common to all mankind, it is not codified in international acts on human rights worked out by the United Nations, particularly in the Universal Declaration of Human Rights and in the international covenants on Human Rights. It is impossible to set up a global strategy of life, protection without codifying in international acts and realising the right of man and the peoples to political, social, economic and cultural choice, i.e. the human and peoples' rights of self-determination.

Justice H.R. Khanna has described about human rights as follows:

> "It is in an ambience imbued with the sanctity of human rights that Society is assured of the rule of law, an essential ingredient, and a postulate, of which is the existence of independent courts. It bears reiteration that equality before law and the equal protection of the laws are among the most vital human rights. It is basic to the effectiveness of these rights that the courts are independent. Independence of courts thus necessarily flows from the Charter of Human Rights."

Secretary-General of the International Commission of Jurists Sri Niall-Macdermot explained about human rights in following words:

Such knowledge as I have of human rights has been gained during the past 18 years as an activist, with no claims to any qualifications as an academic. Accordingly, I have chosen as my subject the role of Non-Governmental organizations in the promotion and defense of human rights, illustrating what I have to say by drawing on my experience as Secretary-General of the International Commission of Jurists.

Sri N.A. Palkivala has described human rights as follows:

> "The case for human rights is so strong that it almost argues itself. It is an instance of what lawyers call *res ipsa loquitur*—the thing speaks for itself. To attempt to define Human rights definitively, would be merely to illustrate how the human mind tries, and tries in vain, to give a more precise definition than the subject-matter warrants. Human rights may be summed up in one 'word-Liberty'. But Isaiah Berlin noted that there are more than 200 definitions of liberty; and, as Abraham Lincoln

observed, the world had never had a good definition of Liberty.

Soli J. Sorabjee has opined about human rights, which is as Protection of human rights of individuals, an abiding concern of every civilized state, assumes vital importance in the time of emergency when there is invariably vast concentration of power in the executive and considerable dilution of safeguard in which ensure protection of fundamental rights. Suspension of human rights is a concomitant feature of emergencies, there violation an inescapable consequence."

E.S. Venkataramiah has expressed his views about human rights as follows:

"The concept of human rights is very much the product of history and of human civilization and as such is subject to evolution and as change. Every person born in this world however is entitled to certain minimum rights which ought not to be curtained in any manner. It is in this spirit, the United Nations General Assembly adopted about forty years ago, on 10 December, 1948, the Universal Declaration of Human Rights. Subsequently, it has enacted many conventions and protocols relating to human rights and placed them before the member countries for their acceptance and implementation. A large number of States have ratified them. The year 1968, which came twenty years after the Universal Declaration of Human Rights was adopted, was declared by the United Nations General Assembly as the International year of human rights and the then Secretary-General of the United Nations Mr. U. Thant requested all the member-countries to take appropriate action to uphold the human rights. Now that forty years have passed since the adoption of the Universal Declaration of Human Rights, there is reason to take stock of the position and status of human rights the world over. In doing so, we find that the picture is not really rosy. In many countries of the world people continue to be denied even the basic freedoms.

M.H. Beg, former Chief Justice of India has defined human rights as follows:

> "Human rights imply justice, equality and freedom from arbitrary and discriminatory treatment: These cannot be subordinated to the interests of the rulers.

No one can be subjected to coercion for holding particular religious beliefs. The doctrine of national sovereignty cannot justify violation of human rights."

As Paul Sieghart has stated, the distinction between human rights and other rights give rise to three consequences. The human rights are not acquired, nor can they be transferred, disposed of or extinguished by any act or event because those rights inhere universally in all human beings. The primary co-relation of duties in connection with human rights fall upon the state and their public authorities. Because of these two distinctions, says Sieghart, three between consequences follow.

One is non-discrimination between individuals belonging to different groups; second is the rule of law whereby people are governed by law and not by men; and thirdly there are remedies available for the violation of human rights. If these three tests are applied, one must say that nation has come a long way towards the realization of human rights. But there is still a long distance to be covered, before we can say that we have done all that is possible.

Shree Shridath, S. Ramphal, Secretary-General of Commonwealth Nations has described about human rights as follows:

> "We have come a long way since 1948; but we have a long way to go before we translate the commitments implicit in the Universal Declaration into performance. The record to date is far too deficient both within nations and between them, and it is also deficient at a much more personal level in terms of relations between individuals. Furthering human development is a process in which everyone has a role to play: international organizations" but perhaps, most of all, people the world over. In the pecking order of decision-making, people may seem the most lowly and ineffectual. In reality, it is people who represent our best hope for truly furthering human development and advancing the goal of the Universal Declaration."

Shree P.P. Rao has defined human rights:

> "The inherent dignity and inalienable rights of all members of human family recognizing them as the foundation of freedom, justice and peace in the world".

Basic to human rights is the concept of non-discrimination. But if we look into the pages of the history of mankind there has always existed and continues to exist a wide gap between precept and practice, between abstract principles and their application or implementation.

Human rights have been no exception but this has not deterred humanity from repeating and reiterating the principles which govern human rights. According to Sir Hersch Lauterpacht, a noted protagonist of human rights and one of the most eminent international law jurist of post-world war era, observed, "the protection of human personality and of its fundamental rights is the ultimate purpose of all law, national and international." Indeed, characteristic features of the post-world war international relations and represents a revolutionary development."

"The question of human rights if looked at somewhat unconventionally is, in fact, an admixture of political expediency and legal realism marked with humane traditions. In real sense they are not the rights of an individual not to be the society. However, there is nothing in itself to be derogatory in the notion of dependence. There is dependence at all the levels of human existence."

Justice Fathima Beevi has observed about human rights as "The concept of human rights has assumed importance globally during the past few decades and has international significance as every country is subject to international scrutiny by the world body which indicts member-states for violations, while there is increasingly widespread concern for universal respect and observance of human rights, gross violation of internationally recognized norms continue unabated in almost all parts of the world. The overall situation has been characterized by large scale breaches of civil and political rights, as well as economic, social and cultural rights.

The rights to life, to an adequate standard of living, to freedom of expression, to protection from torture, arbitrary arrest and many of the common standards of achievements for all people and all nations, are as far from realization now, as ever. The obligations set out in the course of international conventions and multilateral treaties for, the promotion and protection of human rights and accepted by most of the governments are flouted by them with impunity."

Justice R.N. Misra, Former chair-person of National Human Rights' Commission of India, has observed as follows:

> "It is an obligation which all of us have to perform. Man, wherever he lives, whatever religion he professes, whatever food he takes, is a member of one family. All of us must learn to live like a member of one family. The whole world is one family. One then we will be able to develop the culture of Human Rights. In the absence of Human rights, Societies, individuals and families are disintegrating in the modern era. It is a challenge to human process. We should all be prepared and united to face the challenge of the indiscipline. 1, therefore, call upon you all whether you are in a company, industry, factory, university to face this challenge and help the commission in meeting this challenge. Every one must realize that what is prescribed by law is not for next man, or the man to follow, but for you."

D.D. Raphoel has described human rights as follows:

> "What are human rights? In a general sense they denote the rights of humans. However, in a more specific sense, human rights constitute those very rights which one has precisely because of being a human being. Pertinently the term human rights' received wider acceptance in place of 'the rights of men' in post-world war liberal terminology as it conveyed equal concern for the rights of both sexes. Moreover, the usage of the term 'human rights' also reveals their source: humanity, nature, being a person or human being."

The genesis of the concept of human rights can be traced into the emergence of classical liberalism. Classical liberalism made a passionate defense of the principles like competitive individualism, private property and market ethics, etc. It cherished the realization of Individual's liberty, his development and human progress through the functioning of the above principles. The ideas of the rule of law, limited government and individualism characterized the seventeenth and eighteenth century anti-nationalist school of political liberalism."

Dobbelly has defined human rights "Just as legal rights have the law at their source and contractual right arise from contracts, humanity, human nature or some such aspects of all persons would seem to be the source of human rights".

Human rights are not merely ideals or aspirations, nor are they some rights granted to us by the existence of particular set of laws. They are claims made by virtue of the fact that we are human beings with an inalienable right to human dignity. Therefore, we cannot delegate the authority to a group of persons to define these lights. All individuals and all peoples have these rights to self-directed development. Mr. Lakayan describes the human rights in the following words:"

"Human rights remain with both a statement of reality and an ever expending set of objectives waiting to be actualized and their realization is possible only through a process of constant struggle. Thus, while recourse to law, or appealing to the state to enforce the law, or legislate new ones will and possibly must remain an important and even the primary strategy to transform the human condition, equally important is to evolve a social proxies, rooted in the need of the most oppressed communities, that seek to create the shared norms of civilized this a shared vision of how we want to live as a collectivity that can provide us the moral basis for evolving our own conduct."

Justice Venkatchaliya, Chairperson", Human Rights Commission has defined "Human rights are rights in own nature and without which we cannot live as human beings".

Professor Baidyanath Labh of Jammu University in Budhist studies has considered human rights concept in Budhististic religious approach. Let us consider his view:

> "The notion of Human rights has occupied dominant place in the international deliberations on peace and security for the human beings. The human rights concept has been predominantly western liberal concept which has come to be widely accepted by rest of the world. Thus, though Buddhism has got acquainted with this concept of human rights in imbibing the very ethos of the concept of human rights in the form of defense of human essence and dignity. It may properly be understood if we refer to the seminal norms and principles of Buddhism. The present article makes an attempt to look for the compatibility between the norms and doctrines of Buddhism and the notion of human rights.

Human rights concept ensures that an individual living in a Society will be guaranteed of his position. In this view, human rights emerges as a legal concept. However, for proper realization of human rights, it is essential that the society as a whole accept the basic norms of human rights and that one needs to address to the relevance of Buddhism does not believe in discrimination or inequality simply on the basis of one's birth, caste or colour. In other words. a person is neither a Sudra nor a Brahmana (low or high) simply by virtue of his birth, but only by virtue of his bad or good actions. Not only that, if a person feels false pride over his caste, wealth or origin and treats others as inferior to him, he insults the basic human dignity and consequently declines in his life.

The Buddha has taught to honour parents, brothers, sisters, children, other relatives and other persons in the society. If someone hurts anybody physically or even vocally, he may be treated as a person lacking—the basic human qualities. Regard for human dignity is the basic social message of Buddhism. Every person is suggested to treat others just as he or she has love and attachment for himself or herself. Buddhism as a philosophical position as well as a moral way of life, has been concerned with spiritual salvation whereas human rights aims a natural salvation, i.e. safety of the rights of equality, dignity and freedom at worldly level.

However, Buddhism does not talk of imaginary idealism as misunderstood sometimes by some people. It is very much based on the experiences of day-to-day life. It advocates for observance of moral duties towards one another among people in the Society. It is a fact that each and everyone cannot give up worldly life and become a recluse. The Buddha was well aware of this fact. Therefore, he prescribed a moral code of conduct for householders as well as for homeless recluses, which ensures safeguard of human dignity, of course. Buddhism lays more emphasis to the attainment of spiritual salvation.

On the other hand, cultural background of the western societies (where natural rights concept was given by the seventeenth and eighteenth century classical liberals like Hobbes and Locke has been traditionally different from the social and cultural milieu in which Buddhism developed. Thus, Buddhist thought has comparatively a wider spectrum of the modern notion of human rights claims. Therefore, there may be a good scope of reconciliation between the two concepts emanating from altogether different historical backgrounds.

V.R. Krishna Iyer he has described "Human rights and fundamental freedoms are indivisible, the full realization of civil and political rights and cultural rights, is impossible. This process of realization calls for legal positivisation, not political polemics nor diplomatic clap-trap but normative formulation. But what are human rights? We may discover that the Religion of Man is located in the Vedas, Buddhist Texts, Bible, the Quran or the holy literature or other authentic teachers to upholds human divinity. Every human being is a divine being and has title to dignity, liberty, equality and other basic rights. We cannot understand or evaluate human rights divorced from the historical and social context. Idle ideals and empty assertions cut no ice.

The status of human rights takes us to the life-style of a society. That is why the Indian constitutional approach is soaked in the social milieu and human conditions. India is plural Society and the concept of the human rights in such society has a different and unique position." With regard to the position of human rights Scarman has said "an article that the problem is old".

Today we tend to think in terms of ethic origin or skin colour when we take of a plural society. But there are other social divisions just a difficult to bridge that most unitary of Societies, the greek city state was a plural society, incorporating the rightless slave as well as the fully entitled citizen and the Roman world was a compiles plural society as any in the history of mankind, but human rights are they as prevalent or as old established as the plural society? That is another story. For most of mankind's human rights have and continue today to be, more conspicuous in the mouth of men than in their practice.

These fundamental minorities in a democratic society are to be won and protected. A constitutional safety value has to be designed to relieve men of the pressures of excess of power. It is, we hope helpful to take a lock at the various solutions to the constitutional problem attempted in the western world. The countries, whose legal systems derive from the Roman, built the necessary restraints into the very exercise of executive or administrative power. This was the Roman way of governing their world a plural society of immense complexity based on a rigid class structure ranging from the privileged Roman citizen to the slave labour force which had no civil rights at all.

The western world of our time is making an honourable endeavor to cope with the problem. There is no single blue-print, for success. But we believe that modern experience shows that there is one essential feature of every solution, a constitution mechanism strong enough to prevent absolute power from lodging in any one group of Society or in any institution coupled with a plain declaration of the rights and duties of man in Society.

Their rights and duties are those which are so fundamental that civilized man cannot survive without them; they are the just natural of mankind the just genuine of all races. The story of Human Rights is thus the story of human wrongs. God divided the light from the darkness and the waters from the land. And man divided his fellow man into those who were considered to possess none. And he came to the conclusion that all men had certain rights which other man had no right to natural law and natural rights. These concepts were developed by the Greek and Roman.

Let us consider the view of Justice RN. Bhagwati on Human Rights, who is now Vice-Chairman of U.N. Human Rights, Committee:

> "Fundamental rights are of great importance for individual, freedom, but these fundamental

> rights are a very minimal set of rights and therefore, human rights, which are derived from the inherent dignity of the human person and cover every aspect of life and not just a small number of preferred freedom against the state, have tremendous significance. For the large number of people in a developing country like India, who are only solution for making fundamental rights meaningful would be restructure the social and economic order so that they may be to able to realize their economic rights. Human Rights Conference called by the United Nations General Assembly in 1968 declared that "since human rights and fundamental freedoms are indivisible, the full realization of civil and political rights without the enjoyment of economic, social and cultural rights is impossible".

Protection of Human Rights' Act, 1993 has defined the term "Human rights under section 2(D) as follows:

> "Human rights means the rights relating to life, liberty, equality and dignity of the individual guaranteed by the constitution or embodied in international covenants and enforced by courts in India".

The concept of human rights has gradually evolved over the past several centuries. It is immaterial whether you call these rights as inherent rights, fundamental rights or by some other name. These rights by themselves have no fixed content as has been rightly remarked by Justice Mathew and most of them are empty vessels into which each generation has poured its content in the light of its experience.

Human rights, as conceived in the last few decades of the twentieth century, are justifiable claims on behalf of all men to corporate action. They are owed to the individual by the State as well as by the organized social and economic groups which are the center of power and authority. The concept of human rights has a dynamic nature in reference to time and space. Human rights have existed, in however, nascent a form, ever since man as a gregarious animal has lived in communities; family, clan, tribe, village, town or nation, and now in an independent, world community.

The superstitious acceptance by the ignorant masses of their object poverty, of human miseries, hunger and disease, of callous discrimination and exploitation of man-by-man, and of the age-old apathy of the elite in power in large parts of this globe, has further complicated the problem of human rights. The U.N. Charter has provided a Constitutional basis on which the United Nations can bring about changes in the status of the individual vis-a-vis his own State. The United Nations have been deeply involved in the furtherance of the cause of human rights ever since its inception.

Human Rights could thus be defined to be the rights of an individual and the interest to be protected collectively both at international and national level by the coordinated efforts with the intervention of the States in pursuance of intended objectives collective wisdom is utilized for formulating basic policies on a uniform pattern which are given recognition jointly so as to adopt and enforce them in the form of so-called human rights and in this process even if there is any conflict of interest among various nations but it occupies insignificant position and having least regard to national boundaries, common consensus is arrived at for the purpose of upliftment of mankind, in general and for improving the lot of downtrodden masses, in particular. In this context, it could be rightly said that a man is a human-being first and foremost irrespective of where he is born to live and it is indeed a welcome development.

The basic problem that arises concerning human right relates to their proper enforcement and this aspect varies today from State to State. This is indeed so because the first initial step in the direction of enforcement of human rights is very much confined to the national frontiers of the state where the individual resides. It would be certainly justified to presume that so far as the basic job of drafting the human rights is concerned, this job has been successfully accomplished by the efforts of member states of United Nations Organization but the basic problem has been the effective enforcement of human rights so as to eradicate poverty and improve standard of living of mankind, in general and the worker, in particular. It is apparent that any concept of human rights which can be acceptable to the modern liberal democratic societies must fulfil two basic assumptions. First, the rights must be equal in an effective manner. Second, there must be an obligation on others to accept each notion of natural rights does not meet these requirements.

Writing primarily in the concept of classical political philosophies Hobbe's and Locke's views on natural rights. Macpherson explains this failure in the following manner: "The inability of either doctrine to meet our requirement is due to the same basic postulate about the nature of man and society; and it is this postulate which makes it impossible that any extension or reshaping of their concepts of natural rights could produce a new acceptable theory of human rights. Both writers imputed to the nature of society a permanent conflict of interests between individuals. Hobbe's men necessarily sought power over others. Locke's national men sought unlimited property, which he assumed must be at the expense of others'. Thus classical liberalism, which lies at the heart of natural right tradition, cannot be acceptable to modern liberal democratic as it rested on the sanctification of bourgeois self-interest.

Although these natural rights were supposed to express the human essence, and . . . were claimed in the name of human freedom, they are not now regarded as a sufficient statement of human essence or freedom, even in the countries where they originated. The liberal democratic concept of human rights in the second half of the twentieth century has come to mean defense of the rights of the human being against abuses of power committed by the organs of the state with the help of institutionalized means. It also involves the promotion of the establishment of human living conditions and the overall development of the human personality. What are the main contentions of the twentieth century human rights theory? Briefly stated, they are among others; First, the validity of human rights is established by specific legislation.

The inherent dignity of human being is not sufficient. Thus the whole concept has acquired a juridical character; second, within the bourgeois legal system the human rights issue receive an extended treatment by two branches of law, i.e. constitutional and International Law; third, the human rights are vested in all individuals and only in individuals, not in professional groups, Social groups, communities, tribes, races, classes, castes, nations or other entities.

Furthermore, a human being enjoys his or her human rights both as an individual and a citizen; fourth, the human rights concept remains immutably valid wherever human beings lead a collective life. The above concept of human rights has been gaining wider significance and acceptance in the western liberal democratic countries who have reached the stage of advanced capitalism. As discussed above, liberal democratic theory of human rights has not been accepted both by the socialist countries as well as the developing countries.

The socialist theory, whose roots are essentially traced back to Marx, has argued against the individualism of human rights theory. Making a scathing attack on natural rights concept, Marx in 'On the Jewish question' considers it as the ideological expression of bourgeois egoism and social atomization. 'The so-called rights of man . . . are nothing but . . . the rights of egoistic man, of man separated from other men and, from the community . . . None of the so-called rights of man therefor, , go beyond egoistic man, as a member of civil society, that is, an individual withdrawn into himself, and separated from the community. Marx goes on to extend his basic postulate by emphasizing the necessary connection between bourgeois society and the notion of human rights.

Writing in the Holy Family, Marx and Engels stated: 'The recognition of the rights of man by the modern state has no other meaning than the recognition of slavery by the ancient state had slavery as its natural basis, the modern state has as its natural basis, civil society and the man of civil society, i.e. the individual man linked with other men only by the ties of private interest and unconscious natural necessity, the slave of labour for gain and of his own as well as other men's selfish needs. It follows that the very notion of human rights, according to Marx and Engels is linked to the competitive struggle that is the hallmark of the bourgeois society and is based on vision of society and the individual as inherently separate and antagonistic units.

Human rights are thus viewed as instruments for carrying out adversary relations between competing, primarily atomistic individuals. Central to Marxism in its concern for human beings and the idea that man, stripped of 'his human essence' when he first fell into the class of the exploited,, confronts 'the destruction of all humanity' in him in a bourgeois society.

The process of bourgeois exploitation, with its natural corollary 'greed and the war between the greedy competition' holds the entire society at the mercy of the market forces. It 'estranges man from nature; from himself, his own active functioning . . . from his universal, essence . . . it makes his essence into a mere means for his existence . . . It estranges . . . his spiritual, his human essence . . . it results in) the alienation of man from man'. Such kind of alienating, depersonalizing and dehumanizing impact of bourgeois system makes the whole context that Marx stated about communism that it is 'the actual phase necessary for the next stage of historical development in the process of human emancipation and recovery. Thus in a Communist Society, Marx argued in the critique of the Gotha Program working class would enjoy the right to compensation for labour. In the early socialist stage the working class would contribute a quantity of labour and in return, would acquire a right to receive back a share of the social product exactly in proportion to its contribution in the production process.

However, in the later phase of communism when subordination to the division of labour would be ended 'only then come the narrow horizon of bourgeois right be crossed in its entirety and society inscribe on its banners' from each according to his ability, to each according to his needs. The liberal democratic theory of human has also invited criticism in the context of its application in the developing stages.

Like the Marxist critique, one common theme in analysis of third world conceptions of human rights is the individualism of the human rights theory, its 'obsessive concern with the dignity of the individual, his worth, personal autonomy and property.' Presenting a view from the periphery, Legesse argues: If Africans were the sole authors of the Universal Declaration of Human Rights, they might have ranked the rights of communities above those of individual's. What is true for Africa is also true for the Arab world.

Writing of the predominantly Islamic societies Yamani criticizes the western liberal democratic tradition as it, according to him, 'is so overzealous in its defense of the individuals freedom, rights and dignity, that it overlooks the acts of some individuals in exercising individual centered and universalist philosophical premises of western liberal human rights concept. Legesse argues that 'any system of ideas that claims to be universal must contain critical elements in its fabric that are avowedly of African, Latin American or Asian derivation'. In a similar vein, Cranston asks: How can the governments of those parts of Asia, Africa, and South America, where industrialization has hardly begun, be social rights . .. secured by fairly simple legislation. Since these rights are largely rights against government interference, the greatest effort will be directed towards restraining the government's own executive arms.

In essence, the western liberal democratic human rights concepts with its emphasis on the natural, inalienable and individualistic rights of human beings favour the empowerment of the state and its organs. The whole idea is that if the human beings are to be empowered to become able to enjoy the human rights, the state and its organs must be correspondingly disempowered. Such an idea if considered in the non-western context leads to an 'acute' and 'real' dilemma, especially if it gets too far fetched. As Upendra Baxi argues: 'The notion of disempowerment makes sense.

But should it be extended all the ways? Obviously not. Activists to ask that new laws may be made addressing the worst forms of violations of human rights in the civil society, usually associated with the most regressive forms of social behaviour associated with a historic revival of religion, culture and ethnicity. Should there not be stricted law and state action, for example, on sati, dowry murders, sex-selective abortions through the abuse of amniocentesis techniques, nutritional sex discrimination which creates new forms of deferred female infanticide, child abuse, familial violence against women, atrocities against dalits, exploitation of bounded, migrant and contract labour? The answer is yes. The difficulty with this answer is that it empowers the state. Baxi's views held true for India as well as other developing countries where there has been wider agreement in favour of the acceptance of the inclusion of group or people's rights along with the individualistic human rights. To quote Donnelly,

'Human rights . . . are held primarily by individual and they are exercised and claimed primarily in relation to Society, usually in the person of the state. People's rights, though, are held by society (again in the form of state) and their operation. Such a concept of human rights which has become increasingly important in the 'new states' subscribe essentially to the populist general-will theory, whose roots are in Rousseau. It would appear to any discernible observer that the above third world concept of articulation between human rights and people's rights may result into the marginalisation of the sentinel character of human rights.

However, one must understand that the unique social, economical and political structures of the developing countries make it imperative that a relatively autonomous 'overdeveloped' state has to play a pivotal role in maintaining human rights with the help of a relatively independent judiciary, while recognizing that the state is an instrument of the class domination, of disorganizing the sub-patterns, of fracturing their emergent unity, and disorienting the masses struggle for justice and rights. We have to retain state and its bourgeois legal system. The solution of the above problem lies in the radical transformation of the society, state and economy which would be accompanied with a vision of counter-law, an alternate legality which will base itself on moralities, ideologies and practices, not merely different from but superior to those of the (existing bourgeois) state law. Until that is realized with the achievement of scientific socialism, the human rights movements in the developing states must not remain observed with the condemnation of state and its relatively autonomous legal system, of course, this does not mean that the repressive laws, agencies, ideology, actions, etc. of the state are not to be combated. All of us belong to one family: mankind. Every member of our fan-lily has the same fundamental and equal rights. Each of us is entitled to have these rights respected and each of us has a responsibility to protect these rights for all others.

Differences of race, sex, language and colour do not change these rights. Nor go differences of property, social origin, political ideas or religious beliefs. Every one regardless of who they are and what they do or think, is born with human rights. It is worth mentioning here that the subject of human rights' is of universal concept of human rights is that of the respect for human personality and its absolute worth regardless of colour, race, sex, religion or other considerations. These rights are essential for the full development of the human personality and for human happiness. Woven into the wrap and woof of human history, the concept of Human Rights has been a variable and dynamic one. It has in fact varied from generation to generation and evolved with the changing times and under the constantly shifting conditions.

Even within the same Society, perception of what human rights are, may vary from state to state. Human rights ought to be for all men and women, general and universal and not linked to any special positions. What shall vary in different situations and at different points will be the extent of implementation and limitation of human rights and not the content or nature of the rights themselves.

Human rights are rights both of individuals and of Society, of groups, of minorities and of majorities.

Dr. S.D. Sharma, the then President of India described about human rights as follows:

> It is important that, from very early times, thinkers and lawmakers in our country had arrived at an extremely clear, specific and comprehensive understanding of the essential elements having a bearing on the life of the individual and his position in society, and also of the desirable relationship between the state and the individual. The most ancient literature that humanity possesses today-the Rig Veda-reveals the enlightened and refined treatment of key issues of important to human being—even in advanced stages of development of human Society.

Such an outlook of humanism, as well as of vigilance, regarding protection of human rights also accounted for the clarity with which Indian thinkers developed the concept of 'Sarva Dharma Sambhav'-providing the freedom of the individual to follow any of different streams of thought, expression, belief and religious preference.

A magnificent expression of this approach comes to us from the great Mauryan Emperor Ashoka, whose stone edicts at Shahbazarhi, Kalsi and Girnar bear the imprint of enlightened philosophy and good law. It is evident that such initiatives followed the realization that it was absolutely essential to recognize and enforce certain rights of the individual if a well-ordered society were to be brought into existence. We would like to mention with emphasis that the linkage between axioms of law and the lives of individuals is a crucial internal elements in organized society. It is this element which reflects how abstract ideas determine the actual lives of the people. The judiciary has thus a position of far-reaching significance in this context, particularly bearing in mind the fact that we follow the common law system. It is a happy feature that human rights declared under the Universal Declaration are no longer the subject of guarantee only of individual nations but are guaranteed by the United Nations for all human beings.

Appropriately the process appears to be evolving towards a mandate which may be called the 'common law of mankind' and of the world which Pt. Jawahar Lal Nehru often spoke of one world which as he said "could no longer be spilt into isolated fragments", because "Peace has been said to be indivisible, so is freedom, so is prosperity".

Jawahar Lal Nehru said:

> 'Hence appropriately the process appears to be evolving towards a mandate which may be called the common law of mankind and of the one world which could no longer be split into isolated fragments because peace has been said to be indivisible so is freedom, so is prosperity'.

Security General U.N.O. Boutrous Gali has highlighted the importance of them in meeting the needs of human rights developments. He has also described that human rights may be said to be rights that are inherent in people by virtue of beings human beings, the rights that are absolutely essential for full and complete development of human personality. Generally, two categories of human rights are recognized, namely, civil and political rights and economic, cultural and social rights. However, third category has also come up but has as yet not been fully established that includes rights to development, right to common heritage of mankind, etc. These rights have been forcefully advocated by developing countries.

Hence it may be concluded that human right is not a new issue. Human right has now been taken by all in a much broader sense. There are various aspects of human rights. Along with disarmament and development, human beings are essential part of the total and holistic peace and human dignity. We mean not only civil and political rights, but the right to live with all the basic, economic, social and cultural rights of fullness, freedom, including religious freedom. The human right signifies both rights and duties which are inter-linked.

The term "Human Rights" means being argued as vital for a democratic society, but also an economic, social and cultural rights as well as the rights are essential component of sustainable development and therefore not possible without respect of human rights. Respect of human rights makes freedom meaningful. Human rights are meaningless in an environment of poverty and deprivation. Human rights are above politics. They are part and parcel of life in society and they concern humanity.

Human rights necessarily signify human values in an absolute senses: but they have greater relevance to the real well-being of the individual if they are applied in the context of society. 'Me human rights are sign and symbol of human development and peace. The whole fabric of society depends upon human rights. Without human rights the society cannot run smoothly, and there could be many chances of crimes and disturbances in the society.

The protection of human rights is a constant struggle which cannot be won unless every man and woman participate in it. In real practice the human rights is the sum of all rights necessary to ensure our rights to be human and it is the duty of all peoples and governments to create the condition headed to exercise our right to be human.

Let us conclude few basic essentials to qualify a particular right to be human rights. These essentials may be counted as follows:

1. It is a right of individual or group of individuals.
2. It can only be executed in a Society for and against state by individual or groups.
3. These rights are inalienable and human beings are entitled to them by birth.
4. It is a permanent universal and legal concept in all spheres of life.
5. These rights are meant to uphold human dignity and equality and to set forth liberty and fraternity to all without any kind of discrimination to all needy.
6. These rights are minimum requirements for survival of mankind or human beings in Societies.
7. These rights are protected and enforced by the Authority of society or state at all levels.

In brief, "human rights comprise rights of individual

or groups in a society in all spheres of life since inception up to the last, i.e. from birth to death. They may be exercised individually or collectively." No specific set of rights can be created universally. These may differ from time to time and place to place, but their applicability is universal. Hence, human rights are "those minimum set of rights of a mankind available in all spheres of life to all individual or groups of Societies individually or collectively which is expected to be permanently inalienable since berth up to last of man or society for the purposes of survival or benefit of mankind, individual or society." Historical Development and Evolution of International Human Rights. According to socio-political theories, the genesis of the concept of human rights can be traced into the emergence of classical liberalism. Classical liberalism made a passionate defense of the principles like competitive individualism, private property and market ethics, etc. It cherished the realization of individual's liberty, his development and human progress through the functioning of the above principles.

The ideas of the rule of law, limited government and individualism characterized the seventeenth and eighteenth century and anti-nationalist school of political liberalism. Macpherson in 'his brilliant study of classical political liberalism refers to the assumptions, inherent in the view it takes of man, society and political society. These assumptions according to Macpherson, and 'peculiarly appropriate to a possessive market society', as 'possessive individualism'. Thus the individual is conceptualized 'as essentially the proprietor of his own person or capacities, owing nothing to society for them.

Freedom is viewed as 'a function of possession'. Essentially the greatness of liberalism was its assertion of the free rational individual as the criterion of the good society. Broadly speaking, these different variants of general political theory can be viewed as deriving their theoretical fundamentals from one of three types. To quote Macpherson, they are: 'the individualist liberal theory, whose roots are generally traced back to Locke, the socialist theory, whose roots are essentially in Marx, and the populist general-will theory, whose roots are in Rousseau. However, in each of these three types of theory there is a problem of fitting the modern notion of human tights into the general lines of the theory.

The individualist-liberal theory has no difficulty accommodating the rights of life, liberty, and property, for it was built largely on the individual, but it finds some difficulty fitting in the modern ideas of economic rights, but do not find it so easy to accommodate the earlier trilogy of natural rights of life, liberty and property, which they have tended to mistrust on the ground that these are essentially bourgeois' rights.

"After centuries of fatalistically enduring political subjugation and suffering, after millennia of accepting social discrimination as a decree of the gods, and economic disparity as an unalterable fact of life, science and technology have awakened mankind all over the world to the realization that this need no longer be so." There is also a difference in thinking and ideas. Everybody has his own ideas and thinking.

Everyone is born with human rights regardless of who he is and to which community he belongs, and wears different culture. Everyone has a right to be protected by the state and the people. Human rights are inherent in and integral to every human beings, basic for human life and its development, and incorporated in the constitutions of every state. The concept of human rights has gradually evolved over the past several centuries. It is immaterial whether you call these rights as inherent rights, fundamental rights of by some other name.

These rights by themselves have no fixed content as has been rightly remarked by Justice Mathew" and most of them are empty vessels into which each generation has poured its content in the light of its experience. Human rights, as conceived in the last few decades of the twentieth century, are justifiable claims on behalf of all men to corporate action. They are owed to the individual by the state as well as by the organized social and economic groups which are the center of power and authority.

The concept of human rights has a dynamic nature in reference to time and space. According to religious philosophical views the basis of human rights is "Dharma" which is vitally concerned with humanity.

Dharma is one word which defines and covers the totality of human experience and existence. Dharma derived from the root, Dhr meaning to uphold, to support, to nourish, to integrate, etc., is the sum total of essential values and ideas on which the political, economic, cultural and religious expression of life are based. Dharma has another dimension when relates to the individual person who contribute society.

Source of Human Rights

There are various theories and sources of human rights. Let us first concern ourselves to the various sources of human rights. These sources can be counted as under:

Religion

It is one of the old. Ancient source, not only of human rights but also to the world at large. Its ambiguity cannot be identified. All basic principles of human rights are derived from all major religions.

Natural Law

Principles of natural justice and Law constitute another old and essential basic of all societies in all respects. Human rights are no exception to it. All universal natural law principles are human rights. These are principles of logic which still govern the conscience of society and man.

Independent Individual

Individuals thinking constitute major thought of human rights. It shall be considered later on.

Positive laws

All codification which provide rights to Individual constitute major modern human rights at present.

State actions

Sometimes Governmental orders, circular orders and executive actions also play a vital role in the field of human rights.

Marxim thoughts

Marxim thoughts also define the human rights in one special society of communism.

Sociological approach

Now the sociological aspect has a key role to play in modern times. Law has been a method of social engineering. Law is meant to progress of society by social actions. It is only possible if all human rights are observed in society.

2

Humanitarian Issues and Human Rights

The root of humanitarian disasters, refugee flows or mass exoduses often stems directly from violations of human rights. Addressing the cause is as essential to preventing humanitarian tragedies similar to those experienced in Rwanda or in the countries of the former Yugoslavia as it is to the search for comprehensive solutions. A continuum between human rights law and humanitarian law is necessary; protection of the victim should be the overriding concern of the United Nations and its agencies and programmes. Since 1948, the UN has developed a comprehensive body of international standards and norms for the promotion and protection of human rights, the major instrument being the international bill of human rights. In 1970, the General Assembly adopted a number of resolutions which recognized that fundamental human rights as accepted in international law and international instruments continue to apply in situations of armed conflict.

While the first World Conference on Human Rights held in Tehran in 1968 did not explicitly refer to humanitarian law in its proclamation, it affirmed that humanitarian principles must prevail during periods of armed conflict. The Vienna Declaration and Programme of Action, the concluding document of the 1993 World Conference on Human Rights, called on all States and parties to armed conflicts to adhere strictly to humanitarian law as well as to minimum standards for protection of human rights as laid down in international conventions. The Conference also recognized the gross violation of human rights as one of the major factors leading to the displacement of people and expressed grave concern over continuing violations of human rights in all parts of the world -in disregard of international standards - and the lack of adequate and effective remedies for the victims.

Human rights and humanitarian law, once clearly distinguishable segments of international law, are increasingly being viewed in an integrated and holistic manner, where the individual has a continuum of protection under human rights law as well as that provided under humanitarian law, as warranted by the specific circumstances.

The Office of the UN High Commissioner for Human Rights (OHCHR), as an institution devoted to the promotion and protection of all human rights, emphasizes the value of early warning and preventive action aimed at deterring human rights violations and defusing situations with the potential for humanitarian disasters. The information and findings of UN human rights experts (special rapporteurs, special representatives, experts of human rights treaty-based bodies), complemented by those submitted by UN human rights field offices, represent a valuable contribution to an early warning mechanism of the UN in this area.

OHCHR recognizes that the wealth of information at its disposal needs to be systematically organized and analyzed if it is to be an effective and useful tool.

The objectives are to strengthen the early warning capacity of the UN in the humanitarian field, enhance the substantive exchanges between OHCHR, the Office for the Coordination of Humanitarian Affairs (OCHA) and other Departments and Programmes, and to integrate human rights concerns before crises arise, thus guaranteeing effective cooperation both in terms of preparedness and response.

Human Rights training should be considered part of the overall training back-round of all UN humanitarian staff. The Office of the High Commissioner is developing a human rights manual for all UN staff members which will be available soon. The manual will cooperate with the Complex Emergency Training Initiative (CETI) as well as with the UN staff college in Turin on the question of initiatives aimed at familiarizing all UN staff with international human rights standards.

As possible immediate steps, contacts should be established with Human Resources Management (OHRM) and the UN Staff College Project with a view to integrating human rights into the courses held at Headquarters and at the College. Training of UN humanitarian staff in the field, as well as staff at Headquarters and new recruits, in human rights standards, monitoring methodology, technical cooperation procedures and other topics, should be given priority attention. A mechanism could be established so that all newly recruited staff undergo appropriate human rights training. In the case of field staff, one or more officers could be appointed as trainers and delegated the responsibility for providing on-site training to all field staff, based on OHCHR training materials.

In regard to the human rights aspects of UN humanitarian operations, it is important to learn from past experience and to attempt to integrate human rights concerns whenever possible, to include human rights experts in large-scale humanitarian operations, and to emphasize the protection and promotion of human rights, including the creation of viable national human rights institutions capable of preventing the recurrence of similar humanitarian crises.

When a humanitarian operation is considered, the human rights dimension should be part of the planning, requiring close cooperation between OCHA, the UN High Commissioner for Refugees (UNHCR) and OHCHR. While the need and opportunity for inclusion of human rights field officers or advisers within humanitarian operations will vary, an explicit human rights strategy would be pivotal to the planning of major humanitarian efforts. The strategy could be of an advisory nature and/or cover training and institution-building issues.

Humanitarian staff, particularly in the field, should be fully conversant with human rights standards and procedures. The effectiveness of the UN machinery and mechanisms in the field of human rights would be enhanced through more consistent use of these procedures by humanitarian workers, resulting in a greater degree of protection for individuals and other vulnerable groups. Procedures on how this information would be handled could be discussed in-depth between OHCHR and the various humanitarian actors so as to preserve their mandates, independence and specific missions.

OHCHR'S global project For internally displaced persons (IDPs), in the context of its technical cooperation programme, is a good example of' humanitarian and human rights interfacing. According to the Representative of the Secretary-General on IDPs, internally displaced persons are: "Persons or groups of persons who have been forced or obliged to flee or to leave their homes or places of habitual residence, in particular as a result of or in order to avoid the effects of armed conflict, situations of generalized violence, violations of human rights or natural or human-made disasters, and who have not crossed an internationally recognized State border".

Internal displacement constitutes one of the greatest challenges confronting the international community. Unlike refugees, whom IDPs greatly outnumber, there exists no single agency to assume responsibility for the promotion and protection of the rights of IDPs. A Representative on IDPs was appointed by the Secretary-General at the request of the Commission on Human Rights in 1992, his mandate supported by OHCHR. The Representative's mandate is concentrated on three main areas:

— developing an appropriate normative framework for meeting the protection, assistance, reintegration and development needs of IDPs: significant progress has been made in this direction over the past few months with the formulation by the RSG of Guiding Principles on Internal Displacement. The Guiding Principles consolidate in one document the rights and guarantees relevant to the protection of persons from forced displacement and to their protection and assistance during displacement as well as during return or resettlement and reintegration. They are intended to provide practical guidance not only to the RSG but also to States and other authorities, intergovernmental organizations, NGOs and all other groups and persons with a role to play in addressing the needs of IDPs;

Ensuring the rights of IDPs worldwide to protection and assistance presents the international community with one of the most daunting challenges of our time. Under its technical cooperation programme, OHCHR's global project for IDPs, relying on effective institutional arrangements, will be implemented jointly with the Representative of the Secretary-General (RSG) on IDPs, with the objective of making the rights of some 25 million IDPs a reality.

The broad scope of priority activities to be put in place will guarantee the widest possible distribution of the Guiding Principles on Internal Displacement 9 as well as other related materials—a Training Manual and Fact Sheets are examples—in the official UN languages and, as appropriate, local languages; field offices will rely on the Guiding Principles for the technical guidance essential in their monirtoring and reporting functions. Educational and training activities will be provided primarily at the national level, in response to requests from Member States. Workshops on IDP-related issues will be attended by the RSG and his support staff. Interagency needs assessment missions will utilize staff seconded for that purpose. The project will also ensure a focus on IDP activities by the treaty bodies and the mechanisms of the Commission on Human Rights in Geneva.

— fostering effective institutional arrangements for addressing these needs; and

— focusing attention on specific situations of internal displacement with the aim of ensuring that they are effectively addressed. The Secretary-General recognizes that addressing the plight of IDPs is a priority for the international community. Over the past few years. OHCHR, in addition to supporting the work of the Representative, has become increasingly involved with IDPs in its own right.

OHCHR is developing a global project for internally displaced persons (IDPs) in the context of its technical cooperation programme. The aim of the project is to meet the growing operational requirements of the

Representative, particularly in the areas of promotion, education, training, and strengthening of national capacities. The objective is to provide the necessary resource requirements to meet the commitments undertaken by OHCHR on behalf of IDPs. The project also identifies possible future activities of OHCHR which could be initiated on behalf of IDPs, on condition that sufficient institutional capacity for mandated tasks and other commitments is first ensured. It will provide a framework for action by OHCHR and the Representative of the Secretary-General on the basis of individual requests from member states for activities at the national level or occasionally in a regional or sub-regional context.

As long as crimes of torture, rape and murder go unpunished, we cannot hope to prevent their recurrence. Those who contemplate indiscriminately attacking civilians, or forcing them out of their homes simply on account of their ethnicity or religion, must know that there is a price to pay for such actions. This justifies the pertinence of UN efforts to date to demand accountability—the establishment of the ad hoc criminal tribunals for former Yugoslavia and Rwanda is a case in point. Mary Robinson, High Commissioner for Human Rights, addressed the Diplomatic Conference in Rome on 15 June concerning the finalization and adoption of the statute for a permanent ICC.

We look forward to cooperating closely and developing an effective modus operandi with the ICC in due course.

Indeed, the relationship of the ICC and UN human rights and humanitarian actors and institutions is a subject which elicits considerable interest. Discussion and analysis will complement OHCHR's ongoing efforts to facilitate access to the information available from treaty bodies and mechanisms of the Commission on Human Rights, to quantify and measure human rights progress (or lack of it) so that benchmarking becomes possible and readily available within the UN.

There is a broad space for forging effective linkages between humanitarian assistance and human rights programmes. The separate mandates and different methods of work can produce a remarkable added value if perceived as complementary and mutually supportive and if we maintain the focus of all we do to increase the extent of protection for the victims.

3

Children's Rights

Children's victimization in its different expressions is a constant feature of practically all societies. It is common belief that childhood as currently understood is a relatively recent creation. In the old Roman days, the life of the young subjects was strictly monitored. Roman citizens were under the authority of a tutor upto puberty, which was deemed to occur at 14 for males and 12 for females. The period before puberty was divided into two parts.

During infancy, that is to say upto the age of seven, the child was incapable of reason and could perform no legal act. Thereafter, the *pupillus* was granted a limited capacity, in other words it could acquire rights but it was not entitled to alienate them, nor to incur duties. There would follow a long period which young Roman would be regarded as a minor and as such subjected to cura-minorum, only at the age of 25 would it acquire full legal status, yet always under the partria-potestas or father's authority which would lost for its entire life. The juristic concept that child being legal person is entitled to the protection of law, developed during the last two centuries, following industrialisation and the emergence of women's rights.

The advent of industrial revolution brought about the enactment of child labour laws some of them dating back to the first half of 19th century. The progressive liberation of women changed the familys' pattern of power and as a result paternal authority lost absolute decisional power over the children.

Child under International Law

The first conventions indirectly protecting children began in the late 19th and early 20th centuries in the international arena. Geneva Convention IV and the additional protocols incorporated and expand many of the principles contained in the Hague Conventions a specifically provided for the protection of the children. Articles 14, and 24 of the Geneva Convention IV and 76, 77 and 78 of Protocol Article 50 of the Geneva Convention IV affords genera) protection children as well as protects children in occupied territories.

The Force Labour Conventions of 1930 and the Abolition of Forced Labo Convention of 1957, require State parties to suppress and abolish force child labour imposed by either the State or by the private individual and organisations. In 1959 Declaration, "Soft Law" documents enunciates genera principles and entitlements for the care and protection of children. It is mainly concerned with economic, social and cultural rights. Any Convention on the Rights of the child must be read within the frame-work of the International Bill of Human Rights, composed of the 1948 Declaration and the 1966 International Covenant on Economic, Social and Cultural Rights (ICES) and International Covenant on *Civil* and Political Rights (ICCPR) with its optional protocol. Another factor of the utmost importance to the cause of children's protection comes from Article 35 which requires state parties to take all appropriate measures to prevent the abduction, the sale of or traffic in children for any purpose or in any form. The 1979 Convention on the Elimination of all forms of Discrimination Against Women insofar as it singles out a second group of individuals who deserve special protection.

The Convention is divided into three main sections:

— Preamble,

— The substantive Articles (Part 1; Articles 1-41), and

— The Implementation provision (Parts II & III, Articles 42 to 54).

However, the beneficiaries of the Convention are Children. Article I clarifies that, "a child means every human being below the age of 18 years unless under the law applicable to the child, majority is attained earlier." The Convention covers a variety of aspects and does this more or Jess satisfactorily. Among the happiest provisions Article 3 deserves a mention. It states that, "in all actions concerning children the best interests of the child shall be a primary consideration".

Child abuse and neglect have been defined as, "The portion of harm to the child that results from human action or inaction, this is Prescribed proximate and preventable. Child abuse is active, neglect passive maltreatment Children's interests are too any types of violations, which are disruptive elements of childrens growth. There are three main causes of child suffering; war, poverty and social disruption. They all have a common denominator which is the economic impulse that rules on the rules societies.

The 1989 UNICEF report on the conditions of children in the world reveals that during the 80s in the 37 poorest countries there has been a cut of 50 per cent on health expenditure and of 25 per cent on education. As a result, the average weight of these children has lessened, the proportion of children between 6 and 11 years attending school is family. Separation from family, community and the routines of normal life can be devastating to the children. An idea that may find its realization through the future Conventions on Right of the Child is that of stigmatizing as unlawful forms of neglect that result in an implicit denial of a positive right enshrined by the law. For instance, it would be illegal to employee a child in a job which would prevent it from attending school, thus affecting its right to education.

With regard to child's health care, a necessary warning needs to be issued, to meet these ends, on 20th November, 1989, the United Nations General Assembly has adopted by unanimity the Convention on the Rights of the Child which entered into force on 2nd September, 1990. The expression is so wide a consensus upon the opportunity of establishing a binding legal instrument for the global protection of children is the goal of an increased awareness concerning the many problems that affect children worldwide. The final affirmation of children's lights, which would ensure the world a prosperous future, can be achieved only through international cooperation, that is to say the sound implementation of the rights to development.

I. A Landmark for Children and Their Rights.

The Convention on the Rights of the Child was adopted by the General Assembly of the United Nations by its resolution 44/25 of 20 November 1989.

This was the end of a process which had begun with the preparations for the 1979 International Year of the Child. That year, discussions started on a draft convention submitted by the Government of Poland.

Children had been discussed before by the international community. Declarations on the rights of the child had been adopted by both the League of Nations (1924) and the United Nations (1959). Also, specific provisions concerning children had been incorporated in a number of human rights and humanitarian law treaties. Nevertheless, some States argued that there was a need for a comprehensive statement on children's rights which would be binding under international law.

That view was influenced by reports of grave injustices suffered by children: high infant mortality, deficient health care, limited opportunities for basic education. There were also alarming accounts of children being abused and exploited as prostitutes or in harmful jobs, of children in prison or in other difficult circumstances, and of children as refugees and victims of armed conflict.

The drafting of the Convention took place in a working group set up by the United Nations Commission on Human Rights. Government delegates formed the core of the drafting group, but representatives of United Nations bodies and specialised agencies, including the Office of the United Nations High Commissioner for Refugees (UNHCR), the International Labour Organisation (ILO), the United Nations Children's Fund (UNICEF) and the World Health Organisation (WHO), as well as a number of non-governmental organisations, took part in the deliberations. The original draft submitted by the Polish government was extensively amended and expanded through the long discussions.

The unanimous adoption of the Convention by the General Assembly paved the way for the next stage: ratifications by States and the setting up of a monitoring committee. Within less than a year, by September 1990, 20 States had legally endorsed the Convention, which thereby entered into force.

In the same month, the World Summit for Children was held in New York on the initiative of UNICEF and six States (Canada, Egypt, Mali, Mexico, Pakistan and Sweden). The Summit encouraged all States to ratify the Convention. By the end of 1990, 57 had done so, thereby becoming States parties. In 1993, the World Conference on Human Rights held at Vienna declared that the goal was universal ratification by the end of 1995. By 31 December 1995, no less than 185 countries had indeed ratified the Convention. This number is unprecedented in the field of human rights.

Universal and Forward-Looking Principles

The Convention on the Rights of the Child has the same meaning for people in all parts of the world. While laying down common standards, the Convention takes into account the different cultural, social, economic and political realities of individual States so that each State may seek its own means to implement the rights common to all.

There are four general principles enshrined in the Convention. These are meant to help with the interpretation of the Convention as a whole and thereby guide national programmes of implementation. The four principles are formulated, in particular, in articles 2, 3, 6 and 12.

Non-discrimination (art. 2): States parties must ensure that all children within their jurisdiction enjoy their rights. No child should suffer discrimination. This applies to every child, "irrespective of the child's or his or her parent's or legal guardian's race, colour, sex, language, religion, political or other opinion, national, ethnic or social origin, property, disability, birth or other status."

The essential message is equality of opportunity. Girls should be given the same opportunities as boys. Refugee children, children of foreign origin, children of indigenous or minority groups should have the same rights as all others. Children with disabilities should be given the same opportunity to enjoy an adequate standard of living.

Best interests of the child (art. 3): When the authorities of a State take decisions which affect children, the best interests of children must be a primary consideration. This principle relates to decisions by courts of law, administrative authorities, legislative bodies and both public and private social-welfare institutions. This is, of course, a fundamental message of the Convention, the implementation of which is a major challenge.

The right to life, survival and development (art. 6): The right-to-life article includes formulations about the right to survival and to development, which should be ensured 'to the maximum extent possible'. The term 'development' in this context should be interpreted in a broad sense, adding a qualitative dimension: not only physical health is intended, but also mental, emotional, cognitive, social and cultural development.

The views of the child (art 12): Children should be free to have opinions in all matters affecting them, and those views should be given due weight 'in accordance with the age and maturity of the child'. The underlying idea is that children have the right to be heard and to have their views taken seriously, including in any judicial or administrative proceedings affecting them.

Highlights of the Convention

Every child has the inherent right to life, and States shall ensure to the maximum child survival and development.

Every child has the right to a name and nationality from birth.

Children shall not be separated from their parents, except by competent authorities for their well-being.

States shall facilitate reunification of families by permitting travel into, or out of, their territories.

Parents have the primary responsibility for a child's upbringing, but States shall provide them with appropriate assistance and develop child-care institutions.

States shall protect children from physical or mental harm and neglect, including sexual abuse or exploitation.

States shall provide parentless children with suitable alternative care. The adoption process shall be carefully regulated and international agreements should be sought to provide safeguards and assure legal validity if and when adoptive parents intend to move a child from his or her country of birth.

Disabled children shall have the right to special treatment, education and care.

Children are entitled to the highest attainable standard of health. States shall ensure that health care is provided to all children, placing emphasis on preventive measures, health education and reduction of infant mortality.

Primary education shall be free and compulsory. Discipline in schools shall respect the child's dignity.

Education should prepare the child for life in a spirit of understanding, peace and tolerance.

Children shall have time to rest and play and equal opportunities for cultural and artistic activities.

States shall protect children from economic exploitation and from work that may interfere with their education or be harmful to their health or well-being.

States shall protect children from the illegal use of drugs and involvement in drug production or trafficking.

All efforts shall be made to eliminate the abduction and trafficking of children.

Capital punishment or life imprisonment shall not be imposed for crimes committed before the age of 18.

Children in detention shall be separated from adults; they must not be tortured or suffer cruel or degrading treatment.

No child under 15 shall take any part in hostilities; children exposed to armed conflict shall receive special protection.

Children of minority and indigenous populations shall freely enjoy their own culture, religion and language.

Children who have suffered mistreatment, neglect or exploitation shall receive appropriate treatment or training for recovery and rehabilitation.

Children involved in infringements of the penal law shall be treated in a way that promotes their sense of dignity and worth and aims at reintegrating them into society.

States shall make the rights set out in the Convention widely known to both adults and children.

II Constructive Monitoring

A number of international human rights bodies contribute to improving respect for the rights of the child in their particular areas of competence. In addition to the Commission on Human Rights, the Sub-Commission on Prevention of Discrimination and Protection of Minorities and its Working Group on Contemporary Forms of Slavery, which deals with aspects of the exploitation and mistreatment of children, relevant international human rights bodies include the following:

Human Rights Committee;

Committee on Economic, Social and Cultural Rights;

Committee on the Elimination of Racial Discrimination;

Committee on the Elimination of Discrimination against Women;

Committee against Torture.

These five committees are commonly referred to as treaty bodies, since they were established to monitor the implementation of particular United Nations human rights treaties by States which have ratified or acceded to the instruments in question. The creation of the Committee on the Rights of the Child, established under article 43 of the Convention, reinforced the activities of these bodies on behalf of children.

Committee on the Rights of the Child

In early 1991, a meeting of representatives of States

parties to the Convention on the Rights of the Child was convened for the first election to its monitoring body: the Committee on the Rights of the Child. Some 40 candidates had been nominated for the 10 seats. The experts elected on this first occasion came from Barbados, Brazil, Burkina Faso, Egypt, Peru, the Philippines, Portugal, the former Soviet Union, Sweden and Zimbabwe. Six were women, four men. They represented a variety of professional backgrounds, including human rights and international law, juvenile justice, social work, medicine, journalism and governmental and non-governmental work.

The Committee on the Rights of the Child currently holds three sessions a year, each of four weeks' duration. The last week is always reserved for preparation of the next session. The Committee is serviced by the United Nations Centre for Human Rights in Geneva.

Under article 44 of the Convention, States parties accept the duty to submit regular reports to the Committee on the steps they have taken to put the Convention into effect and on progress in the enjoyment of children's rights in their territories. First implementation reports are to be submitted within two years of ratification of or accession to the Convention and thereafter every five years. The first initial reports were due in September 1992. More than 70 State reports had reached the Committee by December 1995.

At its first session, in October 1991, the Committee adopted guidelines to help States parties writing and structuring their initial reports. Governments are recommended to prepare their reports according to these guidelines, which stress that the report should indicate 'factors and difficulties' encountered by the State in the implementation of the Convention—in other words, that it should be problem-oriented and self-critical. States are also asked to specify 'implementation priorities' and 'specific goals for the future'. Relevant legal texts and statistical data are to be submitted with the report.

In establishing its procedures, the Committee has emphasised the importance of a constructive dialogue with government representatives. In this context, it has also made clear that it seeks close cooperation with relevant United Nations bodies and specialised agencies, as well as with other competent bodies, including non-governmental organisations.

Working Procedure

A working group of the Committee meets prior to each of its sessions for a preliminary examination of reports received from States parties, and to prepare the Committee's discussions with the representatives of reporting States. In addition to State reports, the working group considers information provided by other human rights treaty bodies. The Committee also receives information from mechanisms established by the Commission on Human Rights to investigate human rights problems in specific countries or on thematic issues, for example the Special Rapporteurs on torture, on extrajudicial, summary or arbitrary executions, and on violence against women. A key partner in this context is the Special Rapporteur on the sale of children, child prostitution and child pornography.

General Discussions and Studies

A procedural innovation was introduced by the Committee in January 1993 when it recommended to the General Assembly that it request the Secretary-General to undertake a study on the protection of children in armed conflicts. This request was the result of a full-day 'general discussion' on the subject organised by the Committee in 1992, in which United Nations bodies and non-governmental organisations were invited to participate.

General discussions have since been held on economic exploitation of children, on the rights of the child in the family context, on the rights of the girl child, and on juvenile justice. Such thematic discussions are held about once a year and may lead to requests for studies, but can also serve as a basis for work on interpreting the articles of the Convention.

United Nations bodies and specialised agencies may take part in the deliberations of the working group and provide information. On the basis of written information received from relevant non-governmental organisations, the Committee has also often invited such organisations to take part in the preparatory meetings on State reports.

The end result of the pre-sessional working group's discussion on a State report is a 'list of issues'. This list, which gives a preliminary indication of the issues which the Committee considers to be priorities for discussion, is sent to the government concerned with an invitation to participate in a forthcoming plenary session of the Committee at which its report will be considered. The government is invited to respond to the issues in writing, before the session.

This approach gives governments the opportunity better to prepare themselves for the discussion with the Committee. Other points not included in the list of issues may emerge during the discussion, which is one reason why the Committee prefers to discuss with high level officials, such as ministers or deputy ministers, rather than with representatives who lack the authority to make decisions.

Discussions with States parties are concrete and detailed, and tend to deal with both results and processes. Although all Committee members usually take part in the deliberations, in most cases two members take the lead on each country as 'rapporteurs'.

At the very end of the process, the Committee adopts 'concluding observations', which are a statement on its consideration of a State's report. Concluding observations are meant to be widely publicised in the State party and to serve as the basis for a national debate on how to improve the enforcement of the provisions of the Convention. They therefore constitute an essential document: governments are expected to implement the recommendations contained therein.

Notes are taken at the meetings of the Committee. The United Nations publishes both press releases on the discussions and more detailed summary records of the proceedings. The Committee encourages the publication of the State party's report, the summary records and the concluding observations on each country as a consolidated document. Some governments whose reports have already been discussed have undertaken to do so.

The whole process of discussion of States parties' reports is designed to promote public debate. The Committee's discussions are normally open to the public; only the preparatory discussions of the pre-sessional working group and the drafting of the Committee's concluding observations are conducted in private. Likewise, it is important that the national reporting procedure be open and transparent; the Committee encourages such an approach.

The reporting procedure is constructive and oriented towards international cooperation and exchange of information. The aim is to define problems and discuss what corrective measures should be taken. The Committee can also transmit requests for assistance to the specialised United Nations bodies and agencies, including UNHCR, ILO, UNICEF, WHO, the United Nations Educational, Scientific and Cultural Organisation (UNESCO) and other competent bodies.

Urgent Procedure

There is no procedure outlined in the Convention for individual complaints from children or their representatives. The Committee may, however, request "further information relevant to the implementation of the Convention" (art. 44, para. 4). Such additional information may be requested from Governments if, for instance, there are indications of serious problems.

III. Making Children's Rights a Reality

General Measures of Implementation

In drafting its reporting guidelines for States, the Committee on the Rights of the Child placed emphasis on concrete implementation measures which would make a reality of the principles and provisions of the Convention. More specifically, the Committee paid special attention to necessary reforms within the spirit of the Convention and procedures for constant scrutiny of progress.

Under article 4 of the Convention, States parties are required to undertake all appropriate legislative, administrative and other measures to implement the Convention. With regard to economic, social and cultural rights, they must "undertake such measures to the maximum extent of their available resources and, where needed, within the framework of international cooperation."

An early step in the implementation process is for a State party to review its legislation and ensure that laws are consistent with the Convention. For instance, laws are needed for the protection of children against exploitation, in both the formal and informal labour market, and to ensure free and compulsory primary education.

Mechanisms may be introduced at the national and local levels to coordinate policies and monitor the implementation of the Convention, including through an ombudsman's office. The political decision-making process is important. What procedures are there to ensure that children's affairs are taken seriously in all relevant governmental structures, as well as in both the parliament and local assemblies? Are there opportunities for children themselves and their representatives to make themselves heard?

The gathering of reliable and relevant information on the situation of children is another important step to be taken. With precise data, discussions regarding remedies will be better informed and focused. Improvement of the capacity of the national statistical office can therefore be an essential contribution to the implementation of the Convention.

Other means of genuine realisation of the principles and rights enshrined in the Convention are education and training of personnel working with children, such as nursery school and other teachers, child psychologists, paediatricians and other health personnel, the police and other law enforcement personnel, social workers and others. A broader awareness and knowledge of the Convention among people at large can also serve as a basis for implementation. It is an obligation under the Convention (art. 42) for States parties to disseminate such information—to both children and adults-in understandable languages. States' reports on implementation must also be made 'widely available to the public' (art. 44, para. 6).

What is meant by the wording that States should implement economic, social and cultural rights "to the maximum extent of their available resources" (art. 4)? How does the Convention relate to financial constraints?

The Convention recognises that some of the more costly reforms cannot take place overnight. It specifies, for instance, that the rights to health care (art. 24) and education (art. 28) may be achieved 'progressively'. It also makes it clear that there is an international duty to assist other States in their efforts to protect children's rights—although each State party always has its own obligations. Rich or poor, a State must allocate the maximum extent of its available resources for the implementation of the Convention: priority should be given to children.

Donor countries are encouraged to review their development cooperation programmes in the light of the Convention. At the same time, developing countries may identify a need for international cooperation in their reports on their implementation of the Convention.

Advisory Services

The Convention on the Rights of the Child and the Committee on the Rights of the Child attach special importance to international cooperation and assistance as ways of achieving the effective protection of children's rights. Article 45 (b) authorises the Committee to transmit to the relevant agencies and bodies any reports from States parties that contain a request or indicate a need for technical advice or assistance, along with the Committee's observations and suggestions. The Committee often makes recommendations for technical cooperation in its concluding observations addressed to States parties as an outcome of the reporting dialogue.

The United Nations High Commissioner for Human Rights, whose mandate includes the enhancement of international cooperation for the promotion and protection of all human rights, is providing assistance in this regard and encourages governments to respond favourably to the Committee's recommendations.

ANNEX III

General guidelines regarding the form and contents of initial reports to be submitted by States parties under article 44, paragraph 1 (a), of the Convention on the Rights of the Child.

Introduction

1. Article 44, paragraph 1, of the Convention on the Rights of the Child provides that:

"States parties undertake to submit to the Committee, through the Secretary-General of the United Nations, reports on the measures they have adopted which give effect to the rights recognised herein and on the progress made on the enjoyment of those rights:

"(a) Within two years of the entry into force of the Convention for the State Party concerned;

"(b) Thereafter every five years."

2. Article 44 of the Convention further provides, in paragraph 2, that reports submitted to the Committee on the Rights of the Child shall indicate factors and difficulties, if any, affecting the degree of fulfilment of the obligations under the Convention and shall also contain sufficient

information to provide the Committee with a comprehensive understanding of the implementation of the Convention in the country concerned.

3. The Committee believes that the process of preparing a report for submission to the Committee offers an important occasion for conducting a comprehensive review of the various measures undertaken to harmonise national law and policy with the Convention and to monitor progress made in the enjoyment of the rights set forth in the Convention. Additionally, the process should be one that encourages and facilitates popular participation and public scrutiny of government policies.

4. The Committee considers that the reporting process entails an ongoing reaffirmation by States parties of their commitment to respect and ensure observance of the rights set forth in the Convention and serves as the essential vehicle for the establishment of a meaningful dialogue between the States parties and the Committee.

5. The general part of States parties' reports, relating to matters that are of interest to monitoring bodies under various international human rights instruments, should be prepared in accordance with the "Consolidated guidelines for the initial part of the reports of States parties", as contained in document HRI/1991/1. The present guidelines, which were adopted by the Committee on the Rights of the Child at its 22nd meeting, held on 15 October 1991, should be followed in the preparation of the initial reports of States parties relating to the implementation of the Convention on the Rights of the Child.

6. The Committee intends to formulate guidelines

for the preparation of periodic reports that are to be submitted pursuant to article 44, paragraph 1(b), of the Convention in due course.

7. Reports should be accompanied by copies of the principal legislative and other texts as well as detailed statistical information and indicators referred to therein, which will be made available to members of the Committee. It should be noted, however, that for reasons of economy they will not be translated or reproduced for general distribution. It is desirable, therefore, that when a text is not actually quoted in or annexed to the report itself, the report should contain sufficient information to be understood without reference to those texts.

8. The provisions of the Convention have been grouped under different sections, equal importance being attached to all the rights recognised by the Convention.

I. General measures of implementation

9. Under this Section, States parties are requested to provide relevant information pursuant to article 4 of the Convention, including information on:

   a) The measures taken to harmonise national law and policy with the provisions of the Convention;

   b) Existing or planned mechanisms at the national or local level for coordinating policies relating to children and for monitoring the implementation of the Convention.

10. In addition, States parties are requested to describe the measures that have been taken or are foreseen, pursuant to article 42 of the

Convention, to make the principles and provisions of the Convention widely known, by appropriate and active means, to adults and children alike.

11. States parties are also requested to describe those measures undertaken or foreseen, pursuant to article 44, paragraph 6, of the Convention, to make their reports widely available to the public at large in their own countries.

II. Definition of the child

12. Under this section States parties are requested to provide relevant information, pursuant to article one of the Convention, concerning the definition of a child under their laws and regulations. In particular, States parties are requested to provide information on the age of attainment of majority and on the legal minimum ages established for various purposes, including legal or medical counselling without parental consent, end of compulsory education, part-time employment, full-time employment, hazardous employment, sexual consent, marriage, voluntary enlistment into the armed forces, conscription into the armed forces, voluntarily giving testimony in court, criminal liability, deprivation of liberty, imprisonment and consumption of alcohol or other controlled substances.

III. General Principles

13. Relevant information, including the principal legislative, judicial, administrative or other measures in force or foreseen, factors and difficulties encountered and progress achieved in implementing the provisions of the Convention, and implementation priorities and specific goals for the future, should be provided in respect of :

a) Non-discrimination (art. 2);

b) Best interests of the child (art. 3);

c) The right to life, survival and development (art. 6);

d) Respect for the views of the child (art. 12).

14. In addition, States parties are encouraged to provide relevant information on the application of these principles in the implementation of articles listed elsewhere in these guidelines.

IV. Civil rights and the freedoms

15. States parties are requested to provide relevant information, including the principal legislative, judicial, administrative or other measures in force; factors and difficulties encountered and progress achieved in implementing the relevant provisions of the Convention; and implementation priorities and specific goals for the future, in respect of:

a) Name and nationality (art. 7);

b) Preservation of identity (art. 8);

c) Freedom of expression (art. 13);

d) Access to appropriate information (art. 17);

e) Freedom of thought, conscience and religion (art. 14);

f) Freedom of association and of peaceful assembly (art. 15);

g) Protection of privacy (art. 16);

h) The right not to be subjected to torture or other cruel, inhuman or degrading treatment or punishment (art. 37 (a)).

V. Family environment and alternative care

16. Under this sectioon, States parties are requested to provide relevant information, including the principal legislative, judicial, administrative or other measures in force, particularly how the principles of the "best interests of the child" and "respect for the views of the child" are reflected therein; factors and difficulties encountered and progress achieved in implementing the relevant provisions of the Convention; and implementation priorities and specific goals for the future, in respect of:

    a) Parental guidance (art. 5);

    b) Parental responsibilities (art. 18, paras. 1 and 2);

    c) Separation from parents (art. 9);

    d) Family reunification (art. 10);

    e) Recovery of maintenance for the child (art. 27, para. 4);

    f) Children deprived of a family environment (art. 20);

    g) Adoption (art. 21);

    h) Illicit transfer and non-return (art. 11);

    i) Abuse and neglect (art. 19), including physical and psychological recovery and social reinte-gration (art. 39);

    j) Periodic review of placement (art. 25).

17. In addition, States parties are requested to provide information on the numbers of children per year within the reporting period in each of the following groups, disaggregated by age group, sex, ethnic or national background and rural or urban environment: homeless children, abused or

neglected children taken into protective custody, children placed in foster care, children placed in institutional care, children placed through domestic adoption, children entering the country through intercountry adoption procedures and children leaving the country through inter-country adoption procedures.

18. States parties are encouraged to provide additional relevant statistical information and indicators relating to children covered in this section.

VI.Basic health welfare

19. Under this section, States parties are requested to provide relevant information, including the principal legislative, judicial, administrative or other measures in force; the institutional infrastructure for implementing policy in this area, particularly monitoring strategies and mechanisms; and factors and difficulties encountered and progress achieved in implementing the relevant provisions of the Convention, in respect of :

    a) Survival and development (art. 6, para. 2);

    b) Disabled children (art. 23);

    c) Health and health services (art. 24);

    d) Social security and child-care services and facilities (art. 26 and art. 18);

    e) Standard of living (art. 27, paras. 1-3).

20. In addition to information provided under paragraph 9 (b) of these guidelines, States parties are requested to specify the nature and extent of cooperation with local and national organisations of a governmental or non-governmental nature, such as institutions of social workers, concerning

the implementation of this area of the Convention. States parties are encouraged to provide additional relevant statistical information and indicators relating to children covered in this section.

VII. Education, leisure and culture activities

21. Under this section, States parties are requested to provide relevant information, including the principal legislative, judicial, administrative or other measures in force; the institutional infrastructure for imple-menting policy in this area, particularly monitoring strategies and mechanisms; and factors and difficulties encountered and progress achieved in implementing the relevant provisions of the Convention, in respect of:

    a) Education, including vocational training and guidance (art. 28);

    b) Aims of education (art. 29);

    c) Leisure, recreation and cultural activities (art. 31).

22. In addition to information provided under paragraph 9 (b) of these guidelines, States parties are requested to specify the nature and extent of cooperation with local and national organisations of a governmental or non-governmental nature, such as institutions of social workers, concerning the implementation of this area of the Convention. States parties are encouraged to provide additional relevant statistical information and indicators relating to children covered in this section.

VIII. Special protection measures

23. Under this section, States parties are requested to

provide relevant information, including the principal legislative, judicial, administrative or other measures in force; factors and difficulties encountered and progress achieved in implementing the relevant provisions of the Convention; and implementation priorities and specific goals for the future, in respect of:

a) Children in situations of emergency:

   i) Refugee children (art. 22);

   ii) Children in armed conflicts (art. 38), including physical and psychological recovery and social reintegration (art. 39);

b) Children in conflict with the law:

   i) The administration of juvenile justice (art. 40);

   ii) Children deprived of their liberty, including any form of detention, imprisonment or placement in custodial settings (art. 37 (b), (c) and (d);

   iii) The sentencing of juveniles, in particular the prohibition of capital punishment and life imprisonment (art. 37 (a));

   iv) Physical and psychological recovery and social reintegration (art. 39);

c) Children in situations of exploitation, including physical and psychological recovery and social reintegration (art. 39):

   i) Economic exploitation, including child labour (art. 32);

   ii) Drug abuse (art. 33);

   iii) Sexual exploitation and sexual abuse (art. 34);

iv) Other forms of exploitation (art. 36);

v) Sale, trafficking and abduction (art. 35);

d) Children belonging to a minority or an indigenous group (art. 30).

24. Additionally, States parties are encouraged to provide specific statistical information and indicators relevant to the children covered by paragraph 23.

4

Women's Rights

Violence affects the lives of millions of women worldwide, in all socio-economic and educational classes. It cuts across cultural and religious barriers, impeding the right of women to participate fully in society. Violence against women takes a dismaying variety of forms, from domestic abuse and rape to child marriages and female circumcision. All are violations of the most fundamental human rights.

In a statement to the Fourth World Conference on Women in Beijing in September 1995, the then United Nations Secretary-General, Boutros Boutros-Ghali, said that violence against women is a universal problem that must be universally condemned. But he said that the problem continues to grow.

The Secretary-General noted that domestic violence alone is on the increase. Studies in 10 countries, he said, have found that between 17 per cent and 38 per cent of women have suffered physical assaults by a partner.

In the Platform for Action, the core document of the Beijing Conference, Governments declared that "violence against women constitutes a violation of basic human rights and is an obstacle to the achievement of the objectives of equality, development and peace."

The Work of the Special Rapporteur

The issue of the advancement of women's rights has concerned the United Nations since the Organisation's founding. Yet the alarming global dimensions of female-targeted violence were not explicitly acknowledged by the international community until December 1993, when the United Nations General Assembly adopted the Declaration on the Elimination of Violence against Women.

Until that point, most governments tended to regard violence against women largely as a private matter between individuals, and not as a pervasive human rights problem requiring State intervention.

In view of the alarming growth in the number of cases of violence against women throughout the world, the Commission on Human Rights adopted resolution 1994/45 of 4 March 1994, in which it decided to appoint the Special Rapporteur on violence against women, including its causes and consequences.

As a result of these steps, the problem of violence against women has been drawing increasing political attention.

The Special Rapporteur has a mandate to collect and analyse comprehensive data and to recommend measures aimed at eliminating violence at the international, national and regional levels. The mandate is threefold :

— To collect information on violence against women and its causes and consequences from sources such as governments, treaty bodies, specialised agencies and inter-governmental and non-governmental organisations, and to respond effectively to such information;

— To recommend measures and ways and means, at the national, regional and international levels, to eliminate violence against women and its causes, and to remedy its consequences;

— To work closely with other special rapporteurs, special representatives, working groups and independent experts of the Commission on Human Rights.

Incest, Rape and Domestic Violence

Some females fall prey to violence before they are born, when expectant parents abort their unborn daughters, hoping for sons instead. In other societies, girls are subjected to such traditional practices as circumcision, which leave them maimed and traumatised. In others, they are compelled to marry at an early age, before they are physically, mentally or emotionally mature.

Women are victims of incest, rape and domestic violence that often lead to trauma, physical handicap or death.

And rape is still being used as a weapon of war, a strategy used to subjugate and terrify entire communities. Soldiers deliberately impregnate women of different ethnic groups and abandon them when it is too late to get an abortion.

The Platform for Action adopted at the Fourth World Conference on Women declared that rape in armed conflict is a war crime and could, under certain circumstances, be considered genocide.

Secretary-General Boutros-Ghali told the Beijing Conference that more women today were suffering directly from the effects of war and conflict than ever before in history.

"There is a deplorable trend towards the organised humiliation of women, including the crime of mass rape," the Secretary-General said. "We will press for international legal action against those who perpetrate organised violence against women in time of conflict."

A preliminary report in 1994 by the Special Rapporteur, Ms. Radhika Coomaraswamy, focused on three areas of concern where women are particularly vulnerable: in the family (including domestic violence, traditional practices, infanticide); in the community (including rape, sexual assault, commercialised violence such as trafficking in women, labour exploitation, female migrant workers (etc.); and by the State (including violence against women in detention as well as violence against women in situations of armed conflict and against refugee women).

In the Platform for Action adopted at the Beijing Conference, violence against women and the human rights of women are two of the 12 critical areas of concern identified as the main obstacles to the advancement of women.

Commitments by Governments

Governments agreed to adopt and implement national legislation to end violence against women and to work actively to ratify all international agreements that relate to violence against women. They agreed that there should be shelters, legal aid and other services for girls and women at risk, and counselling and rehabilitation for perpetrators.

Governments also pledged to adopt appropriate measures in the field of education to modify the social and cultural patterns of conduct of men and women. And the Platform called on media professionals to develop self-regulatory guidelines to address violent, degrading and pornographic materials while encouraging non-stereotyped, balanced and diverse images of women.

Defining Gender-based Abuse

The Declaration on the Elimination of Violence against Women is the first international human rights instrument to exclusively and explicitly address the issue of violence against women. It affirms that the phenomenon violates, impairs or nullifies women's human rights and their exercise of fundamental freedoms.

The Declaration provides a definition of gender-based abuse, calling it "any act of gender-based violence that results in, or is likely to result in, physical, sexual or psychological harm or suffering to women, including threats of such acts, coercion or arbitrary deprivation of liberty, whether occurring in public or in private life."

The definition is amplified in article 2 of the Declaration, which identifies three areas in which violence commonly takes place :

— Physical, sexual and psychological violence that occurs in the family, including battering; sexual abuse of female children in the household; dowry-related violence; marital rape; female genital mutilation and other traditional practices harmful to women; non-spousal violence; and violence related to exploitation;

— Physical, sexual and psychological violence that occurs within the general community, including rape; sexual abuse; sexual harassment and intimidation at work, in educational institutions and elsewhere; trafficking in women; and forced prostitution; and

— Physical, sexual and psychological violence perpetrated or condoned by the State, wherever it occurs.

The importance of the question of violence against women was emphasised over the last decade through the holding of several expert group meetings sponsored by the United Nations to draw attention to the extent and severity of the problem. In September 1992, the United Nations Commission on the Status of Women established a special Working Group and gave it a mandate to draw up a draft declaration on violence against women.

The following year, the United Nations Commission for Human Rights, in resolution 1993/46 of 3 March, condemned all forms of violence and violations of human rights directed specifically against women.

The World Conference on Human Rights, held in Vienna in June 1993, laid extensive groundwork for eliminating violence against women. In the Vienna Declaration and Programme of Action, governments declared that the United Nations system and Member States should work towards the elimination of violence against women in public and private life; of all forms of sexual harassment, exploitation and trafficking in women; of gender bias in the administration of justice; and of any conflicts arising between the rights of women and the harmful effects of certain traditional or customary practices, cultural prejudices and religious extremism.

The document also declared that "violations of the human rights of women in situations of armed conflicts are violations of the fundamental principles of international human rights and humanitarian law," and that all viola-tions of this kind—including murder, systematic rape, sexual slavery and forced pregnancy—"require a particularly effective response."

Kinds of Violence against Women

Violence against women in the family occurs in developed and developing countries alike. It has long been considered a private matter by bystanders—including neighbours, the community and government. But such private matters have a tendency to become public tragedies.

In the United States, a woman is beaten every 18 minutes. Indeed, domestic violence is the leading cause of injury among women of reproductive age in the United States. Between 22 and 35 per cent of women who visit emergency rooms are there for that reason.

The highly publicised trial of O. J. Simpson, the retired United States football player acquitted of the murder of his former wife and a male friend of hers, helped focus international media attention on the issue of domestic violence and spousal abuse.

In Peru, 70 per cent of all crimes reported to the police involve women beaten by their husbands. In Pakistan, Prime Minister Benazir Bhutto strongly defended a 35-year-old mother of two who was severely burned by her husband in a domestic dispute.

"There is no excuse for such a behaviour," the Prime Minister declared after visiting the hospitalised victim. "My presence here is to send a message to all those who violate Islamic teachings and defy laws of the land with their inhuman treatment of women. This will not be tolerated."

According to the Human Rights Commission of Pakistan, in the 400 cases of domestic violence reported in 1993 in the province of Punjab, nearly half ended with the death of the wife. According to the Special Rapporteur's report, many governments now recognise the importance of protecting victims of domestic abuse and taking action to punish perpetrators. The establishment of structures allowing officials to deal with cases of domestic violence and its consequences is a significant step towards the elimination of violence against women in the family.

The Special Rapporteur's report highlights the importance of adopting legislation that provides for prosecution of the offender. It also stresses the importance of specialised training for law enforcement authorities as well as medical and legal professionals, and of the establishment of community support services for victims, including access to information and shelters.

In many countries, women fall victim to traditional practices that violate their human rights. The persistence of the problem has much to do with the fact that most of these physically and psychologically harmful customs are deeply rooted in the tradition and culture of society.

According to the World Health Organisation, 85 million to 115 million girls and women in the population have undergone some form of female genital mutilation and suffer from its adverse health effects.

Every year an estimated two million young girls undergo this procedure. Most live in Africa and Asia, but an increasing number can be found among immigrant and refugee families in Western Europe and North America. Indeed, the practice has been outlawed in some European countries.

In France, a Malian was convicted in a criminal court after his baby girl died of a female circumcision-related infection. The procedure had been performed on the infant at home.

In Canada, fear of being forced to undergo circumcision can be grounds for asylum. A Nigerian woman was granted refugee status since she felt that she might be persecuted in her home country because of her refusal to inflict genital mutilation on her baby daughter.

There is a growing consensus that the best way to eliminate these practices is through educational campaigns that emphasise their dangerous health consequences. Several governments have been actively promoting such campaigns in their countries.

Son preference affects women in many countries, particularly in Asia. Its consequences can be anything from foetal or female infanticide to neglect of the girl-child over her brother in terms of such essential needs as nutrition, basic health care and education.

In China and India, some women choose to terminate their pregnancies when expecting daughters but carry their pregnancies to term when expecting sons.

According to reports from India, genetic testing for sex selection has become a booming business, especially in the country's northern regions. Indian gender-detection clinics drew protests from women's groups after the appearance of advertisements suggesting that it was better to spend $38 now to terminate a female foetus than $3,800 later on her dowry.

A study of amniocentesis procedures conducted in a large Bombay hospital found that 95.5 per cent of foetuses identified as female were aborted, compared with a far smaller percentage of male foetuses. The problem of son preference is present in many other countries as well. Asked how many children he had fathered, the former United States boxing champion Muhammad Ali told an interviewer: "One boy and seven mistakes."

Dowry-related Violence and Early Marriage

In some countries, weddings are preceded by the payment of an agreed-upon dowry by the bride's family. Failure to pay the dowry can lead to violence.

In Bangladesh, a bride whose dowry was deemed too small was disfigured after her husband threw acid on her face. In India, an average of five women a day are burned in dowry-related disputes—and many more cases are never reported.

Early marriage, especially without the consent of the girl, is another form of human rights violation. Early marriage followed by multiple pregnancies can affect the health of women for life.

The report of the Special Rapporteur has documented the destructive effects of marriage of female children under 18 and has urged governments to adopt relevant legislation.

Violence in the Community

Rape can occur anywhere, even in the family, where it can take the form of marital rape or incest. It occurs in the community, where a woman can fall prey to any abuser. It also occurs in situations of armed conflict and in refugee camps.

In the United States, national statistics indicate that a women is raped every six minutes. In 1995, the case of a Brazilian jogger raped and murdered in New

York City's Central Park drew international attention once again to the problem. The incident occurred only a few years after an earlier sensational jogger-assault case in which the victim— an American assaulted in the same general area of the park —barely survived after her assailants left her for dead.

Relations between residents of the Japanese island of Okinawa and American GIs were thrown into turmoil in 1995 after two marines and a sailor allegedly kidnapped and raped a 12-year-old girl.

The Special Rapporteur's report underlines the importance of education to sensitise the public about the special horrors of rape, and of sensitivity training for the police and hospital staff who work with victims.

Sexual Assault within Marriage

In many countries sexual assault by a husband on his wife is not considered to be a crime: a wife is expected to submit. It is thus very difficult in practice for a woman to prove that sexual assault has occurred unless she can demonstrate serious injury.

The report of the Special Rapporteur noted that light sentences in sexual assault cases send the wrong message to perpetrators and to the public at large: that female sexual victimisation is unimportant.

Sexual harassment in the workplace is a growing concern for women. Employers abuse their authority to seek sexual favours from their female co-workers or subordinates, sometimes promising promotions or other forms of career advancement or simply creating an untenable and hostile work environment. Women who refuse to give in to such unwanted sexual advances often run the risk of anything from demotion to dismissal.

But in recent years more women have been coming forward to report such practices—some taking their cases to court.

In her report, the Special Rapporteur stressed that sexual harassment constitutes a form of sex discrimination. "It not only degrades the woman," the report noted, "but reinforces and reflects the idea of non-professionalism on the part of women workers, who are consequently regarded as less able to perform their duties than their male colleagues."

Prostitution and Trafficking

Many women are forced into prostitution either by their parents, husbands or boyfriends—or as a result of the difficult economic and social conditions in which they find themselves. They are also lured into prostitution, sometimes by 'mail-order bride' agencies that promise to find them a husband or a job in a foreign country. As a result, they very often find themselves illegally confined in brothels in slavery-like conditions where they are physically abused and their passports withheld.

Most women initially victimised by sexual traffickers have little inkling of what awaits them. They generally get a very small percentage of what the customer pays to the pimp or the brothel owner. Once they are caught up in the system there is practically no way out, and they find themselves in a very vulnerable situation.

Since prostitution is illegal in many countries, it is difficult for prostitutes to come forward and ask for protection if they become victims of rape or want to escape from brothels. Customers, on the other hand, are rarely the object of penal laws. In Thailand, prostitutes who complain to the police are often arrested and sent back to the brothels upon payment of a fine. The extent of trafficking in women and girl children has reached alarming proportions, especially in Asian countries.

Many women and girl children are trafficked across borders, often with the complicity of border guards. In one incident, five young prostitutes burned to death in a brothel fire because they had been chained to their beds. At the same time, sex tours of developing countries are a well-organised industry in several European and other industrialised countries.

The Special Rapporteur has called on governments to take action to protect young girls from being recruited as prostitutes and to closely monitor recruiting agencies.

Female migrant workers typically leave their countries for better living conditions and better pay—but the real benefits accrue to both the host countries and the countries of origin. For home countries, money sent home by migrant workers is an important source of hard currency, while receiving countries are able to find workers for low-paying jobs that might otherwise go unfilled.

But migrant workers themselves fare badly, and sometimes tragically. Many become virtual slaves, subject to abuse and rape by their employers. In the Middle East and Persian Gulf region, there are an estimated 1.2 million women, mainly Asians, who are employed as domestic servants. According to the independent human rights group Middle East Watch, female migrant workers in Kuwait often suffer beatings and sexual assaults at the hands of their employers.

The police are often of little help. In many cases, women who report being raped by their employers are sent back to the employer—or are even assaulted at the police station.

Working conditions are often appalling, and employers prevent women from escaping by seising their passports or identity papers.

The report of the Special Rapporteur draws attention to the fact that there are many international instruments that can be used to prevent abuse against migrant women and suggests some measures to protect the human rights of migrant women.

Pornography

Another concern highlighted in the Special Rapporteur's report is pornography, which represents a form of violence against women that "glamorises the degradation and maltreatment of women and asserts their subordinate function as mere receptacles for male lust."

Violence against women by the very people who are supposed to protect them—members of the law enforcement and criminal justice systems—is widespread.

Women are physically or verbally abused; they also suffer sexual and physical torture. According to Amnesty International, thousands of women held in custody are routinely raped in police detention centres worldwide. The report of the Special Rapporteur underlines the necessity for States to prosecute those accused of abusing women while in detention and to hold them accountable for their actions.

Rape has been widely used as a weapon of war whenever armed conflicts arise between different parties. It has been used all over the world: in Chiapas, Mexico, in Rwanda, in Kuwait, in Haiti, in Colombia.

Women and girl children are frequently victims of gang rape committed by soldiers from all sides of a conflict. Such acts are done mainly to trample the dignity of the victims. Rape has been used to reinforce the policy of ethnic cleansing in the war that has been tearing apart the former Yugoslavia.

The so-called 'comfort women'—young girls of colonised or occupied countries who became sexual slaves to Japanese soldiers during the Second World War—have dramatised the problem in a historical context. Many of these women are now coming forward and demanding compensation for their suffering from Japanese authorities. "Such rape is the symbolic rape of the community, the destruction of the fundamental elements of a society and culture—the ultimate humiliation of the male enemy," the report by the Special Rapporteur noted. It stressed the need to hold the perpetrators of such crimes fully accountable.

Women and children form the great majority of refugee populations all over the world and are especially vulnerable to violence and exploitation. In refugee camps, they are raped and abused by military and immigration personnel, bandit groups, male refugees and rival ethnic groups. They are also forced into prostitution.

In her report, the Special Rapporteur proposes the following measures to be taken for the protection of women and girls in refugee camps: improvement of security, deployment of trained female officers at all points of the refugees' journey, participation of women in organisational structures of the camps and prosecution of government and military personnel responsible for abuse against refugee women.

In recent years some countries have taken significant steps towards improving laws relating to violence against women. For example :

— In July 1991, Mexico revised its rape law in several important ways. A provision was eliminated that allowed a man who raped a minor to avoid prosecution if he agreed to marry her. Now judges are required to hand down a decision regarding access to an abortion within five working days.

— On 9 June 1994, the Organisation of American States adopted the Inter-American Convention to Prevent, Punish and Eradicate Violence against Women (also called Convention of Belam do Para), a new international instrument that recognises all gender-based violence as an abuse of human rights. This Convention provides an individual right of petition and a right for non-governmental organisations to lodge complaints with the Inter-American Commission of Human Rights.

— In Australia, a National Committee on Violence against Women was established to coordinate the development of policy, legislation and law enforcement at the national level as well as community education on violence against women.

— In 1991, the government of Canada announced a new four-year Family Violence Initiative intended to mobilise community action, strengthen Canada's legal framework, establish services on Indian reserves and in Inuit communities, develop resources to help victims and stop offenders, and provide housing for abused women and children.

— In Turkey, a Ministry of State for Women was established whose main goals are, among others, to promote women's rights and strengthen their role in economic, social, political and cultural life. Legal measures are being adopted towards the elimination of violence against women. The establishment of special courts to deal with violence is envisaged. Psychological treatment for abused women is also planned, along with the establishment of women's shelters around the country. Specially trained female police officers could provide assistance to victims of violence.

— In Burkina Faso, a strong advertising campaign by the government as well as television and radio programmes on the unhealthy practice of genital mutilation were launched to educate and raise public awareness about the dangerous consequences of such an 'operation'. A National Anti-Excision Committee was established in 1990 by the present head of State. Today, the practice of genital mutilation has been eliminated in some villages of Burkina Faso. In others, there has been an incredible drop in the number of girls excised: only 10 per cent of the girls are excised compared to 100 per cent 10 years ago.

— Some countries have introduced police units specially trained for dealing with spousal assault. In Brazil, specific police stations have been designated to deal with women's issues, including domestic violence. These police stations are staffed entirely by women.

These examples illustrate some steps taken at the national level towards the eradication of violence against women. Combating and eradicating this scourge require enhanced and concerted efforts to protect women at the local, national and international levels.

States have tended to adopt a passive attitude when confronted by cases of violations of women's rights by private actors. Most laws fail to protect victims or to punish perpetrators. Passing laws to criminalise violence against women is an important way to redefine the limits of acceptable behaviour. States should ensure that national legislation, once adopted, does not go unenforced. State responsibility is clearly underlined in article 4 of the Declaration on the Elimination of Violence against Women, which stipulates that "States should exercise due diligence to prevent, investigate and, in accordance with national legislation, punish acts of violence against women, whether those acts are perpetrated by the State or by private persons."

Any approach designed to combat violence must be twofold, addressing the root causes of the problem and treating its manifestations. Society at large, including judges and police officers, must be educated to change the social attitudes and beliefs that encourage male violence.

The meaning of gender and sexuality and the balance of power between women and men at all levels of society must be reviewed. Combating violence against women requires challenging the way that gender roles and power relations are articulated in society. In many countries women have a low status. They are considered as inferior and there is a strong belief that men are superior to them and even own them.

Changing people's attitude and mentality towards women will take a long time—at least a generation, many believe, and perhaps longer. Nevertheless, raising awareness of the issue of violence against women, and educating boys and men to view women as valuable partners in life, in the development of a society and in the attainment of peace are just as important as taking legal steps to protect women's human rights.

It is also important in order to prevent violence that non-violent means be used to resolve conflict between all members of society. Breaking the cycle of abuse will require concerted collaboration and action between governmental and non-governmental actors, including educators, health-care authorities, legislators, the judiciary and the mass media.

Women's Rights, the Responsibility of All

The human rights of women and girl child are an inalienable, integral and indivisible part of universal human rights. The full and equal participation of women in political, civil, economic, social and cultural life, at the national, regional and international levels, and the eradication of all forms of discrimination on grounds of sex are priority objectives of the international community. (The Vienna Declaration and Programme of Action, Part 1, Para 18)

5

Religion and Human Rights

Indian culture and civilisation were based on certain spiritual and ethical values which may be taken as Dharma which is not religious in true sense of the term. The term 'Dharma' etymologically means which upholds, supports and nourishes the society. It maintains stability of the social order and promotes well-being and progress of the mankind. Dharma, is thus, asserts to oneself good conscious and conscientious principles that spring from and aims at increasing one, s happiness and well-being. It relieves from ignorance, fear, disease and other evils and cherishes and moulds fellow-feeling, brotherhood and amity and other good feelings. The Vedas and Puranas contain basic principles of Dharma, Artha, Kama and Moksha.

Dharma was practically dominating other aspects of Indian life in the past. It influenced substantially social, economic and political life and seemed to have moulded and welded into a social order which was a unified configuration of ideas, ideals and practices that are mostly ethical as well as spiritual. The fundamental principles propounded in the Vedas aim at securing happiness to all, which constitute Dharma. These were all basic human rights incorporated in the Smritis 'and Puranas in various rules and regulations, customs and usages. Anything which goes against these principles were rejected as invalid. Dharma as enunciated by Vyas, the author of Mahabharat, also says that when there is conflict between what is Dharma in the Vedas and provisions in the Smritis, Puranas, etc., what is declared in the Vedas shall prevail. These principles enable us to decide what is Dharma and what is Adharma? The principles of Dharma show that human rights are valuable and eternal.

These are identified and are recognised in Indian civilisation from time immemorial as the basic conditions for peaceful and progressive life. These are the values included in the human rights subsequently incorporated in the Universal Declaration of Human Rights and also in various Fundamental Rights contained in Part III of the Constitution of India. Similarly, Artha (Economic Prosperity) and Kama (Pleasure of Sensuous activities) of the ancient India although superseded and dominated by Dharma were not entirely neglected or under-estimated. It, of course, deals with worldly affairs and mundane activities of the mankind but were profoundly influenced by religious pursuits. Dharma was deeply intermingled with political, economic and social activities.

The various purposes of state administration or government was to ensure smooth functioning of Dharma and economic and spiritual well-being of the individual. The King or Head of the State was mainly responsible for providing adequate facilities for material advancement and also to spiritual and ethical well-being of people. Moksha or salvation was the ultimate reality for the Indians, and it aims at not only salvation from the birth but also from ignorance and poverty of all kinds. It was closely related to spiritual and religious pursuits of the people. Dharma also is not aloof from the well-being of the people. Rather all the individuals regard moksha as the most alluring spiritual well-being to be relished and the most valuable, and ethical, metaphysical wealth created through religious activities.

Thus Dharma was taken as the ultimate reality and basic to all spiritual activities of the ancient Indians. The material attainment through Artha and Kama-two most important worldly pursuits were an integral part of Dharma and the purpose of all these achievements was the realisation of the ultimate end of life-Moksha. Individual was considered basic unit of the society and he has to be given all the facilities and conditions for attainment of excellence in all these directions.

These facilities and conditions are the basic human rights. These are regarded as the instruments for achieving objectives of Dharma, Artha, Kama and Moksha. These four cardinal values (chaturbarg) constituted the ancient cultural heritage-of India. Although there were some contradictions and contentions to the basic value, these principles ultimately pre-dominated the spiritual life of Indians. Charvaka was one of the pioneers and powerful exponents of materialism. His words were sweet and alluring for Charu means nice and Vaka means words. But he did not drift away Indians in general.

There were references of Charvaka philosophy in Vedas, Puranas and epics of Ramayana and Mahabharat in an interesting manner but could not have lasting effect on the spiritual life of Indians, incidence of Charvaka's pleasant philosophy is as follows:

> On the whole, Artha and Kama were the main aims of life according to the Charvaka's

> philosophy. The worldly pleasure was rather the ultimate end of or aim of materialism as advocated by this school of philosophy However, Vedas and vedic philosophy did not accept the materialism of Charvaka and as such it was mostly rejected by the vedic culture of India. It was rather criticised and condemned by most of the philosophical schools of India, as it was gross egoistic hedonism. It was also felt that such individualistic and gross material interest would destroy social structure and frame of human relations. The pleasure seeking worldly pursuit would spoil the ethical and cultural values which are the bases of human rights.

The materialistic philosophy of Charvaka was, however, refined by some thinkers. For instance, Vatsayana, the famous author of Kamasutra was called materialist alongwith a few others. He pleaded for pleasures of life and believed in the positive aspects of life of desirable happiness in a civilised manner. Charvaka laid emphasis on spiritual discipline, self-control and self-sacrifice to some extent which are the basic human rights i.e., restraint of one's pleasure for allowing others to live gracefully.

The entire ancient Indian civilisation was based on a kind of realistic idealism. The sweet reconciliation was made between secular and spiritual spheres and compromises made in between. Rather both of them were wonderfully blended into a harmonious whole. Gupta has rightly observed, "Indian life in all its respects both in daily course and more important relations was bound up with religious observation called to bring about the realisation of the ultimate truth by progressive course of mental and moral discipline.

Physical body was looked upon as a scared duty. Chaturbarg or four types of principles viz., Dharma,

Artha, Kama and Moksha ensure and promote a cluster of human rights like Right to Happiness, Right to Equality, Right to Religion, Right to Protection, Right to Education, Right to Social Security, Right to Humane Treatment and Right to justice, etc. All these human rights are duty-based and the society cannot guarantee such rights without reciprocal duties. These rights are discussed as follows:

Right to happiness

Man is apt to avoid unhappiness and seeks happiness. Hence, it is a natural human right to be happy and without happiness life becomes dull and dreamy. Right to Happiness is, therefore, essential for every individual and has been recognised as salt of life. Since it is the most important human right and comprises all rights relating to self-fulfilment and satisfaction, it is very much comprehensive. Every human being has the capacity to fulfil his/her desires through his/her efforts and secure happiness for himself/herself and for others who are his near and dear ones to him/her.

Human life is full of sorrows and sufferings and pleasure and happiness. Happiness which is beyond one's reach may create unhappiness. Some unhappiness is created by one's inadequacies and some are by various accidents and accumulated whether man made or natural. Miseries which can be avoided create more unhappiness and miseries which cannot be avoided are tolerated easily. Individual being rational has to take decisions judiciously and discharges his/her responsibilities for achieving his pleasure and happiness. It is natural that every human activity has certain objectives which may be personal or otherwise and man performs his work as a result of the impulse of his desire, or Kama.

The force behind man's every action is his/her desire or Kama whether for getting good food or cloth or wealth and for other valuables i.e., Artha for securing comfort and pleasure.

The cause of unhappiness of human being was to be wrong or evil actions of their own or those of other human beings. The reckless desire of human beings to earn more wealth and more material pleasure gives rise to conflicts and controversies and clash of interest among individuals". To get rid of all these man-made miseries is an eternal issue confronting mankind. By that we can ensure the realisation of right to happiness. Every human activity, good or bad is motivated by certain desire. Centuries back, Manu, has rightly said, "There is no act of man which is free from desire. Dharma or righteous conduct ensures happiness among the people treading the path of Dharma. The people are overpowered by sensual desires, Passion and Greed. Manu has, therefore, laid down tri-varga i.e., Dharma, Artha and Kama for promoting welfare and happiness among the people.

This is the basic philosophy of Indian life and this doctrine was introduced to strike a balance between the interest of individuals and that of public. The objective was to secure right tic) happiness through supremacy of Dharma over Artha. The advocates of Dharma also observed that the fulfilment of desire was an essential aspect of human life. Without it, life was meaningless. But such desires are to be regulated by the Principles of Dharma.

Peace is the outcome of happiness and if peace is sought and found, then naturally happiness is ensured. In Mahabharat also a stateless society was contemplated where, human rights were protected by others confirming to Dharma, Kautilya, in its Arthasastra incorporated Rajadharma emphasising the right to happiness of all individuals and the righteous duties of the King.

The principle of Dharma is inculcated in the hearts of every individual. The principles should also prevail in the modem democratic society which stands for the ideal "Sarve Bhavantu Sukhinah" (Let all people be happy). This doctrine was also adopted in the Constitution of India and has been reinforced through various Acts and Policy decisions of the modem Government.

Right to Equality

The very foundation of Indian culture is laid on the principles of equality, equity and other egalitarian tenets. The Right to Equality (Samanata) or Samya is regarded as an important right without which happiness is not available. The discrimination led to inequality that resulted in discontent and miseries. Vedas preach Dharma and a charter of equality is incorporated in the Rig Vedas and also in the Atharva Veda. In the Rig Veda, it has been rightly said, "No one is superior or inferior.

All are brothers and all should strive for the interest of all and progress collectively". Similarly in Atharva Veda, it has been pointed out, "All have equal rights in articles of food and water". Yoke of the chariot of life is placed equally on the shoulders of all. All should live together with harmony supporting one another like spokes of a wheel of the chariot connecting its ring and the hub". Hence Right to Equality of all human beings has been said and reiterated in so many hymns of the Vedas.

All individuals are regarded as the children of God and there should be no discrimination and disparity in the human society Rig Veda and Atharva Vedas are vociferous about the equality of man which is taken as an integral part of Dharma. It is also interesting to see the Article 1 of the Universal Declaration of Human Rights, 1948 in this context, "All human beings are born free and equal in dignity and right. They are endowed with reason and conscience and should get Act towards one another in a spirit of brotherhood. It has also been reinforced in the Article 7 of the same document, "All are equal before law and are entitled without any discrimination of equal protection of the law.

All are entitled to equal protection against any discrimination in violation of this Declaration and against any incitement to such discrimination. In explaining Rajadharma, Manu says, "Just as the mother Earth gives equal support to all the living beings so also a King should give support to all without any discrimination." Hence it is emphasised that a King should give equal treatment to all the citizens in the same manner as a mother towards her children. Article 14 of the Constitution of India has also aptly says, "State shall not deny to any person equality before law or the equal protection of law within the territory of India.

Article 14 of the Constitution is regarded as the fundamental right to equality which secures equality of the individual before law and equal protection to all on the part of the state. The Supreme Court and High Courts of India in different states have also ensured Right to Equality of the Indian citizens through their various judgements. The latest incidence in this context is the transfer of Ex-Chief Ministers of Bihar Shri Laloo Prasad Yadav and Dr. Jagannath Mishra from Bihar Military Police Guest House to Beur Central Jail at Patna in response to Public Interest Litigation filed before the Supreme Court of India.

Right to Education

Through ages education regarded as a means of equality and potential instrument for social change. An individual can improve to the maximum mainly through education. Therefore, the Vedas laid stress on three pious obligations as Dharma, namely 'gratitude' in which every individual has an obligation to the source of all benefits received by him including his own existence.

One should acquire knowledge by studying hard and by painstaking effort through concentration of mind and devotion. It can not be acquired by easy methods. One may obtain degrees and diplomas by malpractice in the examinations but cannot acquire genuine knowledge. Rather by getting certificates through unfair means put him to various embarrassing and undesirable situations.

A student who has genuine desire to acquire knowledge must put in hard labour and great effort. A man may become rich by easy ways but cannot acquire knowledge which is possible only through self-efforts. To impart knowledge is also equally regarded as an obligation towards teachers. If it has been discharged faithfully over thousands of years in this country, it has therefore been possible to conserve knowledge and desire to succeeding generation.

The Great Sanskrit Poet Bhartruhari of the 1st Century has rightly observed, "Education is the special manifestation of the man, education is the treasure which can be preserved without fear or less, education secures material pleasure, happiness and fame, education is the teacher of teacher; education is the friend when one goes abroad, education is God incarnate, education secures honour at the hands of the state, not money. A man without education is equal to animal i.e., he can be truly called "Vidya Bihinah Pashuh".

Patanjali highlighted four aspects of education with necessary duties to every individual:

(i) acquire knowledge/ education from parents and teachers,

(ii) study and improve knowledge on your own,

(iii) impart value-based education to every individual and to your children as parents and to others as teachers, and

(iv) use that knowledge for the benefit of the family and the society through your profession or avocation.

These four aspects of education have been emphasised not only for improving the education but also for developing the society. He also added that potential energy of an individual would be unfolded and could help an individual to lead a purposeful life. Importance of education thus cannot be overestimated and it has been rightly emphasised for development of the child. Right to Education has, therefore, been guaranteed to every child.

The Constitution of India says, "State shall endeavour to provide within a period of ten years from the commencement of this Constitution free and compulsory education for all children until they complete/attain the age of 14 years". However, this goal has not yet been fully realised and all attempts are being made to reach to target of Education for All by 2000 AD. The UNICEF and UN have also declared Education as an important right of the child and have been emphasising its realisation in all the countries of the world.

Right to Religion

Irrespective of the degree of our belief in God, religion

has been playing an important role in human life since time immemorial. We have our religious practices and rituals according to our family background or various other factors. There are a lot of differences in the religious practices of man and for that we have to maintain tolerance and positive attitude towards all these religions. But Indians believe in God from the ancient times and they are very liberal and universal. That is why some people name it as Sanathan Dharma. Only foreigners have given it the name Hinduism as this religion prevailed in the area on the bank of river Sindhu. It is said in our ancient scriptures that, "just as the rain water comes down to Earth from the sky and reaches Ocean, we pay obeisance to God. Whatever may be its name, the destination is the same.

We differ in the modes of worshipping God and we address God in various names whether it is Ishwar or Allaha. Therefore, eminent sages and saints and sadhaks of India have been emphasising on the religious equality and harmony and the Right to Religion has been recognised as an integral part of harmony. The above rule of Dharma is very unique to Indian culture and civilisation. It required the State to give equal protection not only to believers of God but also to disbelievers of God.

The broad concept of religion ensures freedom of thought, belief and faith in India. Article 18 of the Universal Declaration of Human Rights reads, "Everyone has the right to freedom of thought, conscience and religion. This Article includes freedom to change his religion or belief and freedom as that alone or in community with others and in public or private, manifest his religion or belief in teaching practice, worship and observation. The Constitution of India has also recognised freedom to religion as one of the fundamental rights. It is Article 21 which reads, "freedom of conscience, free profession, practice and propagation of religion subject to public order and health and to other professions.

All these parts of business are equally entitled to freedom to conscience and the right to freely profess, practice and propagate religion". Thus secularism has been given a significant place in our religion. But such religion is not neutrality but freedom to religious practices subject to Public Order and Peace.

Right to Protection

It is the basic responsibility of the state to ensure protection to its individuals from insecurity and oppression. The State has to see that all its citizens live happily in peace and tranquility. As already discussed in the Mahabharat, Rajadharma should emphasise such protection as an important responsibility of King or the ruler. It has been said therein, "to punish wicked to protect Good; to enrich treasury by fairmeans; to be impartial in the litigation and to protect the Kingdom-these are five yajnas (selfless duties) to be performed by a King.

The paramount duty of the state is to protect its people. It is the responsibility to protect helpless and the deceased or diseased; to protect be life and personal liberty is equally important for enabling people for leading a comfortable life and to live with dignity and happiness. It has, therefore, been included as a fundamental right under the Article 21 of the Constitution of India. It has also been declared as one of the human rights.

Convention of the Right of the Child has included the Right to Survival and Right to Protection as important rights of every child. According to UN, Right to Survival includes Right to live, the highest attainable standard of health, nutrition and adequate standard of living and the Right to protection includes freedom from all forms of exploitation, abuse; inhuman or degrading treatment and neglect including Right to special protection in situations of emergency or armed conflicts. India alongwith other countries of the World has accepted the Convention and has affirmed its commitments in its National Policy for Children since 1974. Under the Right to Protection, Child Labour has been banned in order to protect the children of India-the future citizens of the nation from economic exploitation, physical as well as psychological oppression.

Right to Humane Treatment

Humane Treatment is pervasive and comprehensive if we will allow equality, equity, happiness and social security, it is implied that we have to be humane and considerate. Employees enjoy the Right to Humane Treatment if he has been given fair wages and decent facilities, bonus and other incentives. Similarly, deceased employee's son or daughter is to be given preference for the appointment.

This Right has been an integral part of mankind. Article 23(3) of Human Rights Declaration says, "Everyone who works has the right to just and favourable remuneration ensuring for himself and his family an existence of worthy human dignity and supplemented, if necessary, by other means of social protection". Similarly, an individual in custody or in prison deserves humane treatment.

The officer in charge of prison and lock up should be aware of this basic right and ensure protection to the prisoners. Even any misconduct by them was described by Kautilya as punishable offence, who says, "Superintendent of a jail is liable to be punished for his acts of, omission and commission as follows:

(a) for putting a person in jail without disclosing the ground for his detention;

(b) for subjecting prisoner to unjust torture;

(c) for transporting the prisoner to any other place or deprive him of food and water;

(d) for causing trouble to prisoner or receiving bribes from them;

(e) for beating the prisoner resulting in his death;

(f) for having sexual intercourse with the wife of a thief or prisoner who is dead; and

(g) for having sexual intercourse with an arrested woman in lock up.

It is also interesting to note that the clever Kautilya not only laid down these offences, but also gave the punishment according to the degree or seriousness of the offences. At present such offences are found to be rampant in the society and there are frequent instances of violation of human rights by the police who are entrusted with the duty to enforce law and order.

Although there is specific provision in the Constitution requiring production of a prisoner or an arrested person by the police before the Magistrate within 24 hours, there are several instances which depict/reveal that it is not adhered to. Fortunately the modem Indian judiciary has been taking many laudable steps in giving justice to the suffering. The Supreme Court of India has declared that Human Rights should be a subject matter of Public Interest Litigation and in a given situation, if an individual whose-human rights are violated is not able to approach the Court, any individual/ public spirited person has right to move the Court on his behalf or on behalf of the former.

Right to Justice

It is the duty of the King or the ruler to give/offer justice to the oppressed and those who are deprived. Rajadharma included this duty as a very pious of the King. Narada Muni has said that the King should try cases with great care, should give decision according to the Law and should adhere to the opinion of the Chief justice.

The King was required to decide all such cases impartially and in accordance with the relevant laws. But such justice should be rendered speedily. Similarly, Katyayan has very aptly observed, "The King should not delay in examining the witnesses. A serious defect, namely, miscarriage of justice would result owing to delay in examination of witnesses". The King was to desist from greed and anger in deciding cases. It is therefore rightly said that, "Justice delayed is justice denied"'. Utmost care should be taken for examining the cases and giving final judgment from the view point of speed and impartiality.

Article 10 of the Universal Declaration of Human Rights says, "Everyone is entitled in full equality to a fair and public hearing by an independent and impartial tribunal, in the determination of his rights and obligations and of any or all criminal charges against him". Hence the speedy and objective disposal of litigation has been recognised as one of the basic human rights not only in the Universal Declaration of Human Rights but also in the Constitution of India and therefore various acts have been legislated from time to time. Human Rights should be regarded as sacrosanct and maximum opportunity should be allowed in ensuring human rights to all citizens. This kind of protection has been eulogised and confirmed through multifarious Indian epics.

The very idea of universalistic norms is viewed by some as nothing more than the imposition of some particular set of religio-cultural values on the other peoples of the world. That is due to the fact that in most of human history and in much of the world still today, ethical norms are rooted in religious orientations that seldom embrace human rights except insofar as they advance the particular religion.

The idea of ethical principles standing beyond religions, cultures, and societies, and able to evaluate and alter them, is to many a strange and hostile notion. Such an understanding of ethics requires that we tie thought and faith together in a philosophical theology, which is able to defend itself in public discourse, critically evaluate the relative adequacy of various religions on key questions, and provide the deep guidance system for complex societies and cultures. What an irony we face.

Modern articulations of human rights were born out of the attempt to constrain the great barbarisms of the twentieth century. In this context, ancient insights, which had been obscured or suppressed, were retrieved and made the basis for what is today called human rights. For the most part, the surge of interest in human rights that occurred after World War II turned to the formulations of human rights and democracy that grew out of the Enlightenment. However, it was only sometimes noted that these developments were themselves rooted in previously established theological assumptions that derive from antiquity—which the Enlightenment had claimed to overcome. While the great thinkers of the Enlightenment were familiar with the ancient sources, their heirs were not.

Hence, the interpretations of human rights that have come to triumph in the West are both derived from and opposed to their deeper religious roots. They nearly always ignore the greatest contribution of faith to human rights: namely, that some religious positions in alliance with selected philosophical traditions developed a transcendental view of the world and began to conceive of it as a whole, and thus to recognize that there is a perspective which is beyond the time and space, culture and society, religion and morality which we inhabit when we imagine the unity. If we grasp something of this perspective, or are grasped by it, we think and experience theologically, and see the nature of justice more clearly, for we see it sub species aeternitatis. If the world is a unity, and we can conceive of if as a whole-this, of course, means that we transcend it in some degree and do not simply live within it, trapped by its horizons-then we begin to suspect that it is governed by a unified moral law, even though the customs and habits of many people in the world and their ways of modelling the whole differ. Further, these customs, habits, and models can be altered according to a more ultimate and reliable pattern.

The most pertinent developments of modernity, in this view, have to do with the recovery, radicalization, propagation, and relative institutionalization of an ethical vision of this sort. The late twentieth century has been the period in which these principles have become spread throughout the world.

Human rights provisions are now built into the constitutions of more peoples than any previous civilization could have imagined, and are among the decisive criteria as to whether a religion, a culture, a regime, or a society should be honoured or altered, isolated or revolutionized. However, this has also been the century in which we have faced dramatic challenges to these ideas. These challenges have taken and continue to take many forms—most notably the quests for the solidarity of a particular community against such universal and transcendental claims. Indeed, the greatest struggles of the twentieth century are of this order one against the pagan anti-modernism of Hitlerian-Fascist National Socialism, another against the secularist hyper-modernism of Marxist Leninist Proletarian Socialism.

Each manifested itself in massive political military movements that became the chief threats to human rights and to modernity in this century. Both have, in substantive measure, been defeated, although, like ail great terrors, they writhe in their bonds and threaten to reappear from their graves in new forms. For instance, a direct challenge to human rights from these defeated forces appeared in new conspiracy of anti-modernists and hyper-modernists who, while having apparently abandoned the Nazism of Hitler's politics and Communism of Stalinist economics, now join the internal entrepreneurs of Asia's "liberalizing" economic policies and the business interests of the West who want access to Asia's cheap labour and vast markets to echo the defeated arguments.

In 1993, China led a coalition of nations, including Indonesia, Vietnam, Burma, Syria, and Iran that posed concepts of national sovereignty and state-supported development against democracy and human rights, as stated in the "Bangkok Declaration," which became 'the basis for their postures in the U.N. conference on human rights in Vienna. The triumph of these developments in the long run is unlikely, unless the fundamental conception of human rights itself begins to collapse.

The maledictive of political or economic gain may be decisive in many matters of indeterminate policy, but the deeper theological and ethical influences shape determinate matters of polity, and over time polity guides, leavens, and sets boundaries for policy.

The more profound threat to the idea of human rights as a determinate of polity, thus, is an attack from both it detractors and, unwittingly, from many of its defenders. A number of contemporary philosophers, social theorists, and religious thinkers of note have begun to doubt that there are such things a human rights, or have attempted to defend them in such terms as to make them impossible to sustain.

On the other side of the ideological spectrum, a major attempt to defend human rights from a "liberal" point of view has been advanced by Rhoda E. Howard and Jack Donnelly. They use sociological and anthropological theory to argue that human rights involve the affirmation of the autonomy and equality of every individual, in contrast to all the tribalisms, feudalisms, socialisms, communisms, and Communitarianisms, old and new, that view the individual as a part of a whole.

They argue that the idea of rights "is rooted in structural changes that began to emerge in late medieval and early modern Europe, gained particular force in the eighteenth and nineteenth centuries, and today are increasingly the norm throughout the world. The creation of the private individual separate from society is closely linked to the rise of a new, more complex division of labour, the resulting changes in class structure... and [thus] a new vision of the individual's relationship to God, society and the state. Leaving aside historical questions as to whether Abraham, Moses, Sara, Ruth, Jeremiah, Amos, Jesus, and Paul, or for that matter, Cleopatra, Socrates, Plato, Aristotle, Confucius, or the Buddha were in any serious sense individuals, we do not view human rights as an imaginative literary or political fiction on the order of unicorns. Instead, we view ethical norms such as human rights as the cultural by-products of socio-evolutionary processes.

Thus, human rights (and the persons and groups to which they apply) are seen to be an historical artifact, pertinent only insofar as social conditions stand at a particular stage of development, and subject to disappearance if those conditions do not obtain or eventually pass away. These philosophical and sociological views would be a great comfort to those in closed societies who use torture as a policy of governance or allow slave labour, for they can claim that they are at a particular stage of development. And neither are these scholars alone.

Literally hundreds of social commentators and clergy share this understanding of morality, even if they read the "signs of the times" of societal evolution differently. What is missing in these philosophical and sociological views is an account of why such matters as human rights, which cannot be derived from the empirical analysis of the world, prudentially or socio-historically, are plausible or why people should be committed to them, since it is empirically obvious that human rights are violated often and not everyone believes in them.

Two things are required for a full analysis: (1) a social hermeneutical theory of how such things come into consciousness- a matter that shall take us into questions of religion and social theory; and a way of evaluating which kinds of normative, but non-empirical, matters like human rights might be valid-a matter that requires theology. This is not to suggest that we can abandon all philosophy and social theory. Some forms of them can be extremely useful when they are stabilized or undergirded by a theological perspective-a perspective that they can help analyse, but which they can neither generate nor surpass.

An historically and cross-culturally comparative view of these questions suggests that ideas of human dignity, human rights, and the great liberties of speech and association derive from certain kinds of religious views, indeed, a distinct set of religious views developed in dialogue with key strands of philosophy and particular theories of social life that are different from, and in fact contended against, positions analogous to the ones we have just noted. In fact, it is quite likely that human rights are based on nothing less than decisive theological convictions, distinct from but incorporating and utilizing some of the best insights of philosophy and social theory. The challenges to human rights today, thus, are more subtle than the threats of Nazism and of Communism, for what we face is not likely to be overcome so quickly as these rose and fell-in a mere century or so.

The three great challenges for human rights in the next century are these (1) the decay of philosophy, and the consequent suspicion of any onto-theological account of how things are; (2) the attempt to establish normative principles for civil society on the basis of social description alone—the sadly unfulfilled promise of the social sciences; and (3) the power of resurgent, ancient religions, particularly Islam and Hinduism, which have a normative metaphysical-moral vision and which have shown their capacity to organize complex and vast civilizations over long periods of time. In their present forms, it is doubtful that any one of these three car sustain the idea of human rights in the long run—although it may turn out that Islam and Hinduism, or at least key strands of them, like key strands of Christianity critically refined by theology, will come closer than philosophy and sociology insofar as these try to remain detached from religion and theology.

To be sure, all of these are potential companions of the kind of ethic that could sustain human rights, if and when they develop a "public theology" in the sense that they seek to discern, under God, the moral and spiritual architecture whereby just and humane civilizations can be constructed. But it is also the case that if any one of them should become the dominant view without substantial reform, human rights are likely to be subordinated or lost.

Instead, the discussion has focused domestically on the removal of discrimination based on sex, race, and culture,... the enhancement of freedoms of speech, press, and association.... [and] the safeguarding of criminal and cultural rights." Similarly, the international debate has centered on the "democratic/socialist" polarity, with each. It tempting to show that it can best provide for "the eradication of sexual, cultural, and ethnic discrimination" and economic injustice. And, throughout this recent period, the place of religion in human rights has been relatively muted, except that religion became one item on the list of sociocultural factors to be protected, and the hegemony of any one religion became something to be feared. The remarkable resurgence of the question of religion in relation to human rights over the past few years, however, has many causes.

Perhaps the most profound cause is that societies and souls cannot flourish without a deep substratum of awareness about the moral basis of life, a substratum that generally does not occur without a religious orientation. This is not to say that all religious orientations are good or equal or supportive of human rights, 'They are not; some religions are quite destructive of all that human rights stands for, and the very intensity and potency of religion makes the destructiveness all the more vicious. It therefore makes a good deal of difference what sort of religion is at hand. But the key point here is that such intensity and potency has at times been supportive and even generative of human rights, and that the commitment to a moral substratum which can guide the common life seems to appear most strongly in those societies informed by certain kinds of religious influence, and to be least vigorous in those societies shaped by other religious traditions or by anti-religion.

We have a situation, thus, in which the freedom and vitality of religion at one level appears to depend on human rights, but in which the intensity and viability of human rights in society at another level seems to depend on the extent of certain kinds of religious influence. In the vast literature on religion and human rights, this second aspect is the least discussed and often the most superficially treated. Although there is considerable evidence that human rights are deeply and fundamentally dependent on religion and specifically on certain kinds of theological issues, it is equally clear that not all are convinced of this rather substantive point.

Indeed, it is probable that for human rights to be recognized and sustained in the common life, two things are necessary: a theological understanding of normative reality, and a set of concrete institutional channels to actualize these normative visions in society and make them accessible in a civilization.

The Central Issue of Religion and Human Rights

The main contentions of this chapter are (1) that the very idea of human rights is rooted in a theological ethic; and (2) that this ethic needs to be defended from contemporary challenges-philosophical, sociological, and religious—in order that, as an ethical norm, human rights may more fully be actualized in societies, and so that philosophy, social theory, and religion supportive of human rights may flourish among all peoples.

The challenges to human rights are based upon doubts about the nature of theology as well as the confusion between confessionalism and theology. Religion is often treated as a strictly personal, cultural, or historical experience, and theology is understood to be its formal, dogmatic articulation. Thus, to root human rights in religion or theology is seen as a form of personal, cultural, or historical imperialism.

Further, since we have come to wider awareness of the variety of religions in the world, it is hard for some to imagine that not all the religions contribute equally to moral matters. Although the world religions have been around for centuries, they did not seem to many to be present as living options or necessarily related to human rights. Yet historically, the evidence is rather clear, as Brian Tierney has, already suggested.

The deep roots of human rights ideals are rooted nowhere else than in the biblical tradition, for it is here that we find the decisive unveiling of a perspective in which moral first principles demanding the respect for the neighbour are made known to humanity by a reality that is universal and absolute. This reality, which the Western traditions call "God," is neither a figment of human imagination, a projection of our personal needs or tribal consciousness, nor a product of human creativity. Nor is this God morally neutral. This is an ethical God, the source and norm of a kind of justice and righteousness and contends against what we often find as we look around the world. Richard Deats puts it this way:

> The universal implications of this faith in the righteous God, creator of the earth and all living things... [permeated] the life of Israel, expanding their faith to widened horizons of inclusiveness and compassion. "Am I my brother's keeper?" and "Who is my neighbour?" are questions that never ceased to stir the conscience of the people of God.... [T]he universality of this faith.... is to be a "light for all the peoples."

This heritage was applied to all the peoples of the world in the prophetic traditions, when the prophets protested the exploitation of the poor and weak, and demanded that the various nations, especially those who claimed to be most loyal to this God, must submit to a moral law not of their own making. Some things simply ought not be done by one human to another, even if they are approved or commanded by an impious political authority. In this context, Christianity arose and radicalized the prophetic point of view, carried it into the Graeco-Roman world, and linked it to philosophical and jurisprudential theories that, on quite other grounds, also had begun to articulate a -notion of a universal normative moral order.

This interaction of faith and philosophy created theology and ethics as basic modes of discourse to guide thought and action on the most universalistic bases Possible." These developments remained a minority tradition for centuries, and were often suppressed by pagan tendencies, power interests, and forms of myth and magic that could not be said to be universalistic, moral, faithful, or philosophically sound. But periodically this tradition was retrieved and made central, to attempts to reform life, and to establish it on a more universalistic, more humane, and more godly foundation.

This we can see in the revolutionary transformations of law and society so central to the history of the West, in the theological theories of "conciliarism" that anticipated and approximated constitutional democracy and especially in parts of the Reformation that influenced the modern formation of human rights.

However, it was periodically the case that precisely this tradition was distorted by both the ideological use of religion at the hands of political power to legitimate its interests, and the betrayal of the rational and ethical character of theology by religious leaders who made Christianity into a series of arbitrary dogmas to be accepted on blind faith, without intellectual justification, moral rigor, or a sense of what it meant to be "a for all peoples." When the wars of religion of early modern Europe combined these perversions, the heritage was discredited in the eyes of all sorts of post-Christian views of human moral a *priori*, self-evident truths and natural rights were developed to attempt to guide and strain political authority without religion, and to develop a cosmopolitan ethic that would allow the various obscurantist religions to hold their own dogmas-albeit only as private preferences.

Theology, in-a public sense, was destroyed in favour of apolitical or pietistic fideism, on one side, and an ontologically free-floating rationality, on the other. The destruction was called Enlightenment. However, the Enlightenment col not carry the full load of what it attempted, and its rational fruits became instruments of oppression, even as it struggled to establish and maintain a sense of universal moral order. Its godless foundations could not bear the weight of all that the Enlightenment philosophers confidently placed upon them.

The Enlightenment's initial success depended upon the deeper, but hidden, foundations which had been laid by theology, Apart from them, philosophy began to deconstruct—into romanticism, historicism, existentialism, and now postmodernism. Our argument is not only that we need to get and keep our history straight, although that would be a very good idea. Our argument is a Is that it is quite possible for an idea that is generated out of one context to be found valid in another, and to become contextualized in forms of thought and life in ways that enhance possibilities within those adopted forms of thought and life that were only latently central to the new host. This, of course, produces "revisionist" history in the secondary tradition as happened to Greek philosophy and Roman law when they were wedded to biblical insights to form a theology which surpassed these original sources.

Our argument is, in brief, that today human rights can best be seen as a part of the process of the recognition of the validity of decisive ethical concepts that, while offered and made actual by a particular tradition, are recognizably valid for all people and are essentially true for the world. Human rights are a modern way of speaking about cross-cultural ethical concepts that actualize certain valid theological presuppositions and in turn legitimates constraints on what humans or states can do to each other, where theology is understood to be the critically examined and systematically stated interpretation of what humanity is sinful creatures not driven entirely by nature and nurture, that know we live under a God who establishes moral laws and ends and contexts of life we cannot attain alone. Theology, in this view, is not merely the rationalized form of a social or cultural view legitimated by a privileged religion. It is also a necessary partner of philosophy and the social sciences, and a critic of religions, in clarifying, and establishing universal and valid ethical norms for an emerging global civilization.

Theology tells us whether this or that religion, our own or someone else's, is valid or whether it ought to be challenged on the grounds of its truth or its justice. This hypothesis then bears within it an ironic implication: it suggests the likelihood of religious, philosophical, and social conflict, for not all religions are equally capable of developing or sustaining a theology that can generate a universalistic ethic of jurisprudential importance.

Indeed, in its strongest form, this argument suggests that it is doubtful whether human rights can be sustained without a theology that has certain definable characteristics, which we will attempt to indicate. Yet, as the threats of the anti-modernists on the right and the hyper-modernists on the left fade, increasingly frequent attacks are made upon the theological genealogy of human rights and the very possibility of anything being universal especially anything with normative content.

A new surge of pragmatic anti-Enlightenment and anti-theological philosophy has attempted to deconstruct all aspects of culture, including language, with the reductive techniques of the social sciences, and to view the great world religions as evidence against the possibility of developing and sustaining a universalistic theological ethic. These deconstructive arguments suggest that both theology and modernity are to be faulted for trying to supply a basis for human rights, for they rest on strictly untenable universalistic claims. In what follows, first consider aspects of these deconstructive philosophical arguments, and then we use a preliminary discussion of postmodern social theory as a segue into a consideration of Islam and Hinduism as interlocutors in the rights dialogue.

We argue (1) that the postmodern case against universalistic theological principles is inconsistent and not convincing; (2) that certain postmodern social theories already realize this; and (3) that aspects of classical Hinduism and Islam can be enlisted as allies in the struggle for the global recognition of human rights, even if aspects of them, along with aspects of historical Christianity, also are judged to contain features which could potentially subvert human rights.

Postmodern philosophy and human rights

Philosophers since the Enlightenment have frequently argued that only human reasoning carried out as philosophy adequately grounds human rights, for religions are usually enemies of rights, unless they relegated to optional personal preference. Theology, in this view, is less passe for it is but the rationalization of fideist belief.

The serious work of establishing ethical and political values is accomplished by philosophy. This view, it is widely acknowledged, is in considerable difficulty today, and it is doubted whether human reasoning carried out philosophy can justify anything, let alone human rights. Reason no longer speaks with the booming confidence of Archimedes, nor even in the conversational and receptive tones of Hermes. Both the "clear and distinct" arguments of epistemology and subtler shades of hermeneutics are thought to be maniacal ravings of the pompous predicament of Enlightenment reason. Modern philosophy here thought to be a kind of pretentious insanity, as was religion and theology.

The substantiality of this view is not at all clear, for human rights are by definition both universalistic, practical, and highly theoretical. Rorty has argued that it is possible to "de-universalize" and "de-theorize" both democracy and human rights, and yet to maintain them as a good way to live. As ways of life, democracy and human rights are prior to philosophy. Enlightenment philosophy's most profound self-deception, he argues, was to believe that its theory of rights was foundational and Prioi to the form of democratic life.

Rorty argues, to the contrary, that Enlightenment justifications were always justifications of this way of life; and this way of life can be "justified," or made sense of, in a number of ways. But, better yet, it needs no justification. In lieu of a theoretical defence of rights and democracy, one has to say merely that these forms of life work well; they have helped us to stop killing one another. That pragmatic justification, if one can call it that, involves certain understandings about what is desirable, but these understandings should be recognized as strictly contingent products of our historical experience. Rorty is surely correct that the Enlightenment justifications were not prior to democracy and human rights, for in fact it was key theological and ecclesial traditions that established them for at least parts of the human community, long before the Enlightenment.

Furthermore, it can easily be argued that democracy and human rights were based upon universalistic theories of right and wrong that were, in fact, resisted by particular local traditions, stories, biographies, and group identities that would have lost the arbitrary power they held over people if rights and democracy were acknowledged. Also, Rorty's theory presupposes a touching vision of a naturally harmonious state of affairs for all life that is not touched by the sin of grand theory. This wonderful polytheistic paradise, with no trees of knowledge since it is "beyond good and evil," is as universalistic and religious a theory as any he rejects, although it is not theological and thus has no grounding beyond arbitrary preference.

Finally, he cannot provide a reason why we would stop killing one another, especially if it is to the great advantage of some that the killing continue. Lyotard also believes, echoing aspects of Heidegger and Neitzsche, that the fundamental error in Western philosophy is that grand narratives storm through history by swallowing up and silencing alternatives and otherness. Grand narratives reign by "terror," even though they are guided by a profound humanism.

This humanism is supported by the grand narratives of Marxism and liberalism, which measure all things by their ability to produce results for humanity. Marxism promises a catastrophic liberation of humanity; liberalism promises humanity's gradual unfolding and flowering. Yet both liberalism and Marxism agree that human beings stand at the center of history, and that history told rightly tells the story of the ineluctable emancipation of humans from tyranny and need. The idea that some universally conferred dignity stands behind the Enlightenment doctrine of human rights is, in this interpretation, the product of a false consciousness.

The recurrence of grand narratives, or bold declarations like claims c natural rights, are a sign that cultural psychotherapy has gone badly awry-that the therapeutic process has mistaken the content of it- conversation for an authoritative and normative remembering of "history. Spinning grand narratives, like theoretical defences of universal human rights, entail a "primal repression" all such attempts are tied to a philosophy of consciousness, which is doomed to repeat the horrors of the past. In Western history, the chief example is the Jews:

> What is most real about the Jews is that Europe, in any case, does not know what to do with them: Christians demand their conversion; monarchs expel them; republics assimilate them; Nazis exterminate them.

The grand narratives of the Enlightenment, with their promise of equality, did nothing in Lyotard's view to protect the Jews from extermination. Their most benevolent face was to require the abandonment of all of the distinctive features of judaism. Lyotard wants human rights to be much less than a theoretically comprehensive articulation of the rights and duties of humanity, and so to provide much more of a shield for simply being human. At the core, human rights are about the right to talk with others, and to tell one's own stories. One's stories ensure that one is always "other," not reduced to some alien scheme:

> [T]he strangeness of the other seems to escape any totalization.... It is precisely when we think we have reduced the abject or the sacred to transparent meanings that it becomes most opaque. The discontent from which contemporary societies are suffering, the postmodern affliction, is the foreclosure of the Other. It is the reverse of the triumphant identification with the Other which effects modern republics at their birth.

Lyotard is surely correct that the Enlightenment conception of the Self, as autonomous, complete, whole, and unique, is unconvincing. But his view of the socially and narratologically constituted person is equally unconvincing, and it is doubtful that his view can provide the shield from "terror" that he wants. Lyotard recognizes one of the emphases of the biblical and theological tradition, namely, that humans are creatures made from the dust, to which they return after a brief life.

The biblical and theological tradition, however, also affirms that humans are created in the image of God. The self does not have an automatic dignity; it has a conferred dignity. The weak, the fragile, the foolish, the faulty also are to be treated with dignity. The biblical view is paradoxical; these creatures from the dust, made in the image of God, may not be violated-in prophetic voice, their heads may not be crushed-at least not without incurring God's wrath.

Just as Rorty falls into an unwitting romantic and presumptively harmonious polytheism, Lyotard falls into a soulless vacuity of chatter. Rorty needs God; Lyotard needs the image of God. Their arguments are insufficient, even though they have helped us see more clearly the insufficiency of key philosophical arguments of the Enlightenment.

Nonetheless, if it comes to it, the world would probably be wise to choose the Enlightenment views over their efforts, for in the notions of a universal moral law and a self with inherent dignity, there is a closer approximation to what these two philosophers want to protect than in what they themselves proffer as alternatives. Several other lines of argument could be marshalled against this vision of Rorty and Lyotard.

— Plurality does not take care of itself, in a structural and historical form, plurality without a larger sense of unity is tribalism. Various forms of ethnic exclusiveness and pluralism constitute themselves in terms of "the other" by constant hostility, and it is romantic and historically blind to argue otherwise.

— The so-called totalistic impulses of the Enlightenment can be criticized, along the lines laid out by Rorty and Lyotard, without denying the importance of inclusivistic narratives.

The problem is that the Enlightenment was not inclusive enough. Its narrative was petty, not grand, for it lacked depth. The Enlightenment conception has only selves, not souls; it has humanism, but neither God nor creation. Rorty and Lyotard are right, then, that the Enlightenment does not deliver on its promise to secure some kinds of particularity and plurality, and thus these are subject to deconstruction, because they have no ground for being honoured. Yet that has as much to do with the Enlightenment's denial of the theological foundations of its own presumptions as anything else.

The doctrine of the trinity, for example, enables the articulation of ultimate reality, marked by a non-reductive inclusivity, with principles and freedom, otherness and identity.

— It is possible to see vestiges of the "Enlightenment" all through Rorty's and Lyotard's writings, especially when they are read from a Christian theological point of view. The premature dismissal of theology as a voice in public discussion represents the Enlightenment in its most dubious philosophical aspect, and they accept the dismissal at face value.

— It is not at all clear how one can have a non-theoretical practice or form of life, without falling prey to self-referential inconsistencies. It is a noble impulse that should be nurtured, one that has people pause and ask, "Is this practice just, and therefore theoretically justifiable?" Human rights apply to more than one form of practice, because they are highly theoretical, Yet, beyond these issues, there is reason for a deeper critique of Rorty and Lyotard from the perspective we are advancing here.

In short, theology is an indirect, and often a direct,

target of their critiques, as it is for enlightened liberals. Moreover, their focus upon the smaller fragments of life leads them to ignore a manifest feature of the ethos of our time, namely that the world's increasingly unified economic, political, ideational, and legal global ethos can support a nonviolent plurality. Rorty and Lyotard spool together these features of bad theology and a misunderstood ethos because they believe that the Enlightenment best spoke for its own presuppositions and correctly analysed the nature and character of religion.

But, since they have challenged the Enlightenment on a dozen points, it is not clear why they remain dependent on it for this one. Rorty and Lyotard simply assume that theology is inherently heteronomous and that an irreducible plurality is better than the stifling singularity which theology ostensibly desires. The social hermeneutic of Rorty and Lyotard blinds them to the emerging global ethos, or to view it as some demonic Leviathan, and no more. The fate of human rights as a sustainable cluster of doctrines is likely to require the apologetical refutation of these sorts of claims.

For, on the one hand, if theology cannot enter into first-order dialogue about the nature of humanity, without being destructive or heteronomous, it is hard to see how religious human rights can mean anything. On the other hand, if they show that classical and enlightenment philosophy and all of theology is inherently dehumanizing, it is also hard to see where substantive accounts of "humanity" will come from, since nearly all of the current human rights proclamations depended, directly or indirectly upon the normative anthropotogical assumptions of biblically influenced philosophical theology. Rorty's denial of "metanarratives" turns out to be a particular metanarrative that systematically denies the reality of the world. In fact, both Rorty and Lyotard presume a metaphysical and epistemological ethically normless polytheism at the level of experience.

Their social hermeneutic has decided a priori that it will see nothing other than fragments which are threatened by comprehensive unities. That means that, the bases for rights which might be used to stave off intrusions on inviduality are undermined. To be sure, in the emerging global ethos, there is an intensive plurality that which cannot be denied and that which often be celebrated, but there is also a quite real unity. There is one system with multiple climates, one global economy with highly differentiated markets, one emerging cosmopolitan global civilization with many cultures and subcultures, and one need to communicate with many languages.

Human rights as a normative concept adds that there is one humanity with a rich variety of individual lives, traditions, community and religions that ought not be violated. This is a theological hermeneutic that includes unity and difference. Rorty and Lyotard undermine the dialectic by focusing upon difference; this is quite directly related to their denial of theology as a form of public discourse, since theology join unity to difference and articulates the real differences found in and under ultimate unity.

Social Theory and the Religions

The course travelled by these postmodern philosophers is odd. Rorty and Lyotard tacitly accept several key presumptions of the Enlightenment, turn them on the greatest achievements of modern humanistic thought, and thus destroy the foundations of the very values that they want to affirm. Further, they finally have to rest their case on a socio-historical reading of how things work in the common life and on a priori convictions about what is valuable. Yet they can defend neither, some thing they disavow at the outset, in any event. Rorty and Lyotard, however, are not the only contemporary philosophers to address human rights.

Terry Nardin and David Maple of the Thikon Institute, for example, are editing a major volume on the Constitution of International Society, in which both classical (conservative) and Enlightenment (liberal) theories of law, in dialogue with certain theological positions, are being tetrieved and revised to guide the common life in ways that support and sustain human rights. Similarly, certain self consciously "conservative" and "liberal" moral philosophers, and some self-consciously liberal, and conservative "Christian philosophers," are making very similar arguments against both the reductionism of the Enlightenment and the moral emptiness of many postmodern alternatives. The Enlightenment thinkers would surely have found it odd that some of the most serious arguments against human rights come not from religion or theology but from philosophy.

That may not be enough, were we able to discuss these matters with the Enlightenment thinkers, to turn them to a reconsideration of religion and theology. For a number of social theorists in our day, however, it has been enough, even if the turn these theorists make to religion is not always fully adequate. The work of Jdrgen Habermas, for example, represents an attempt to go beyond the narrowness of both Enlightenment philosophy and sociology by commingling their insights in a program of critical theory. He joins Rorty and Lyotard by rejecting a philosophy of consciousness, monological justifications of the social contract, and the foundationalism of Enlightenment philosophy; he also joins them by turning to language and communication theory. Yet here is precisely where Habermas turns away from Rorty and Lyotard, for he attempts to extract a normative justification for rights out of the very nature of communication.

Communication theory is the venue through which Habermas engages the functionalist focus on the "life world", an I themes of rationalization and disenchantment articulated by Max Weber. Habermas remains tied to unnecessarily reductive analyses of religion, and his account of a communication requires the abandonment, of theology and teleology in rights discourse. But he comes closer than the postmodernists of our day to providing a sustainable, normative framework for human rights. Scholars in the sociological tradition of Weber, Emile Durkheim a Talcott Parsons, such as Robert Bellah, are also increasingly, though cautiously, engaging in dialogue with religion. This move is not without controversy. Some writers in this tradition challenge the use of the sod sciences as a companion to religion and theology."

Others, such a Peter Berger, question whether sociology alone can provide any guidance, about human rights as normative claims. To the contrary, other sociologists argue that social sciences are the only disciplines that can provide normative guidance to post-religious civil society. It is not clear whether contemporary sociology, any more than contemporary philosophy, can offer normative guidance about human rights, though both discipline point to the necessity of dealing with religions as decisive factors in human rights discourse. It may be that the more urgent approach to human rights is to raise, the question of the world religions directly. To do so, however, we need a method that both focuses directly on religious realities and joins the study of religion to philosophy and social theory. Such a method is found in theological ethics, or what some traditions call social theology, philosophical theology or natural theology.

Theological ethics, along with certain forms of philosophy of religion and jurisprudence which are alert to theological issues, goes to the deepest normative perspective in which human rights can be talked about without sacrificing concrete socio-historical institutions. Surely, human rights would be on a more secure footing if we could place them on a foundation that has both a sustainable normativity and a concrete, institutional footing.

The theological ethical considerations of the world religions bring these concerns together, because all of the axial religions express metaphysical-moral visions that entail normativity, and their civilizational expansiveness verifies their sustainability. The major religions also interactive the chief and indispensable social structures—familial, political, economic, and cultural. Indeed, in many classic societies, religion is identified with one or more of these social structures, so that it is not strange to speak of a tribal, clan, or caste religion, an imperial, political or civic religion, a religion focused around the hunt, the harvest, or the expected "cargo, or a religion of a cultural-linguistic grouping.

In some societies, however, where religion is focused upon a culture-transcending, ethical reality, it becomes distinguished from these so that it is not to be identified with any one of them. There, quite often, we find the formation of voluntary associations-centers of bonding and meaning that are intentionally not tied to any of these, even if these associations continue to influence any or all of them. When this begins to happen, we find also the emergence of other independent institutions of society-law, science, medicine, and business-which also segregate particular activities into distinctive institutions and shape the fabric of the whole society. Historically, it has been in certain kinds of traditions—those which on ecclesiological grounds, have spawned voluntary associations, an thereby institutional pluralism—nearly always populated by minorities at the outset, that we find the most promising institutional focus for the creedal recognition, affirmation, and nurture of human rights."

Voluntary associations are also created in secular forms, once the space is established and rationalized by religious groups, and these associations can transmit the ethical ideas in routine institutions, quite often in forms which are not recognized as religious. Anthony Giddens' thesis may be promising here with some modification, for he argues that globalization is the "radicalization of modernity," the realization of its consequences Giddens' "discontinuist" account, however, does not sufficiently engage the question of the religious and theological antecedents of modernity.

It is likely that the global radicalization of modernity is the most recent actuation of the deep fount of modernity, that is, of what Max Weber saw in his treatment of "the city," and more fully in his study of the spirit of capitalism-the "secular" rationalizations of life prompted by religious transformations. But Giddens' thesis holds that we are now experiencing the consequences of that ethic in ways that Weber did not and could not envision. Newly emerging global patterns, reflected in international law, media, and markets, but largely evoked and facilitated by new forms of the multinational corporation, concretely shape the world in which we live and in which human rights are recognized or violated.

We should investigate what drives these new patterns, because they harbour the ability to create inclusive institutions and to nurture normative ideas about what is true and just, at least latently. This raises the question: do global institutions, since they are universal in scope, bear within them an ethic which can be allied to that of human rights? If so, with theological ethical guidance, they may support human rights more securely than either philosophy or sociology alone, that is, of either an uninstitutional normativity or an institutional anomie.

Answering that question requires a consideration of the chief fount of voluntary associations, the world religions. It requires a theological ethical consideration of them, a consideration that seeks to articulate which religious claims are true, and how one could know their truth. In sum, important as philosophy and sociology are, both finally depend upon religion the investigation of which finally requires theological analysis, if a universalistic ethic such as human rights is to be sustained by religion. For our purposes, only some religions are interesting those that have demonstrated a capacity to shape large scale civilizations. Only these religions can reach toward human rights in the relevant respects; only these make claims to universality.

The world's major civilizational religions are, to use postmodernism's contemptuous phrase, totalizing theories. God's covenant with Israel commissions it to be a prophet to the nations. The Christian gospel is to be taken into all the world. The Qur'an is the Arabic words of Allah. The sounds of the Sanskrit words preexist the cosmos itself. These traditions know something about what Christians also say, "In the beginning was the word." Indeed, in what Karl Jaspers called the religious, of the axial age (*Achsenzeit*), several traditions discovered that the cosmos could be comprehended as a single whole thousands of years before such an idea could begin to make empirical sense, as it does now in what social theorists call globalization, internationalization, or the world system.

Three distinct elements are present in the ethics of each of these religions; these need to be sorted if we are to find out where and how we are similar, and where and how we are different in regard to human rights.

— The world religions are allies in identifying a fundamental need to transform reality as we now find it, and together they form a cluster of formal deontological claims that categorically address all humans and all human societies. Every religion has something like universal moral laws that condemn murder, rape, lying, stealing, dishonouring religion and proper authority, and commanding truth-telling, promise-keeping, and upright living. In broad terms, members of the religions can agree with each other, and often with philosophies that also seek to know the "right order" of things, and can cooperate on these bases about many matters concerning human rights.

— However, all the great religious traditions have a way of interpreting and guiding the social context of life. There is considerable tension on this point, although it does not perhaps involve ultimate differences. This second area of ethics has to do with the ways in which commonly held first principles and final aims become embedded in the necessary contexts of life. Frequently, they become attached to a socially and historically conditioned ideal, which determines what the most fitting context of life ought to be, and what kinds of concrete social arrangements best allow the right order of things to be actuated.

Religious institutions and loyalties have been, and presumably always wilt be, closely allied with these, but how that connection is made from- the standpoint of the religion will be decisive for the actual functioning of the first principles of right and wrong, including the ways in which human rights operate. Islam was led by Mohammed, of blessed memory, who was not only professionally given to commerce, but also a political-military leader who, by being the mediator of the Qur'an and the first judge in legal cases, established a direct and immediate connection between the faith and political and legal rule. It would, indeed, be very strange if religious organizations in that tradition did not draw a close connection between political, military, and legal principles, especially as they dealt with property, trade, and agreements among the heads of households, clans, tribes, and nations.

Over the centuries, that has been quite characteristic, from the rise of the Caliphate, to the Iranian Revolution, to the new militancy nearly every Islamic country is now facing. Religion encouraged political and military expansion and thereby the establishment of the Shari'a and of trade. When political and military expansion went well, religion flourished, marked by wider establishment of the sacred law and commercial success. When any one these declined, the others fell into frustration or disrepair. To be sure, there have been grand moments in the history of Islam, when issues of cultural and philosophical genius, medicine, science, commercial fairness, and generosity to the poor have surpassed most other civilizations, and these "arenas of life" remain highly regarded by many devotees of the tradition. And, of course, Islam, has quite distinctive teachings about family life, presumably born out of the political, military, and legal history of the faith, and quite supportive of an ethic which nourished their common life.

In general it might be said that the of Islam" basically supports the "nation of Islam," and that both bring political power, law, and religion into intimate proximity. In contrast, Hinduism is organized by a priestly caste that is viewed as superior to the military-political-legal custodians of public order, and they, in turn, are superior to those given to commerce and production.

The fact that priestly domination triumphed over political and military rule in India is of basic significance; the priests have first-order contact with the first principles of morality, in a way that no other vocational group does. A casted hierarchy, determined by birth, sets the extended familial patterns at the core of religious association in a way that has no real analogy in Islam or Christianity.

Thus, dynastic institutions, guided by a marriage-conscious and highly educated literate dynasty tends to dominate life in those areas where Hinduism is predominant. Both traditions have elements of transcendence, of the dignity of the human soul, and of the necessity of legal protections for life. But neither has developed a general theory of human rights. However, these deeply embedded social orders are not beyond change, any more than the imperial and feudal structures of medieval Christianity were.

Further, once the concept of human rights is presented to these traditions, and once the possibilities of a pluralistic and open civil society becomes accessible to them, and people within these faiths begin to adopt patterns of organization that are neither totally given to political-legal militancy or to familiar-dynastic hierarchy, elements in their own traditions can be found that support the notion of human rights. Human rights can be used to catalyse growth in the latent depths of these traditions which are already have profound universalistic dimensions.

Third, the world religions offer constructive, forward-looking visions or teleologies, that is, guidance about how to discern good from evil consequences of our actions by considering them in reference to ultimate aims. This third, teleological dimension of ethical discourse is rather decisive in this process of selective adoption. As the traditions now stand, they have deeply formed, rich contexts, and these make the deontological and teleological conceptions concretely available to people.

While all the religions deconstruct the world with the absolute spectre of religious criticism and the call to transformation, they all also reconstruct it through imagination, doctrine, practice, and ritual so as to redeem or sanctify the world realities. They acknowledge the moral and spiritual legitimacy of the basic institutions of life, although the kind and character of the religion', and specifically its affinities to particular kinds of institutions, will shape the context in quite distinctive ways. All the world religions also know that without a vision the people perish. Here, however, no hasty synthesis is possible: the Kingdom of God is neither Nirvana nor the Paradise of the Qur'an, and liberation in Latin America means something quite different than the *moksa* and *bhakti*.

Thus human rights find possible support in the metaphysical moral visions of the world religions, though these are indigenized in various contexts, sometimes in ways that suppress the deontological insights. But what shall be made of the world (and what shall become of the soul) is not so clear. It may well be the case, as many human rights advocates argue, that a high degree of agreement and clarity exists about the possible cooperation of religious believers on some matters bearing on human rights.

Most also agree 'hat contexts should be treated with care, although some appeals to context become contextualist ideologies of identity and pluralism that effectively resist every call to transform society toward greater justice. On the question of teleology, however, there is neither agreement nor clarity. Often the role played by teleology ill human rights is ignored, and when it is treated, it usually compromises the deontological character of rights. We are delighted that we can invoke the dharma, the *dhamma*, the Mosaic law, the Qur'an, the Holy Spirit, and, in times past, the proletariat against the injustices we perceive in the world.

A leading scholar in this field observed recently that "for several thousand years the history of religion was marked by religious intolerance and persecution". After mentioning specifically the persecutions of one another by Christians of various persuasions, he added: "Clearly religion and freedom have not been natural allies." This is the situation we have to bear in mind when we reflect on the historical background to the modem idea of religious rights. The Western experience that we want particularly to consider is in some ways paradigmatic, since a doctrine of natural rights-or human rights as we say nowadays-first grew up in the Christian West.

Of course, all the great religious cultures of the world have given expression to ideals of justice and right order in human affairs, but they have not normally expressed those ideals in terms of subjective natural rights. Even in the West, a doctrine of religious rights emerged only painfully and belatedly, out of a tradition that had earlier found it much easier to acknowledge other kinds of rights. Nowadays it has become commonplace to maintain, as Pope John Paul II recently asserted, that religious rights are the "cornerstone" of all other rights. But, viewed in historical perspective, religious rights came last; these rights were the most difficult to conceive of, let alone put into practice.

The Roman Catholic Church was the last of the great Christian denominations to embrace wholeheartedly the principle of religious freedom. This at least had the advantage that its leaders could form a mature and well-considered version of the doctrine. Hence the *Declaration* on Religious Liberty of Vatican Council II, promulgated in 1965, provides an appropriate starting point for our discussion:

> This Vatican Council declares that the human person has a right to religious freedom. This freedom means that all men are to be immune from coercion on the part of individuals or of social groups and of any human power... the right to religious freedom has its foundation in the very dignity of the human person as this dignity is known through the revealed word of God and by reason itself.

This passage of the Declaration referred, in all-embracing fashion, not only to coercion by the state but by "any human power." It defined religious freedom specifically as a "right" and a right inherent in the human person, a natural or human right therefore. This natural right, discernible by human reason, was also said to be rooted in divine revelation and so intrinsic to the Christian faith. The Declaration contained only a bland and innocuous hint that these affirmations represented a radical reversal of a policy of religious repression that the

Catholic church (and the mainstream Protestant churches too) had maintained for centuries.

The hint came in an observation that the demands of human dignity "have come to be more fully known to human reason through centuries of experience." How true these words are can be gathered from a decree of another general council, promulgated in 1215, just 750 years before the Declaration of Vatican Council II. This is from the Fourth Lateran Council:

We excommunicate and anathematize every heresy that raises itself against the holy, orthodox, and Catholic faith.... Seculai authorities, as they wish to be esteemed and numbered among the faithful, ought to take an oath that they will strive in good faith and to the best of their ability to exterminate all heretics pointed out by the church. The idea of a growth of understanding in time is not a novel concept, based on modern historicism. In the thirteenth century the Franciscan theologian Peter Olivi wrote of the need for "new explication in the holy church of God-more and more through the course of time-of the sublime truths of faith." Olivi's master, St. Bonaventure, wrote of "seeds" of truth in scripture that slowly ripened in the minds of men, and he added that "Scripture and its mysteries cannot be understood unless the course of history is known." Such writers were not arguing that divine revelation changes, but that human understanding of scripture deepens in the course of the centuries.

We might add that some kinds of understanding, it seems, can be achieved only by undergoing specific historical experiences, sometimes harsh and bitter ones. This is especially true when we consider the theme of religious rights. In the following discussion I want first to consider some aspects of early Christian teaching and then explain how, even in the medieval church, there were some developments of Christian thought that might seem favourable to the growth of religious liberty.

Next we will try to explain why, for many centuries, such ideas were outweighed by an apparently insuperable body of counterargument favouring coercion of religious dissidents. Finally, we shall need to consider how a new—or renewed—idea of religious freedom took root in the early modern era, with a glance at the relevance of all this historical experience for the global problems of our modern age. From the beginning of the Christian era there were elements in Christian tradition that could lead on either to a doctrine of religious liberty or to a practice of persecution. Jesus himself taught a doctrine of universal love. "I say to you, love your enemies, do good to those who hate you". Jesus disclaimed the role of a political Messiah, lying on coercive force, when he said: "My kingdom is not of this world" (John 18:36). And he offered a new kind of freedom to his followers: "You shall know the truth and the truth shall make you free" (John 2), Paul, too, wrote eloquently of "the freedom wherewith Christ has made us free". And perhaps an ideal of spiritual liberty as always, implicit in the Judeo-Christian understanding, of the human person as a morally autonomous individual, endowed with conscience d reason and free will. But if an ideal of religious freedom was always implicit in Christian thought, it was certainly not always explicitly asserted.

There was always a potentiality for intolerance in the early Christians' disregard for all other religions, their conviction that they alone knew the one true God, that they alone were on the one true path to salvation, that all those outside the church were lost in a world of darkness d sin and error. Still, a belief in the righteousness of one's own cause does not necessarily imply that one should coerce others into joining it. During the early years of the church Christians generally favoured religious toleration, if only because they were so often the victims of persecution; but of course the situation changed dramatically after the emperors themselves became Christians. When Constantine issued the "Edict of Milan" in 313 he granted toleration to the Christian church and to all other religions "so at every man may worship according to his own wish." Later, the emperors adopted a more repressive attitude toward non-Christian realigns; but, in the fourth century, Christian apologists like Hilary of Poitiers d Lactantius still defended the principle of religious freedom.

And toward the end of the century, St. Martin of Tours bitterly condemned a cup of bishops who persuaded the emperor to execute a supposed heretic, Priscillian. Perhaps the case for religious liberty was expressed most eloquently in the words of Lactantius. Liberty has chosen to dwell in religion. For nothing is so much a matter of free will in religion, and no one can be required to worship what he does not will to worship. A decisive turning point in patristic thought came in the teaching of Augustine in 395, when Augustine became bishop of Hippo in north Africa, he found the church in that region divided by a bitter schism between orthodox Catholics and a dissident group known as Donatists.

Religious animosities gave rise to frequent civil disturbances, with riots and street fighting in the cities between the two factions. For years Augustine argued that only peaceful persuasion should be used to end the schism. Finally, however, he accepted the view of his fellow-bishops that the civil power should be called in to repress the dissidents. The works he wrote in defence of this policy seem to contradict his earlier writings where he had emphasized freedom in religious matters. But Augustine always maintained that he was seeking only the salvation of the heretics. "It is better to love with severity than to deceive with indulgence," he wrote.

Augustine justified the use of coercion against heretics by citing the parable of Jesus about a rich man who prepared a great feast. When none of the intended guests would accept the invitations he sent out, the master dispatched his servants to bring in alternative guests.

The key words for Augustine were the last ones (*compelle intrare*). In his interpretation, the guests who refused their invitations were the Jewish people; those who accepted voluntarily were the Gentiles who became Christians; and those who were "compelled to enter" were heretics who had left the church and could licitly be coerced into returning. Modern historians who have studied Augustine sympathetically point out that he always preferred discussion and persuasion in religious controversies; that he did not favour the harshest penalties against heretics—he did not advocate the death penalty, for instance; that for him the purpose of coercion was not to punish but to win back the heretic to the true faith and so to ensure his ultimate salvation.

Less sympathetic historians have designated Augustine as "the prince and patriarch of persecutors" and as "the first theorist of the Inquisition." Certainly his views remained enormously influential throughout the Middle Ages. For a thousand years the church pursued a policy of suppressing religious dissent. Before turning to that theme, however, we need to consider some aspects of medieval religion that could-and eventually did., though only after centuries of struggles and vicissitudes-contribute to a growth of religious freedom.

Church and State

The most obvious way in which the leaders of the medieval church contributed (unintentionally of course) to the emergence of modern religious liberty was by their insistence on the freedom of the church from control by temporal rulers. In the Middle Ages there was never just one hierarchy of government exercising absolute authority, but always two—church and state as we say nowadays—often contending with one another, each limiting the other's power. This duality of government was a rather unusual development in human history. In societies larger than a tribal unit or a city-state the most common form of rulership has been some form of theocratic absolutism. Christianity was different from the beginning. It grew up in an alien culture, the sophisticated classical civilization of Greece and Rome. To become a Christian or to persist in the religion was a matter of free personal choice, often involving considerable self-sacrifice.

There were two authorities in the world; whole areas of religious thought and practice were excluded from the control of the temporal ruler. The text of Gelasius was assimilated into the medieval corpus of canon law and endlessly quoted and discussed in later disputes. The whole issue of empire and papacy arose again when Charlemagne sought to establish a new theocratic empire, and his claims were reiterated by his successors of the Ottoman and Salian dynasties of Germany.

Claiming to be vicars of God on earth, the kings assumed the right to control their churches; they regularly appointed bishops in the lands they ruled and invested them with the ring and staff that were the symbols of spiritual office. When, from time to time, a German emperor invaded Italy and occupied Rome, he chose and appointed popes, just as he appointed other bishops. The church seemed to be drifting into another form of theocratic monism. But a dramatic change came in the pontificate of Gregory VII. Gregory condemned the whole existing order of society as radically contrary to divine justice. He declared himself willing to fight to the death for the "freedom of the church," a phrase he used like a kind of battle-cry. To implement his policy, he forbade the prevailing practice of lay investiture (the appointment of bishops by kings) and so inaugurated a struggle that historians used to call the Investiture Contest but that is now often referred to simply as the Papal Revolution. Henry IV, king of Germany and later emperor, denounced Gregory as a pseudo-pope and a heretic; Gregory responded by deposing Henry from his kingship.

The fight that ensued between pope and emperor was both a war of propaganda and a real civil war in Germany and Italy. At one point Henry had to humiliate himself before the pope at Canossa and humbly beg his forgiveness; but later his armies occupied Rome and drove Gregory into exile. In the end neither side could prevail and, after both of the original protagonists had died, a compromise peace was patched up in the Concordat of Worms. The struggle between popes and kings was reenacted over and over again in the following centuries. After denouncing the theocratic pretensions of kings, the popes were often tempted to assert a theocratic role for themselves.

Freedom of the church from control by the state is one important of modern religious liberty. But it is only a part. 'The libertas ecclesiac that medieval popes demanded was not freedom of religion for each individual person but the freedom of the church as an institution to direct own affairs. It left open the possibility, all too fully realized from the twelfth century onward, that the church might organize the persecution of its own dissident members. And, when the interests of church a state happened to coincide, as they often did in dealing with heresy, there was room for a savage suppression of religious dissent. But, even during the centuries of persecution, there were some aspects of medieval thought and practice that could have been conducive to an alternative tradition of religious toleration. For one thing, medieval canonists and moral theologians often held the overriding value of the individual conscience as a guide to rig conduct.

In the twelfth century, Peter Abelard expanded the argument. He taught that to act against one's conscience was always sinful, even if the conscience erred in discerning what right. A century after Abelard, Thomas Aquinas addressed this same question. It might seem that we are not obliged to follow an erring conscience, he wrote, because we are not obliged to obey the command of a lower authority when it conflicts with that of a higher one; but conscience might favour our acting contrary to the law of God, who was the supreme authority.

In reply, Thomas quoted the Ordinary Gloss to Romans 14:23 and explained that we are only obliged to follow the command of the higher authority when we know that it conflicts with our present judgment. An erring conscience could be formed in good faith if one were ignorant of the higher law. A person was always obliged to do what his conscience discerned as good, even though the conscience might be mistaken. The Ordinary Gloss to the Decretals, a work studied in law schools throughout Europe, explained their implication, "One ought to endure excommunication rather than sin... no one ought to act against his own conscience and he should follow his conscience rather than the judgment of the church when he is certain... one ought to suffer any evil rather than sin against conscience. "

We are not dealing here with a right to religious liberty but with a duty to obey, one's conscience. Still, an emphasis on the primacy of the individual conscience was an important element in later theories of religious rights The medieval position was that a person was right to follow his conscience but that he might suffer at the hands of the authorities if his conscience led him to illicit behaviour.

Similarly, in the modern world, individuals may be led by a sincere conscience to violate the law—as in some forms of civil rights or anti-war protest—but the law will hold them responsible for their actions. There is one further point: medieval moralists did not hold that people should act on mere subjective whims. Everyone was required to use the utmost diligence and every resource of knowledge and understanding to form a correct conscience. Failure to do this was sinful. In practice, it was assumed that most cases where an erring conscience led to illicit behaviour involved culpable ignorance or culpable negligence. In one sphere, the emphasis on individual conscience did lead to a degree of religious toleration.

Medieval doctrine always taught that non-Christians could not be forcibly converted to Christianity. God's grace was a free gift, and it had to be freely accepted. In practice the only substantial populations of non-Christian people scattered throughout the Western church were Jewish communities, and the principle of toleration was explicitly applied to them. The attitude of the medieval church toward the Jews, as toward heretics, was shaped by the teaching of Augustine, though in this case it had a more benign effect.

Augustine held that, although the Jewish people had erred at the time of Christ, still it was God's will that they should always survive. They existed to give permanent independent witness to the divine law revealed in the *Old Testament.* They could also attest to the words of the prophets which Christians understood as foretelling the coming of Christ. (Infidels could not maintain that the Christians had just made up the prophecies about a coming Messiah when the Jews also affirmed their reality.) And accordingly, to fulfil this role, some of the Jewish people would exist until the end of time.

The acceptance of this theology shaped the official attitude of the medieval church toward the Jews. They were indeed discriminated against-made to wear a distinctive dress, excluded from positions of authority in government-but they were allowed to have their own synagogues and to practice their own religion.

Heresy and Persecution

The Wing Interpretation of History, Herbert Butterfield warned historians against "present- mindedness." We should not impose our own ideas on the past, he urged, but rather seek to understand each historical era "in its own terms." The sort of question we ought to ask, Butterfield suggested, is not: How did we get our religious liberty? But rather: Why were people in former ages so given to persecution? It seems to me that both questions are legitimate ones for a historian, but obviously we cannot begin to address the first question until we have considered the second one. And it is not an easy question to answer. In the late Roman empire, laws against heresy, sometimes imposing the death penalty on offenders, were enacted by imperial authority, But in the centuries after the fall of the empire there was little organized persecution, though heretics or people suspected of heresy were sometimes lynched by fanatic mobs. When cases came before church courts, the usual penalty was excommunication.

A more systematic repression began from the twelfth century onward, even as new doctrines of natural rights were growing into existence. This was partly because of the spread of new heresies and partly because of the growing institutionalization of the church. As the church became more aware of itself as an ordered society with its own system of law and organs of government, it became less tolerant of those who rejected its authority. The most threatening heresy of the time was that of the Cathars or Albigensians who had come to dominate substantial areas of southern France. In 1208 Innocent counterattacked by unleashing the Albigensian Crusade, an invasion of southern France by Catholic forces from the north which perpetrated savage massacres in cities that were strongholds of the heretics and effectively destroyed the Cathar civilization in Provence.

Then, in 1215, Innocent's Fourth Lateran Council issued the general condemnation of heretics that I have already quoted. Secular governments also enacted harsh penalties against Heresy. In 1231, Emperor Frederick II decreed that the appropriate punishment was death by burning; the words of his statute indicate the common attitude to heretics: Other rulers enacted similar legislation, and burning at the stake be came the common punishment for heresy.

In some areas of political thought, medieval ideas were not so different from our own. Medieval people had quite well-developed concepts of representation and consent and government under law. But, when we turn to the idea of individual religious rights, their whole mindset was so alien to ours that it takes a considerable effort of historical imagination to enter into their world of thought. The church, he pointed out, had its own institutions of government, its own bureaucracy, its own laws and law courts. In the Middle Ages, secular political power was fragmented. The old Roman empire had passed away, and the attempt to found a medieval Christian empire had failed-partly indeed because of the struggle between popes and emperors that we have considered. National monarchies in France and England were only just beginning to grow into existence. The only bond of unity that held Western Christian society together was the bond of a common religion.

Nowadays the focus of our loyalty is the state; we look to the state to protect our security and our liberty; to be a "stateless person" in the twentieth century is a most unhappy fate. The other side of the coin is that we do not tolerate people who are I perceived of as traitors to the state. We charge them with treason; we punishment on them, sometimes capital punishment in extreme cases. A plea of personal sincerity, that the traitor has acted from good motives, in accordance with his own conscience, is not a sufficient defence.

Medieval people regarded heretics in much the same way, held them guilty of treason to the church, and they treated them as traitors. When a common religion defined the whole way of life of a Society to reject it was to cut oneself off from the community, to become a sort of outlaw—and a dangerous outlaw from a medieval point of view. Medieval people were so convinced of the truth of their religion that they could never see dissent from the accepted faith as arising simply from intellectual error, from a mistake in judgment. They thought that heresy must somehow stem from malice, from a perverted will that deliberately chose evil rather than good, Satan rather than God. Aquinas wrote: "Unfaithfulness is an act of the intellect, but moved by the will." This was the root cause of the medieval hatred of heresy.

The heretics were seen, not only as traitors to the church but as traitors to God. To medieval people it seemed that they had rejected God's truth and God's love out of pride and self-love, the love of their own self-contrived errors. They had set themselves on a path that could lead only to eternal dam nation and, unless they were restrained, they would lure countless others to the same terrible fate. Elementary justice and charity, it seemed, required that they be rooted out.

The Inquisition that pursued this task with increasingly harsh and cruel measures, including the use of torture to extort confessions, was accepted as a necessary safeguard of Christian society. Thinking about the Inquisition may remind us of two aphorisms that Lord Acton quoted. The first is the well-known saying of Mme de Stael: "To understand all is to forgive all." The other, less indulgent, is from the Duke de Broglie: "We should beware of too much explaining lest we end up with too much forgiving." Neither aphorism is altogether satisfying for a historian. Our task is surely to understand and explain as fully as possible; but we do not have to condone everything that we have tried to understand, and, when everything possible has been said in mitigation, the medieval theory and practice of religious persecution will seem abhorrent to most modern people. Over a period of centuries, thousands of persons were hunted down, tortured, and killed for a crime that, to us, might seem a mere eccentricity of personal belief.

A critical observer, looking back over the history of the West for the past thousand years and at the policies pursued in many parts of the world during the present century, might suppose that persecution is a normal pattern of human conduct. He might think that Butterfield had got his question upside down after all. Perhaps the real question a historian has to answer is not: Why were they so given to persecution? But rather: Why are we so committed to an ideal of religious liberty" This the final topic that we have to consider.

6

Prisoners and Human Rights Issues

Rights which are inherent in our nature without which we cannot live as human beings are generally termed as human rights. According to an United Nations publication human rights allow us to fully develop and use our human qualities, our intellegence, our talents and our conscience and to satisfy our spiritual and other needs. They are based on mankind's increasing demand for a life in which the inherent dignity and worth of each human being will receive respect and protection.

The denial of human rights and fundamental freedoms not only is an individual and personal tragedy but also creates conditions of social and political unrest, sowing the seeds of violence and conflict within societies and nations.

However, the concept of human rights does not convey the same meaning and understanding to the matters of different systems of Government. It varies in a democratic government accepting the "Rule of Law" and totalitarian government or to an all powerful monarchy. It does not have the same meaning in India, U.K. U.S.A., C.I.S. and China and it is differently understood in the military and semi-military areas. In fact, all the 190 odd countries of the United Nations deny violation of human rights.

International Instruments

Among the various human rights are the one not to be subjected to torture or other cruel, inhuman or degrading treatment of punishment and the right to freedom from arbitrary arrest or detention. In other words, one is not to be subjected to physical or mental pain or suffering with a view to extracting a confession or information, or to intimidation or punishment for any act allegedly committed. In fact, there are over 30 instruments provided under various United Nations Agencies, concerning crime prevention, specifying and securing human rights in response to specific problems perceived by the various member states. These include the Universal Declaration of Human Rights, the International Covenant on Civil and Political Rights, the Convention Against Torture and other Cruel, Inhuman or Degrading, Treatment or Punishment, the Standard Minimum Rules for the Treatment of Prisoners, the United Nations Standard Minimum Rules for the Administration of Juvenile Justice (Beijing Rules) and the Body of Principles for the Protection of All Persons under Any Form of Detention or Imprisonment.

The United Nations programme on crime prevention and criminal justice system has focused on pre-trail detention in dealing with the treatment of detained and imprisoned persons, although no comprehensive standards for the protection of persons in pre-trial detention, whether in Police or Judicial custody can claim protection under the national legal system as well as under the respective instruments, provided the concerned State adopts any such instrument. Not only absence of torture and ill-treatment are the guiding principles behind the standards on the treatment, but also prosecution of the perpetrators of torture are provided for.

While guaranteeing detainees freedom from torture and arbitrary arrest, the UDHR and ICCPR provides for the presumption of their innocence of any criminal charges till trial, under Article 11 (1) and 10(2) respectively. Similar provisions are also contained in Rule 84(2) of the Standard Minimum Rules of 1955, as well as under General Comment 13(7) of the Human Rights Committee under Article 40 para 4 of the ICCPR.

Article 5 of the UDHR, Article 7 of the ICCPR, Principles 21(1), (2) and Principles 23 of Body of Principles for the Protection of All Persons under Any Form of Detention or Imprisonment, in short the Principles of Detention as well as the General Comment 7(1) and 7(2) of the Human Rights Committee provide that statements found to be obtained by tortures should not be used as evidence against any one and that the allegations of torture should be vigorously investigated and perpetrators prosecuted. It is significant to observe that Article 4 of the ICCPR prohibits the States from derogating under any circumstances of the right of Individuals not to be tortured or to be subjected to cruel, inhuman or degrading treatment or punishment.

In order to prohibit the torture and ill treatment of detainees for the purpose of compelling them to confess to crimes or divulge information under fear or threat by the Torturer, the General Assembly adopted a Declaration on the protection of All Persons from being subjected to torture and Other Cruel, Inhuman or Degrading Treatment in the year 1975. This Declaration was given legal sanction by way of the Convention in 1984.

The Convention not only provides that the States parties will outlaw torture in their national legislation, but also notes explicitly that no order from a superior or one under exceptional circumstances may be invoked as a justification of torture and other cruel, inhuman or degrading treatment or punishment.

The Convention also introduces two new elements of particular importance to combat torture. The first is that a torturor may be prosecuted where ever he is found in the territory of any State Party, since the convention specifies that persons alleged to have committed acts of torture may be tried in any State party or be extradited for trail in any State Party where they have committed their crimes. The other new element is that the Convention contains a provision allowing for an international inquiry if there is reliable information indicating that the torture is being systematically practised in the territory of a State Party. Such an inquiry may include a visit to the State Party concerned, with its agreement.

The State Parties to the Convention also pledge to take legislative, administrative, judicial and other measures to prevent acts of torture in any territory under their jurisdiction. No exceptional circumstances whatsoever, whether a sate of war, internal political instability or any other public emergency, may be invoked as a justification of torture.

The Convention also provides for a Committee Against Torture, to oversee implementation by the State Parties and to resolve any allegations brought to it. This Committee comprising of 10 members are required to consider on measures taken by the member States of the Convention to honour their undertakings. Further, the Committee is also empowered to make confidential inquiries.

In addition, the Committee on Human Rights has a special rapporteur on torture who acts in individual cases and reports to the Commission on the action he has taken with regard to instances of torture in particular countries. There is also the "thematic mandate" on arbitrary detention, besides the right thematic special rapporteurs on related matters, Their reports are submitted to the General Assembly, which are placed for discussion in public sessions and constitute an important element for any decisions the Committee may take on the relevant item.

Further, in the year 1990, the 8th U.N. Congress on the Prevention of Crime and the Treatment of Offenders also called upon the U.N. bodies to assist countries in improving conditions of pre-trial detention, and in developing non-custodial measures as an alternative to the use of pre-trial detention, and request the Secretary General to assist in the task. The Congress inter-alia observed;

(a) Pre-trail detention may be ordered only if there are reasonable grounds to believe that the persons concerned have been involved in the Commission of the alleged offences and these is a danger of their absconding or committing further serious offences, or a danger that the course of justice will be seriously interferred with if they are left free;

  (i) All proceedings concerning persons in custody should be conducted as expeditiously as possible so as to reduce the period of pre-trail detention to the minimum.

The following year, the Human Rights Committee created a working group with the task of investigating cases of detention, imposed arbitrarily or otherwise inconsistently, with the relevant international standards.

Apart from the above Declarations and Conventions the Declaration on Basic Principles of Justice for Victims of Crime and Abuse of Power calls upon the States for providing remedies by way of restitution and compensation, and for providing necessary material, medical, psychological and social assistance to victims of official abuse, as well as for providing access to justice. There are also the Principles on the Effective Prevention and Investigation of Extra Legal, Arbitrary and Summary Executions, adopted by the ESCOC in 1989 and the Declaration on the Protection of All Persons from Enforced Disappearances, adopted by the General Assembly in 1992.

The dignity and humanity of persons in detention Is also sought to be maintained through the Basic Principles on the use of Force and Fire Arms by Law Enforcement Officials, two of which being considered significant are quoted in extension;

Principle 15—Law Enforcement Officials, in their relations with persons in custody or detention, shall not use force, except where strictly necessary for the maintenance of security and order within the institution, or when personal safety is threatened.

Principle 16—Law Enforcement Officials, in their relations with persons in custody or detention, shall not use fire arms, except in selfdefence or in the defence of others against the immediate threat of death or serious injury, or when strictly necessary to prevent the escape of a person in custody or detention presenting the danger referred to in principle (the danger of the perpetration of a particularly serious crime involving grave threat to life.)

Problem of Enforcement

Inspite of the various international instruments, pre-trial detention in Police and judicial custody continue to be a cause of concern to the international community. Although, countries claim of observing the norms of human rights through their domestic legal systems, many countries have not matched the international requirements. The international conventions, particularly the one on torture remains to be ratified by many a state. Inspite of the general agreement to incorporate the basic provisions in the domestic legal systems, many a State have not taken any step towards that end, although signatory states incur a legal obligation to implement the human rights standards to which they subscribe at the international level. This has resulted in the detainees being subjected to the worst conditions of confinement, in antiquated, over crowded, unsafe detention centres. Not to speak of the lack of distinction between convicted and pre-trial detainees, at times three to four times the capacity are confined in the prisons. What is more appaling is that in many a country, persons arrested are never brought before a judicial authority, often times being held in-communicando. Apart from the national prison systems, suspects held are often tortured during Police custody, to extract confession towards their incrimination and to divulge information. This has on occasions resulted in cruel fatalities.

Violation of Custodial Rights

Large number of men, women and children continue to be the victims of torture in custody, due to the lawlessness of the law enforcement machinery. Many of such victims have no remedy for want of corroboration of their torture in police custody, for physical injuries at times do not surface on their bodies. The Police machinery, continue to employ the policy of regression, often by the use of third degree methods, in the form of beating, use of cigarattes butts to burn the skin, denying food, water, sleep drinking urine, putting ice on naked part of human body, head down suspension, electric shock treatment, hot water bottle treatment, parading naked in public, inserting steel or live wires into body crevices. Sereve beating to the extent of fracturing of limbs, hanging upside down and inserting of pins and nails in the sensitive parts of the body, including the private parts, are some of the methods used by the police against women prisoners in custody. Some such, victims of torture suffer mutilation or paralysis, for remaining period of their life for want of proper and timely medical treatment.

Factors which contribute to torture include lack of transparency about what happens in Police custody; Police disregard of legal safeguards regarding policy custody, absence of adequate safeguards regarding interrogation of suspects, lack of accountability; lack of support for police professionalism and prolonged remand in Police custody.

The demand for dignity of the individuals and security of the State at the same time, in the context of rights and liberty of citizens, has to be protected and distinguished from challenges of terrorism and insurgency. Yet, preventing a national institution from investigating violence committed by the Police, severly reduces any such institutions potential effectiveness as a protector of human rights. Similarly, the defence personnel as exempt from the complaint mechanisms may also have a detrimental effect on the institution's effectiveness, particularly in view of the strength of the defence services in many States, and its corresponding potentials to violate human rights by way of torturing the suspects in various ways.

At times victims of torture die in custody, unable to bear the third degree torture of the law enforcement machinery. Such loss of life is a serious cause of concern to the world community. The Human Rights Committee has observed that when a death occurs in custody the State may take steps to ascertain how it occured. In a case where autopsy was given by the military authorities, but the State did not submit any information on the circumstances of death, or the inquiries it had made into there circumstances the Human Rights Committee had held that the State had violated Article 6(1) of the ICCPR by not taking appropriate measures to protect the detainees life in detention *(Wellemmo Igna Çio Dermit Barbato and Hugo Haroldo Dermit Barbuto Vs. Uruguuways* 21.10.82) The Committee held that while it could not determine whether the detainee committed suicide or was killed by others, the State authorities had violated Article 6(1) by not protecting and detainee's life and not investigating how his death occured.

Custodial death may be equated with murder perpetuated by the over enthuastic guardians of law, whose legal duty is to interrogate and keep accused under custody on behalf of the State. The death of a detenu generates some suspicion about the extend of the use of third degree methods of interrogation by the Police all over the world. It amounts to a flagrant violation of human rights in its extreme form which no executive officer should violate under any pretext. It is a disgrace to the entire police profession which is put under a cloud and therefore, calls for condemnation and punishment of those guilty law enforecement officers. Those who exist to protect the freedoms cannot be allowed to indulge in a breach of trust. It calls for strict vigil of the human rights activists all over the world, to ensure the basic liberties to women, children, suspects and even to the proclaimed terrorists.

No nation is free from human rights abuse and therefore, can claim a pre-trial detention system that could riot be improved upon. But at the same time issues of torture are after politicised, giving it an exaggerated form.

Therefore, government should respond to situations of such abuses by streamlining the police force as well as incorporating various provisions of international instruments into their domestic legal system. States have a responsibility to conform to human rights standards setting of the United Nations, by removing the incompatibility of its law with the convention standards.

Situation in India

Coming to the situation in India, it has to be observed that human rights standards find place both in the Constitution Itself as well as various legislations adopted from time to time. Among the significant Constitutional provisions are those incorporated in Articles 14 to 16, 19 to 23, 25, 29 to 32, 136 and 226. Important provisions in the Code of Criminal Procedure are to be found in Sections 173(3), 207, 208 218, 228(2), 235(2), 238, 240(2), 248(2), 273, 304, 306, 313, 314, 317, 374, 379, 380 and 381 etc. However, the Police Act of 1861 is very ancient and needs to be amended to meet the present day demands. Yet, inspite of various provisions, the country is yet to ratify Optional Protocol of ICCPR.

Custodial crimes and Police brutalities are reported to be practiced in various States in India. Due to lack of transparency to the desired extent, the Government has come in for criticism from various national and international organisations, within the country and abroad. Among the international organisations, Amnesty International has been reporting widely on the allegations of human rights violation in certain states in the country.

Amnesty International's current concerns are centred round the use of torture and ill treatment, which is considers to be widespread, leading to deaths of over 50 people in Police custody each year, as a result of such practices. Of the 43 cases of reported deaths in Andhra Pradesh, Karnataka and Uttar

Pradesh between 1986 and 1989, 12 Policemen were reported suspended and only one convicted. However, because of the prolonged procedure of Courts, cases take a long time to be disposed off.

The torture inflicted is often with a view of extract information or towards self incrimination. In the case of women, most allegations of torture concern rape in police custody.

Amnesty International received reports of 517 custody deaths since 1.1.1985 upto 1.3.1994. By November, 1992 it had submitted 455 cases to the Government for their opinion. However, the government submitted fact sheets in respect of 230 of those cases, stating that in more than a third of those cases, there was primafacie evidence that further action was needed against the police allegedly responsible for torturing and killing suspects in police custody. 36 deaths were reported to Amnesty International in 1993 and 64 deaths in custody in 1994. Delhi along accounting for 10 of the 36 deaths during 1993. Although 12 deaths in custody were reported in Kerala between March 1992 and December 1993 the State Police Chief while denying most of them to be caused by torture nevertheless, condemned torture by observing deaths in custody as "the work of devils".

Earlier, in 1992 Amnesty International report on India had observed: "Yet torture is pervasive and a daily routine in everyone of India's 25 States, irrespective of whether arrests are made by the police, para military forces or the army—In all 415 (deaths in custody) there is evidence that the victims who include women and children are brutally beaten or otherwise tortured until they die!"

In the State of Jammu and Kashmir, the Amnesty International listed 706 cases of torture as on 31st January, 1995 but the government has brushed aside the allegations by observing that "generalisation cannot substitute facts". The government held 273 of the 519 listed cases to militants killed in encounter and cross firing. In respect of 81 others go it held that no reports were ever lodged with the police, while 32 persons were considered as intraced. Another 14 were reported to have died due to accident or sickness. Only 85 cases were said to be found involving custodial violence and were said to be under police investigation. However, only in 8 cases charges were framed.

Even though the government has admitted of some custodial deaths having taken place, these are considered to be few and far between. The government has maintained that 225 security forces have been proceeded against. As against this 400 army officers and other ranks are reported killed and over 1000 injured in the hands of the extremists during the last five years. However, provocative grave abuses committed by armed separatists groups can never justify the security forces resorting to arbitrary detentions, torture, extra-judicial killings or "disappearences". It has to be remembered that such practices are prohibited in Indian law and clearly contravenes international human rights standards which the Indian Government is bound to uphold.

The Government facts sheets, responding to the Amnesty International's allegations of "lack of systematic procedure for the independent and impartial investigation", has condemned the, use of torture, terming the incidents as mere abberrations, while denying that the use of torture is wide spread in India. The very fact that the Government has been responding to the allegations of the Amnesty International that the government is taking the issue of custodial violence seriously, by pointing to the action taken to investigate cases of custodial deaths, and prosecute those respondible, is an indication of the problem being addressed to by the Government. Yet, the fact that the situation calls for action is reflected from, the report of the United Nations Special Rapporteur on Extra-Judicial Summary or Arbitrary Executions as observed at Geneva in February, 1995:

"The special Rapporteur notes with concern that, while in most cases investigations are said to be initiated, reports brought to its attention suggest that such proceedings virtually never appear to conclude with a judgment convicting the security forces personnel involved. The length of the investigation procedures is also working in a number of cases, inquiries opened more than two years ago and are still said to be in progress."

But one has to accept that under the existing legal system, the investigative procedures am lengthy and time consuming, resulting in delay in the disposal of cases against police and para-military personnel. Of late, however, the interrogation methods of the army are reported to be streamlined with the imparting of necessary training. Further, the policy of providing some amount of transparancy is also much welcome. In the case of Srinagar, the Amnesty International and others had claimed that there existed a torture camp at Papa Two where captured militants were being tortured, but foreign groups visiting and interviewing the foreign mercinaries lodged at the improvised lock up belie such allegations.

Surprisingly apart from the disturbed frontiers of the country, even in other States them have been allegations of torture (Chart). In the case of West Bengal, 12 custodial deaths are reported to have occured during the current year (1995), taking the total to 217 custodial deaths since 1977. This has invited a strong reaction from the Chief Minister of the State, who has cautioned the police to handle the problem with utmost restraint. Because of the strong public opinion against police excesses, the government initiated action against most of the guilty officials and in others, charge sheets have been submitted and the cases are pending trial.

According to the National Human Right Commission, between April 1994 and May 1995 out of total of 108 custodial deaths, 30 have occured in West Bengal, 14 in Assam, 9 in Rajasthan and 7 in Uttar Pradesh. Around the same time between April 1994 and June 1995 a total of 75 persons lost their lives in Judicial custody, with Delhi accounting for 46 of them. Infact, during the month of June, of the current year alone Delhi has accounted for 10 such deaths, leading the Human Rights Commission to institute an inquiry.

Responding to the situation in the country, the Prime Minister observed on 14.09.92, that action had been taken against 230 officers and security force personnel for violation of human rights in Punjab and Kashmir, and prosecution was being initiated against many others. He observed -

"There can be nothing more revolting and reprehensible than the betrayal of custodial trust by the guardians of law and those appointed to protect the individual. We have to deal with such cases with alacrity and in an exemplary manner and also to ensure that the victims obtain possible and quick response".

He reiterated the nation's commitment In another statement a few months later, on 17.02.93, ensuring that excesses are not committed, specially In custody, stating that "human rights am of paramount importance in a democracy, like ours". According to the Amnesty International this demonstrates that torture practices am not government policy and that there is a recognition at the highest governmental level that India faces a major problem of custodial violence in respect of pre-trial detainees which needs to be addressed is called for, while at the saint time, the existing safeguards are to be properly implemented. For instance, magisterial inquiry into allegations of custodial deaths is provided for mandatory under the law, but is often observed in its breach. Further the Commissions of Enquiry Act, 1952 provides discretion upon the government not to make public, report of nay inquiry commissions, which leads to a feeling of protecting the guilty. A happy augary has been the decision of the Govt. to amend the Criminal Procedure Code, making it mandatory for institution of judicial inquires into cases of custodial deaths. Further jail reforms need to be urgently addressed to as well.

Role of judiciary

The Constitution has assigned a significant role to the judiciary in our legal and constitutional system. It has been playing its role as a sentinel of human rights, not to speak of the constitutional and legal rights. The concept of Public Interest litigation through the process of liberalisation of the concept of *locus standi* has played a humanising role in the sphere of custodial violence, pertaining to pre-trial detainees. This is also evident from the second periodic report of the UNHCR, which has stated that:

"The Supreme Court in India and the various High Courts of the individual states ensured the effective implementation of Human Rights through a liberalised review of administrative action. Such liberalisation has led to the growth of Public Interest Litigation and seizure of Court's jurisdiction in such matter even on the basis of post-cards or telegrams received from individuals or of stories or reports published in magazines or newspapers and the provisions of compulsory legal aid to the needy".

An important role is taste upon the judiciary to see that the police cannot succeed in concealing evidence of custodial violence by falsifying or destroying police records or putting pressure on doctors to manage post mortem reports. Till such time the various conventions are not ratified, the judiciary while implementing the existing legislation in a firm manner should explore the spirit of the international conventions through humanitarian interpretation, atleast under the existing constitutional provisions.

The judiciary is the basic structure for protection of human rights at the national level. The helpless victims of custodial crimes consider it their only my of hope. Therefore, a duty is cast upon the judiciary to help preserve the judicial process for the protection of the rights of individuals in detention.

As observed by the Committee of Ministers of the Council of Europe:

Custody pending trial should be ordered only if there is reasonable suspicion that the accused has committed the alleged offence and that he is likely to absconds, interfere with the course of justice, or commit a serious offence.

The Supreme Court is well as the different High Courts have awarded compensation, even in writ proceedings for violation of human rights. Some of these Important rulings in recent years should certainly help prevent human rights violations, and facilitate effective relief being, granted to the victims of custodial violence as well as to the dependents of the victims of custodial death.

On March 24, 1993 the apex court awarded examplary damages of Rupees one and half lacs to the mother of Suman Behera, a victim of custodial violence from the State of Orissa, who died on 1. 12.87. Similarly, on 19.3.93 the Court awarded monetary compensation of Rupees three lacs to the widow and two children of Joginder Kumar who died in police custody on 6.8.90. The Supreme Court emphasised that the puling did not prejudice the Woman's right to claim further compensation through other legal avenues, and directed to Delhi administration to sanction the prosecution of five police official and a Sub-Divisional Magistrate. The apex Court has even gone to the extent of holding that payment of compensation to a victim of rights violation should be personal liability of the offender and not that of the State. The Court has considered the right against torture, cruel or unusual punishment or degrading treatment and the right against custodial violence as emanated rights, though unenumerated in the Constitution.

Such steps by the apex Court are indeed a positive indication of its serious view on instances of torture and custodial violence. Sentensing the culprits to prison terms and awarding compensation to the victims or their dependents is certainly to have Its effect on the law enforcement machinery. But this has to be matched by the government with equally effective measures to expeditiously bring to book the erring members of the law enforcement machinery. Diseased brains who derive sedastic pleasure in human torture, obviously need to be weeded out of the police force.

The role of the National Human Rights Commission

The National Human Rights institutions have an important role to play in protecting and promoting human rights, aimed at ensuring that they are enjoyed by one and all. In consonance with such objective, the National Human Rights Commission was set up in India on the 1st of October, 1993 under an ordinance, subsequently replaced by the Protection of Human Rights Act 1993, the range of functions being provided under Section 12 of the Act. This is in part a response to the changing social realities and emerging trends in the nature of crime and violence. The Act is also a reflection of the Vienna Declaration of 1993, which expressed the desirability of drawing up a national action plan for the promotion and protection of human rights through a set of priorities and appropriate vehicles for implementation.

Among other activities, the commission has been particularly engaged, either suo-motto or on the basis of complaints with instances of custodial deaths/ violences such as custodial death and rape, disappearance from custody, cruel, inhuman or degrading punishment and torture. Taking a serious view of such violations the Commission has observed that such instances must be boldly and swiftly dwelt with, and accordingly has issued instructions to all State Governments and Union Territories asking for reports from the District Magistrates and Superintendent of Police within 24 hours of the occurance of any such activities. The Commission has further observed that failure to comply will be considered as an attempt to suppress knowledge of any such incident. It has further called for immediate deterrent action against police staff indulging in custodial violence. Going a step further it has also intervened in Court proceedings, apart from holding sitting to probe alleged custodial crimes.

The Commission has given a new direction and added a meaningful perspective in the realisation of human rights in the country. To cite an example/ instance in the case of custodial death of Basudeo Shah a case under Section 302 of the Indian

Penal Code has been registered on the direction of the Commission. The erring officers have been arrested and investigation is in progress. Besides, the Commission has also recommended payment of Rs. 50,000/- to the next of kin of the deceased. The 12 illustrative cases as provided in its 1994-95 annual report indeed reflects a depressing situation with regard to custodial deaths due to police torture, killings of innocent civilians in cross fires between the security forces and the terrorists in the North-East, besides rapes in custody and so on.

While recommending implementation of the recommendation of the National Police Commission, 1979 it has stressed the need for separating the law and order function from the investigative role of police. Another significant recommendation of the Commission relates to accession to the 1984 Convention Against Torture. The Commission has also recommended change in the system with regard to post-mortem in custodial deaths. X Ray analysis has been made mandatory and it would be required to conduct the entire process with video cameras in vigil. Scene of death should be preserved for forensic examination.

The Commission has further been urging the respective State Governments to initiate serious action against allegations of custodial deaths and violence. The data collected by the Commission is being constantly monitored and follow up measures initiated to prevent custodial deaths and ensure that human rights of citizens are not violated.

Further, the Commission has been taking a serious view of deaths in judicial custody. While visiting certain jails, it has made some significant observations besides important recommendations. It has observed that some of the jails are very much over crowded, lacking in proper medical facilities. While citing the instance of Tihar Jail in the capital, it has observed that 30 to 40 persons die in Tihar every year due to TB which is a curable disease. Besides ordering an inquiry into the death of Rajan Pillai, it has also ordered a general probe in respect of deaths in Tihar jail to cover all deaths which have occured in the jail during the last two years. According to the Commission, deaths were related to reasons which could be controlled and the cause removed or properly checked.

In fact, the Chairperson of the Commission has been repeatedly stressing upon the need to sensitise police officials through proper inculcation of human rights values. Towards this end a meeting of 10 Director General of Police was arranged by the Commission in May 1995 to consider, in particular the question of Police training and human rights. This was followed by a recent training programme of police officers of the rank of Deputy Inspector General and above. Further, the Commission has been advising the National Police Academy and the various State governments on various aspects of sensitising the police personnel.

To match the efforts of the Commission, it has also been suggesting to the respective State governments to constitute State Human Rights Commission, who are yet to set up the Commission. Moreover, it has also been emphasising upon the need to sensitise the judicial officers towards human rights values, besides calling upon the State's to constitute human rights courts.

The Commission has also called upon the Government to effect certain changes in the Act to enable the Commission to compel attendance of witness, besides allowing it to initiate proceedings for prosecution as well as for providing interim relief to victims of their dependents. Such measures would enable the Commission to conduct effective investigation through trained personnel and effective and judicative functions.

Sensitising the police and judicial personnel

Prevention of human rights abuses can be properly effected through awareness rising both amongst the public and the law enforcement machinery. This has to be supported through legal measures to counter human rights abuses, particularly in the sphere of custodial violence.

While internal vigilence can be instilled by sensitising an individual to his or her own potential for vindictive behaviour through legal awareness, that of the Police force can be instilled by a behavioural reorientation through training to effect attitudional change in the police force. In fact, a complete restructuring of the police is called for. Training courses concerning law enforcement personnel should be developed which transform knowledge about human rights into operative skills. These courses should aim at fast values and attitudes pertaining to national and international standards, particularly relevant to day to day activities. In other words, the police personnel should be taught to encounter their problems perfectly in consonance with the various instruments relating to torture and other forms of custodial abuses. The process of training and education should aim at motivating the targetted group to continue the training process after completion of course for dissemination of information and free and post course evaluation.

The training process should focus on sensitivity towards observance of human rights, scientific investigation and more intense teaching of the provisions of law dealing with custodial violence and consequences of the policemen. The performance of the officials should be regularly monitored to ensure that they are sensitive to human rights considerations, and that they strictly comply with the relevant provisions of law during the course of investigation. The superior officers should pay surprise visits to police stations to find for themselves any instances of violation of the rights of the accused.

Preventive and punitive measures should be inflicted by way of stringent disciplinary action. For the aforesaid purpose the service rules should suitably incorporate provisions for stringent punishment for violation of human rights. Guilty officials should also be proceeded with under the relevant penal provisions, apart from being made liable to compensate the victim or his family, besides other relief to be provided by the State. Besides the reformative and punitive measures, preventitive measures are also called for. A person under custody should be sent for medical examination and make the reports available to relatives of the accused. Further, the police immediately upon arresting a person should be obliged to provide information of such detention to relatives or any one nominated by the arrested person.

Persons arrested should not be subjected to interrogation for more than a specified period at a stretch. Scientific methods should be adopted by the investigating agency to collect evidence. All modern infrastructure should be made available to the investigation agency, Conditions of police lock ups should be improved without any further delay, and all basic amenities should be provided therein.

.... As soon as an accused is produced before a magistrate, he shall enquire from the detenue if he has any grievance pertaining to physical torture during his police custody. If any complaint is made, he shall take cognisance of the offence and take all other necessary action as may be deemed just and proper."

Thus apart from sensitising the police personnel, the judicial officers should also be provided training, to accord recognition to humanitarian considerations. In fact, as observed by Amnesty International in respect of India, a series of court decisions that have established clear police responsibilty for some custodial deaths and have provided relief to the victims of families, are a further indication of a move towards ending impunity.

The judicial officers should make a conscious effort to prevent torture or maltreatment in police lock-up, or by reducing the length of police custody for investigation, legal assistance should also be provided to the needy at State expense when an accused under custody is produced for the first time before a judicial officer. Further, judicial enquiry in all cases of rape, death and grievious hurt in police custody should be got conducted by Senior Judicial Officers, till such time state level human rights courts are established.

Besides sensitising the police and judicial service personnel to bring about commitment and understanding, increase of public awareness of human rights, particularly matters relating to pre-trial detainees has to be achieved through a process of information and education as envisaged by the Paris principles.

Crimes perpetrated on pre-trial detainees need to he officially condemned and international instruments to be ratified in order to put a stop to custodial violence, besides providing transparency in the functioning of the governmental machinery. Periodic steps are required for implementation of existing standards on the treatment of offenders under a responsive legal system. The lot of the pre-trial detainees would be greatly improved even if existing standards set forth are respected.

Concept of Human Rights

The concept of human rights is not a new phenomenon but it remained a domestic matter failing within the jurisdiction of States until the adoption of the U.N. Charter' by the States at San Francisco in 1945. Under the Preamble to the Charter the Member States reaffirmed faith in fundamental human right; in the dignity and worth of the human person, in the equal rights of man and women and of nations large and small', Article 1 of the Charter has enjoined the United Nations with the responsibility of promotion and encouragement of respect for human rights and fundamental freedoms for all without any distinction.

Besides the United Nations, its Member States have pledged to promote 'Universal respect for and observance of, human rights and fundamental freedoms without distinction as race, sex, language or religion.

While in the early years of the United Nations there was considerable dispute about the nature and scope of the, obligation and the meaning of 'human rights and fundamental freedoms'. Then issues are now by and large settled of the fundamental instruments on Human Rights. The Universal Declaration of Human Rights and the .international Covenant on Civil and Political Rights," have not only created binding legal obligations for Member States in the field of human rights protection but have also provided minimum, definitional guidance on what the international community understands by human rights and fundamental freedoms. The broad human rights guarantees set forth in these instruments have been supplemented and complemented by a series of instruments promulgated by the General Assembly, the UNESCO and other specialized agencies. As a result of these legal developments the matter of human rights as such is no longer a matter essentially within the domestic jurisdiction of individual .States as that concept is set out in Article 2(7)1 of the Charter, the domestic jurisdiction clause.

Some of the international instruments on human rights like the International Convenant on Civil and Political Rights, the Convention against Torture', Mid the Convention oil the Rights of the Child, are multilateral treaties which impose specific human rights obligations oil (he States adhering to them. The international norms and standards laid down in these instruments are concerned with the promotion of' the dignity of all human beings and protection of the rights set out in these instruments.

Human Rights and Criminal Justice

The norms and standards laid down in these instruments are of universal character and touch upon nearly all the important aspects of human life including criminal Justice viz. pre-trial detention, administrative detention, post-trial conviction and imprisonment, Among the international human rights instruments relating to criminal .justice mention call be made of the Convention against Torture and Other Cruel, Inhuman or Degrading Treatment or Punishment, the Convention on the Rights of the Child, the Declaration against Torture, the Code or Conduct for Law Enforcement Officials", the Safeguards Guaranteeing Protection of the Rights of Those Facing the Death Penalty," the Principles on the Effective Prevention anti Investigation of' Extra-Legal, Arbitrary and Summary Executions," the Principles for the protection of persons with Menial Illness and the Improvement of Mental Health Care," Declaration on the Protection of' All Persons from Enforced Disappearance. The Convention for the Protection of Human Rights and Fundamental Freedoms," the Body of Principles for the Protection of All Persons under Any Form or Detention or imprisonment," the Vienna Convention on Consular Relations," the American Convention oil Human Rights, and the African Charier oil Human and Peoples Rights."

While the international instruments which are in the form of multilateral treaties impose legally binding obligations on States, nonbinding instruments are in the form of resolutions, guidelines, code of conduct and declarations. They do not have a binding effect on states, but which might be useful In interpreting broader human rights standards oil crime control and criminal justice and implementing human rights guarantees in national legislation.

Evolution of Human Rights standards on Pre-trial Detention

The first standard-setting specifically relating to criminal justice began with the first U.N. Congress an crime prevention, which adopted in 1955 the Standard Minimum Rules for the Treatment of Prisoners subsequently approved by the Economic and Social Council. The Rules contain detailed provisions on pre-trial detention in a separate section entitled "prisoners under arrest or awaiting trial. These rules are derived from the presumption of innocence of the accused and stipulate that pre-trial detainees shall be kept separate from convicted prisoners and benefit by a special regime laid down in this instrument. Rule 95 was added In 1977 fit order to extend the protection of the Rules to persons under administrative detention." By its resolution 1984/47 of 25 May 1984 the Economic and Social Council offered Governments further guidance on the implementation of the Minimum rules, under the said resolution the Council established procedures for the Secretary-General and Governments to co-operate in reporting and disseminating information on implementation of the Rules.

The 'Body of Principles for the Protection of All Persons under Any Form of' Detention or Imprisonment' adopted by the General Assembly in 1989 is another important instrument relating to protection of pre-trial detainees. It considerably strengthens the rights and status of detained or imprisoned persons by reaffirming and specifying the guarantees contained in the Universal Declaration or Human Rights and the International Covenant on Civil and Political Rights," Of particular importance are rights of the detainees to visits by, persons such as doctors and lawyers" and family members" and the right to effective, recourse to a Judicial or other authority, such as a habeas corpus or recurso de ampero.

In addition to the Standard Minimum Rules for the Treatment of Prisoners, he United Nations Crime Congresses and Crime Programmes have, over the years contributed to the adoption of several other important international instructions referring, inter alia, to pre-trial detention, such as the Declaration against Torture; the Code of Conduct for Law Enforcement Officials; the Principles of Medical Ethics against Torture;" the Convention against, Torture; the Safeguards Guaranteeing Protection of the Rights of Those Facing the Death Penalty.

The creation in 1991 of' the Commission on Human Rights Working Group on Arbitrary Detention with die task of "investigating cases of detention imposed arbitrarily or otherwise inconsistently with the relevant international standards" was a landmark, stop in the aid of the human rights of detainees. The Working Group is authorized to "seek and receive Information from Governments and intergovernmental and non-govern mental organizations, and ... I receive information from the individuals concerned, their families or their representatives. In its First Report to the Commission on Human Rights, the Working Group identified three categories or cases for the purpose of deciding on the arbitrary character of cases submitted to it.' The third category concerns cases in which non-observance or all or part of the international provisions relating to the right to it non trial is such that it confers on the deprivation of freedom on arbitrary character. The Working Group further identified, inter alia, nineteen pre-trial situations in which non-respect of the right to a fair trial could confer on the detention an arbitrary character. Fifteen of these situations apply to both judicial and administrative detention, whereas four apply only to judicial detention, The Working Group has since dealt with many cases where it found arbitrary detention, and in a considerable number of cases the detainees have been released.

With a view to tackle the problem or torture against pre-trial detainees the General Assembly in 1975 adopted the Declaration oil the Protection of All Persons from Being Subjected to Torture and other Cruel Inhuman or Degrading Treatment or Punishment. The provisions of the Declaration acquired the force of international law by virtue of the Convention against Torture and other Cruel, Inhuman or Degrading Treatment or Punishment in 1984. The anti-torture Convention has established the Committee against Torture, to monitor the State's compliance with its provisions. Besides, the Commission on Human Rights has appointed a Special Rapporteur oil Torture, who acts in individual case and sends reports to the Commission oil the actions taken by him oil the cases of torture in particular countries.

Another important development with regard to evolution of standards on torture and ill-treatment was the adoption in 1985 of the Declaration of Basic Principles of Justice for Victims of Crime and Abuse of Power."' The Declaration called upon Member States to provide remedies, including compensation, and necessary material, medical, psychological and social assistance to victims of official abuse.

The Principles oil the Effective Prevention and Investigation of Extra-legal-, Arbitrary and Summary Executions, recommended by the Economic and Social Council in 1989 and the Declaration on the Protection of All Persons from Enforced Disappearance adopted by General Assembly in 1992 prohibit the practice of extra-legal, arbitrary and summary executions and enforced disappearances and set forth a series of measures which States must take to prevent such practices.

The Standard Minimum Rules for the Treatment of Prisoners, 1955 also contain the provisions requiring government authorities to keep records of detainees to prevent their disappearance and to assist in supervision Of places of detention.

The Working Group on Enforced or involuntary Disappearances which was established by the Human Rights Commission in 1980 takes action oil behalf of the victims of' disappearances. It receives information from non-governmental organizations, sends urgent appeals and requests for information to Governments and makes occasional country visits. It also plays an important role in the drafting of the international standards In this area. Similar functions are also to be performed by the Special Rapporteur on Summary or Arbitrary Executions appointed by the Human Rights Commission in 1982.

Provision relating to assistance of' legal counsel find a place of' pride in the International Covenant oil Civil and Political Rights and the Standard Minimum Rules. They are usefully complemented by the Basic Principles oil the Role of Lawyers the Guidelines on the Role of Prosecutors and the Basic Principles on the Independence of the Judiciary.

International law requires States to take measures for the avoidance of pre-trial detention. The relevant standards are laid down in Article 9(3)1 of the International Covenant on Civil and Political Rights and the United Nations Standard Minimum Rules for Non custodial Measures", which interprets the former. Since overcrowding of prisons and lengthy pre-trial investigations are major factors responsible for the abuses of' pre-trial detention, Governments have been urged under these instruments to use it as last resort and make efforts to find out alternative to pre-trial detention.

While instruments discussed thus far seek to protect both the juveniles and adults, there are a few international instruments which specifically deal with the appropriate treatment of juvenile of renders. Among them mention can he made or the United Nations Standard Minimum Rules for the Administration of Juvenile Justice. The standards laid down In the Beijing Rules are interpreted and elaborated upon in the two detailed instruments adopted by the General Assembly in 1990, namely the United Nations Rules for the Protection of' Juveniles Deprived of their Liberty" and the United National Guidelines for the Prevention of Juvenile Delinquency.

Another important international instrument relating to pre-trial detention is the Model Treaty on the Transfer of Proceedings in Criminal Matters. As emphasized in the preamble to this Model Treaty, such transfer not only contributes to effective administration of justice and reducing conflicts of competence, but can also help to avoid pre-trial detention of foreign offenders and reduce the prison population.

Most of the foreign offenders do not have; personal roots in the State of the commission of the crime. For this reason they are frequently detained to ensure their presence at trial. This may result in discriminatory treatment because offenders residing in the State may secure their release on bait even if they have committed an offence of the same severity. The early return of foreign offenders, followed by the transfer of proceedings against them, not only improves social situation, but may also serve as an alternative to imprisonment during the pre-trial stage.

The Eighth Congress also adopted a "Statement of the Basic Principles for the Treatment of Prisoners" which inter alia, encouraged efforts addressed to the abolition of solitary confinement as a punishment and called for the creation of conditions enabling prisoners to undertake meaningful remunerative employment which will facilitate their reintegration.

Mention should also he made of the relevant provisions of the Vienna Declaration on Human Rights, 1993. The Declaration welcomed the ratification by many Member States of the Torture Convention and urged other Member States to ratify the same as early as possible.

It also urged all states to put in immediate end to the practice of torture and eradicate this evil for ever through full implementation of the Universal Declaration of' Human Rights. In addition the, World conference on Human Rights called upon States to co-operate fully with the Special Rapporteur on the Question of Torture in the fulfilment of' his mandate.

Against this background ,in attempt his been made hereunder to discuss and clarify the existing human rights standards relating to pre-trial detention. As international norms in this area cover an the possible aspects of pre-trial detention, the discussion made here focuses only on the following aspects: presumption of innocence, protection from arbitrary arrest, notification of the grounds of arrest, communication by detainees, appearance before a judicial authority, access to counsel and length of pre-trial detention.

Human Rights Standards on Ore-trial Detainees

(a) Presumption of Innocence

The principle of presumption of innocence is a cardinal principle of the human rights law applicable to pre-trial detention. This principle requires that pre-trial detainees should be distinguished from convicted persons and should be provided separate treatment appropriate to their status as unconvicted person." It imposes burden of proof of charge on the prosecution and the accused has the benefit of doubt. No guilt can be presumed against the accused until the charge has been proved beyond doubt.

The principle of presumption of innocence finds a place of pride in Article, 11(1) of the Universal Declaration Article 14(2) of the Covenant and Rule 84(2) of the Standard Minimum Rules. Since pre-trial detainees are presumed innocent, law enforcement agencies may impose only those conditions and restrictions on them as will ensure their appearance it trial, prevent their, interference with evidence, and prevent further commission of offences. They may also impose those restrictions as are necessary to maintain order and security in the place of detention.

(b) Protection from Arbitrary Arrest

The process of detention begins with arrest. Arrest should only occur when authorized by law. Article 9 of the Universal Declaration provides that 'No one shall be subjected to arbitrary arrest, detention or exile.' This principle also finds recognition in the Covenant, the African Charter, the American Convention and the European Convention. Paragraph 1 of Article 9 or the Covenant states: No One shall be subjected to arbitrary arrest or detention. No one shall be deprived of his liberty except on such grounds and in accordance with such procedure as are established by law. This stipulation is applicable to all deprivations of liberty, whether in criminal cases or in other cases such as vagrancy, drug addiction, educational purposes mental illness, immigration control.

The meaning of the word 'arbitrary as used in Article 9 paragraph 1 in the covenant is imprecated. It is unclear whether it means arrest against the existing provisions of law or in violation of the principles of natural justice. The Human Rights Committee' has taken the view that the term 'arbitrary' is used in the Covenant in a wider sense, It is not synonymous with "against the law", but must be interpreted more broadly to include elements inappropriateness, injustice and lack of predictability. The term includes the situation of detainees who are kept in detention after, their release has been ordered by a Judicial or other authority" and those arrested with no criminal charge against them. It follows from this that not only illegal arrest is arbitrary but even an arrest or detention which is ill accordance with law may also he arbitrary. Basing its interpretation upon this wider meaning of the term 'arbitrary' a committee established by the Commission on Human Rights defined arbitrary arrest' as follows:

> "an arrest or detention is arbitrary if it is (a) oil grounds or in accordance with procedure other than those established by law,'or (b) under the provisions of a law the basic purpose of which is incompatible with respect for the right to liberty and security of person."

It has been held that the abduction of a foreign national by a State from the territory of another State constitutes all arbitrary arrest in violation of Article 9(l) of the Covenant. The Inter-American Commission held that the arrest of a person by para-military groups or security forces in civilian dress who presented neither the appropriate identification nor an arrest warrant issued by competent authorities amounted an arbitrary arrest and infringed the Individual's due process rights."

According to Article 5(l) of the European Convention a person may he deprived of his liberty only in certain circumstances and that too only in accordance with a procedure prescribed by law. One of the circumstances in which deprivation of liberty is permitted relates to the lawful arrest or detention of a person for the purpose of bringing him before the competent legal authority on reasonable suspicion of having committed an offence. When arrest or detention of a person is considered necessary to prevent his committing an offence or fleeing after having done so, it will be in accordance with a procedure prescribed by law. According to the European Court, 'a reasonable suspicion' contemplates the existence of facts or information which would satisfy an objective observer that the person in question may have committed the offence.

With a view to prevent the misuse of powers by the arresting authorities Principle 9 of the Principles on Detention" require the authorities which arrest a person to keep him under detention or investigate, to exercise only the powers granted to them under the law. It further lays down that the exercise of those powers should be subject to a judicial or other authority. In other words the lawfulness of' one's arrest and detention must be judged by a competent court. This remedy is vital for protecting a person's liberty from arbitrary arrest and detention. For judicial supervision of arrest and detention to be effective, accurate records of affects must be kept. As it Is also vital for the prevention of disappearances, Principle 12 of the Principles oil Detention stipulates the following:

1. There shall he duly recorded :

   (a) The reasons for arrest;

   (b) The time of the arrest and the taking of the arrested person to a place of custody as well as that of him first appearance before a judicial or other authority:

   (c) The identity of the law enforcement officials concerned; (d) Precise information concerning the place of custody.

2. Such records shall he communicated to the detained person, of his counsel, if any, in the form, prescribed by law.

Notification of the Grounds of Arrest

It is of utmost Importance that any one who is arrested must be informed of' the reasons for his arrest to enable him to prepare a defence and to take immediate steps to secure his release if he believes that the reasons given are invalid or unfounded. The notice requirement is recognized in Article 9(2) of the Covenant on Civil and Political Rights. The Article stipulates that, "Anyone who is arrested shall be informed, at the time of arrest, of the reasons for his arrest and shall be promptly informed of any charges against him."

Thus the Covenant contemplates a two stage notification, firstly, at the time of arrest and secondly, as soon as the charge is framed by a competent judicial authority, The purpose or notice requirement at the stage of arrest is meant to afford the earliest opportunity to the arrested person to remove any mistake or misunderstanding in the mind or the arresting authority and also to know exactly what the accusation against him is, so that he can exercise the second right, namely consulting of his counsel and to he defended by him. In order that notice at the time of arrest, be effective, it must be sufficiently detailed as to the facts and the law authorizing die person's arrest.

As noted earlier, an arrested person is also entitled to be promptly informed of any charges against him. The Human Rights Committee halt Interpreted this requirement of Article 9(2) of the Covenant as follows:

> "....the right to he informed of the charge "promptly" requires that information is given in

> the manner described as soon as the charge is first made by a competent authority .... this right must arise when in the course of an investigation a court or an authority of the prosecution decides to take procedural steps against a person suspected of a crime or publicly names him as such ....

Principle 10 of the Principles oil Detention reiterates the principle laid down in Article 9(2) of the Covenant. Principle 13 of the same instrument extends the notification requirements to the detained person's rights and the means and procedure for availing them. The relevant principle runs "Any person shall, at the moment of arrest and at the commencement of detention or imprisonment, or promptly thereafter, be provided by the authority responsible for his arrest, detention or imprisonment, respectively with information on and an explanation of his rights and how to avail himself of such rights."

The notifications requirement is also emphasized by the European Commission of Human Rights. According to Article 5(2) of the European Convention, anyone who is arrested must be "informed promptly, in it language which he understands, of the reasons for his arrest and of any charge against him". The European Commission his held that the person must he "informed sufficiently about the facts and the evidence which are proposed to be foundation of a decision: to detain him. In particular, he should be enabled to state whether he admits or denies the alleged offence".

Under Article 6(3)(a) of the European Convention, an accused person must he informed of the 'nature' and 'cause' of the accusation against him. The term 'cause' used in the convention refers to the material facts which form the basis of the accusation. The nature of the accusation, however, denotes the legal character or classification of the material facts.

The norms and standards relating to notification can serve their purpose only when notification is made in a language which the arrested person understands. It is therefore desirable that the authorities should make a translator promptly available to notify the person of his and the charges against him, if he is not conversant with the native language. It if also important that arrested persons should be notified of the rights they have under national and international law, particularly or their right to legal counsel. It is equally important that all administrative and Judicial authorities should be made aware of the obligations which the State Party has assumed under the Covenant. To this end States should take necessary steps to familiarize their administrative and judicial authorities with these obligations as a part of their training. In addition human rights education and awareness programmes should be launched to make the people aware of their rights under (he human rights Declarations, Covenants and National laws.

(d) Communication by Detainees

One of the effects of police detention is isolation from friends and family. A person who has been arrested on the street and taken to a police station, may well be concerned that no one will know what happened. Communication with outside world is important for protection of a detainee's rights and is also an, aspect of treatment. For these reasons the various human rights instruments recognize the right to detainees to communicate with the outside world. Any arbitrary interference with his correspondence is a violation of Article 17 of the Covenant on Civil and Political Rights. According to of Human Rights Committee. The practices of detaining persons for an extended period of time without allowing them to communicate with family, friends or legal counsel, and subjecting their correspondence to excessive censorship, are violations of these standards. Those practices violate Articles 10(l) (humane treatment)" and 14(3)(b) (access to counsel) of the Covenant".

Although official may exercise control over a detainee' correspondence to effect the orderly administration of the place of detention, such control must be subject to safeguards against- arbitrary application." Safeguards against arbitrary interference with detainees correspondence is also contained in Principle 15 of the Principles on Detention which provides as follows:

> "Notwithstanding the exceptions contained in Principle 16, paragraph 4 (of the Principles on Mention, relating to delaying notification of family members when exceptional needs of the investigation require such delay), and Principle 18, paragraph 3 (requiring that access of a detained person to counsel be suspended only in exceptional circumstances), communication of the detained or imprisoned person with the outside world, and in particular his family or counsel, shall not be denied for more than a matter of days.

As a general rule on untried prisoners should be allowed to inform immediately his family of his detention. Rule 92 of the Standard Minimum Rules requires that such detainees should be given all reasonable facilities for communicating with his family and friends and for receiving visits from them. The relevant Rule contemplate only those restrictions and controls on the detainee's right to communication with family and friends which are necessary for the security and good order of the place of detention and for serving the purposes of administration of justice. Visits by family members should take place with the minimum restriction compatible with the good order of the place of detention and the need to avoid destruction of evidence. Rule 44(l) of' the Standard Minimum Rules requires authorities to immediately inform the spouse if the prisoner is married or any, near relative of his death or serious illness or serious injury in custody. Authority is also required to inform the relatives of results of the investigation required by the international standards supervision of places of detention any time the death of detained person occurs.

Under the Standard Minimum Rules a prisoner is entitled informed at once of the death or serious illness of any near relatives. In case of the critical illness of a near relative, the prisoner should be authorized, whenever circumstance allow, to 90 to 16 his bedside either under escort or alone. Every prisoner is also entitled to 4 right to inform at once his family of his imprisonment or his transfer to another institution.

Prisoners who are not nationals of the detainer's State have the additional right to communicate with consular officials of the State of their nationality. Rule M(2) requires authority to allow reasonable facilities to such persons for communicating with the diplomatic and consular representative of the State to take charge of their interests or any national or international authority whose task it is to protect such persons. In this context Article 36(l) of the Vienna Convention on Consular Relations which deals with the exercise or consular function relating to nationals of sending State is of great significance. The Article provides:

(a) consular officers shall be free to communicate with nationals of the sending State and to have access to them. Nationals of the sending State shall have the same freedom with respect to communication with and access to consular officers of, the sending State;

(b) if he so requests, the competent authorities of, the receiving State shall, without delay, inform the consular post of the sending State if, within its consular district, a national of that State is arrested or committed to prison or to custody pending trial or is detained in any other manner. Any communication addressed to the consular post by the person arrested, in prison, custody or detention shall also be forwarded by the said authorities without delay. The said authorities shall inform the person concerned without delay of his rights, under this subparagraph;

(c) consular officers shall have the right to visit a national of the sending State who is in prison, custody or detention, to converse and correspond with him and to arrange for his legal representation. They shall also have the right to visit any national of the sending State who is in prison, custody or detention in their district in pursuance of a judgment. Nevertheless, consular officers shall refrain from taking action on behalf of a national who is in prison, custody or detention if he expressly opposes such action.

(e) appearance before a Judicial or Other Authority

Paragraph 3 of Article 9 of the Covenant on Civil and Political Rights requires that in criminal cases any person arrested or detained should be brought promptly before a judicial authority, whose function is to determine the lawfulness of a person's arrest or detention in a given case. Although, this principle Is recognized In the criminal jurisprudence of many countries the drafters of the Covenant considered the requirement so vital for safeguarding the interests of the pre-trial detainees that they recognized it as a fundamental human right of the arrested accused. The purpose of this requirement Is to afford earliest opportunity to a detained person or his counsel / to secure his release if the arrest and detention are in the violation of his rights. Judicial review of detention as required by the Covenant also saves to safeguard the well-being of the detainee and prevents any violation of fundamental rights. It has been found that if the court is not informed of the detention or is informed after a considerable delay, the right of the detainees are not protected.

The principle embodied in Article 90) of the Covenant is also set forth in Article 5(3) of the European Convention. The Principles on Detention also contains elaborate provisions on the judicial oversight of detention. Principle 4 states:

> "Any form of detention or imprisonment and~ all measures affecting the human rights of a person under any farm of detention or imprisonment shall he ordered by, or be subject to (he effective control of, a judicial or other authority."

Paragraph 1 of Principle 11 provides that, "a person shall not be kept in detention without being given an effective opportunity to be heard promptly by a judicial or other authority. A detained person shall have the right to defend himself or to be assisted by counsel as prescribed by law". While paragraph 2 requires that, "a detained person, shall receive prompt and full communication and his counsel, if any therefore", and order of detention together with the reasons of any of paragraph 3 requires that, "a judicial or other authority shall be empowered to review as appropriate the continuance of detention".

Principle 37 is another Important provision which needs to be mentioned here:

> "A person on a criminal charge shall he brought before a judicial or other authority provided by law promptly after his arrest. Such

authority shall decide without delay upon the lawfulness and necessity of detention. No person may he kept under detention pending investigation or trial except upon the written order of such an authority. A detained person shall when brought before such an authority, have the right to make a statement -on the treatment; received by him while in custody".

Paragraph 1 of Article 10 of the Declaration on Disappearance also guarantees to persons arrested on a criminal charge the right to be brought before a judicial authority promptly after detention.

Although precise time-limits for bringing an arrested person before a judicial authority are fixed by law in most States, the provisions of the international instruments discussed above avoided to set the exact time limits to allow the competent. Authorities reasonable time to examine the charge seriously without any justified delay. According to the Human Rights Committee a detention of 49, hours without judicial review does hot fulfil the requirement of promptness, and so violative of Article 9(3) of the Covenant. Similarly, a period of one month between arrest and appearance before a Judicial authority does not conform with Article 9(3). The Human Rights Committee allowed a five day period before judicial field that a legislation which review did not accord with Article 9(3). According to the European Court on Human Rights a detention of, four days and six, hours did not fulfil the requirement of promptness, and so "violated Article, 5(3) of the European Convention."

The provisions of Rule 7 of the Standard Minimum Rules require that authorities keep records of all detainees. The relevant rule as follows:

(1) In every place where persons are imprisoned there shall be kept a bound registration book with numbered pages in which shall be entered in respect of each prisoner received;

(a) Information concerning his identity;

(b) The reasons for his commitment and the authority therefore;

(c) The day and hour of his admission and release;

(2) No person shall he received in an institution without a valid commitment order of which the details shall have been previously entered in the register.

Article 10 of the Declaration on Disappearance requires that detained persons are kept only in official places of detention and records of all detainees are properly maintained and kept. The relevant part of the Article provides: "Accurate Information on the detention of such persons and their place or places of detention, including transfers, shall be made promptly available to their family members, their counsel or to any other persons having a legitimate interest in the information unless a wish to the contrary has been manifested by the persons concerned".

The safeguards discussed above are vital for ensuring effective judicial control of detainees.

(f) Access to Counsel

Article 14 paragraph 3 recognizes the right of access to counsel in connection with the right to a fair trial in the determination of a criminal charge against a person. It is however internationally recognized in human rights circles that access to legal counsel at the earliest opportunity after a person is detained, is essential for the protection of human rights of the detained person. It has been observed that the lack of legal advice at this stage could seriously affect the right to defence of a pre-trial detainee. Ensuring access to in advocate also prevents possible abuse of other fundamental human rights. It is, therefore, desirable that when an accused give it statement or is interrogated, or signs a statement he should be provided access to counsel. The right to counsel recognized by Article 14 of the Covenant Means the right to effective counsel. The person providing legal representation must be qualified to represent the accused. The legal counsel must also fully represent a person's interests and advocates in his or her favour.

The Human Rights Committee has held that, while Article 14 (3) (d) of the Covenant does not guarantee a right to choose one's own appointed counsel provides effective representation for the accused.

A pre-trial detainee is not only entitled to have the assistance of a legal counsel but also have the right to be informed of this right by the competent authority promptly allow arrest. It is the responsibility of the Government to provide reasonable facility for exercising it. If a detained person does not have a legal counsel of his own choice, he is entitled to have a legal counsel assigned to him by a judicial or other authority in all cases where the interest of justice so requires and without payment by him, if he does not have sufficient means to pay.

Rule 93 of the Standard Minimum Rules recognizes the entitlement of an untried prisoner to apply for free legal aid where such aid is available, and to receive visits from his legal adviser with a view to his defence and to prepare and hand over to him confidential instructions. For these purposes, he shall, if he so desires, be supplied with writing material. Interviews between the prisoner and his legal adviser may be within sight but not within the hearing of a police or institution official.

Principles on Lawyers" usefully compliment the above mentioned standard by recognising a number of safeguards

Firstly, Governments shall ensure the provision of sufficient funding and other resources for legal services to the poor and; as necessary, to other disadvantaged persons professional associations or lawyers shall co-operate in the organization and provision of services, facilities and other resources.

Secondly, Government form the public about their rights and shall promote programmes to inform the public about their rights and duties under the law and the important role of lawyers in protecting their fundamental freedoms. Special attention should be given to assisting the poor and other disadvantaged persons so as to enable them to assert their rights and where necessary call upon the assistance of lawyers.

Thirdly, Governments shall ensure that all persons are immediately informed by the competent authority of their right to be assisted by a lawyer of their own choice upon arrest or detention or when charged with a criminal offence.

Fourthly, any such persons who do not have a lawyer shall in all cases in which the interests of justice so require, be entitled to have a lawyer of experience and competence commensurate with the nature of the offence assigned to them in order to provide effective legal assistance without payment by them if they lack sufficient means to pay for the services."

Fifthly, Governments shall further ensure that all persons arrested or detained with or without criminal charge, shall have prompt access to a lawyer, and in any case not later than forty-eight hours from the time of arrest or detention.

Sixthly, all arrested, detained of Imprisoned persons, shall be provided with adequate opportunities, time and facilities to be visited by and to communicate and consult with a lawyer without delay, interception of censorship and in full confidentiality. Such consultations may be within sight, but not within the hearing, of law unforcement officials.

Seventhly, Governments shall recognize and respect that all communications and consultations between lawyers and their clients within their professional relationship are confidential.

Eightly, Governments shall ensure that lawyers (a) are able to perform all of their professional functions without intimidation, hindrance, harassment or improper interference, (b) are able to travel and to consult with their clients freely both within their own country and abroad; and (c) shall not suffer, or be threatened with, prosecution or administrative economic or other sanctions for any action taken in accordance with recognized professional duties, standards and ethics."

And finally, it is the duty of the competent authorities to ensure lawyers access to appropriate information, files and documents ill their possession or control in sufficient time to enable lawyers to provide effective legal assistance to their clients. Such access should be provided at the earliest appropriate time.

The State must also provide effective counsel and, has an obligation to see that the appointed counsel is carrying out his dudes. The authorities must, if necessary, supervise the appointed counsel, replace him, or cause him to fulfil his duties adequately.

If the pre-trial detainee is not fluent In the language of the detaining country and his counsel is not fluent in the detainee's native language (especially where such counsel is court-appointed), States should protect the rights of the accused to prepare a defence and to receive adequate representation by endeavouring to provide a translator for all visits between the detainee and his counsel.'

(g) Length of Pre-trial Detention

International law prohibits indefinite pre-trial detention and requires States to establish a maximum period of time during which a person may be detained without trial, The relevant standards In," regard are to be found in Article 90) of the Covenant which guarantees the rights to trial within a reasonable time or to release. Similar provision is, also embodied in Principle 38 of the Principles on Detention which runs: A person detained on a criminal charge shall be entitled to trial within a reasonable time or to release pending trial. .

It must be recognized that unreasonable delay in the completion of a trial is just as much a violation of the above mentioned standards as delay in the beginning of a trial. But the reasonableness of the delay before trial must be distinguished from the reasonableness of the length of detention before trial, while delay trial may be reasonable under Article 90) of the Covenant, detention for that period may not be. To put it tersely if the time a detainee is hold before trial exceeds the period he would save If convicted and sentenced, such distention is unreasonable, although delay in the commencement of trial may be justified in the circumstances of that case.

Undertrials: Their Rights and Reality

A visitor from some outer planet to this earth will be elated to learn About progressiveness of our legislation and further overwhelmed by the radical interpretation of laws by the Supreme Court. But alas, if he were to tarry it little longer, and devote time to find About the implementation of these laws, he will immediately realise the wide gap existing between laws and implementation. This will be true above all, about our laws regarding undertrials.

It is broadly Accepted that the treatment given to its prisoners Is one of the important test of a civilised and humane content of any nation.

Thus former Chief Justice Y.V. Chandrachud said, "Convicts are not, by mere reason of the conviction, denuded of all the fundamental rights which they otherwise possess ... Likewise, even 4 convict is entitled to the precious right guaranteed by Article 21 of the Constitution that he shall not be deprived of his life of personal liberty except according to procedure established by law".1

Similarly, 1. Krishna Iyer, speaking on behalf of the Court observed "the jurisdictional reach and range of this court's writ to hold prison caprice and cruelty in constitutional leash is incontestable. Thus it is now clear law that a prisoner wears the amour of basic freedom even behind liars and that on breach thereof by lawless officials the law will respond to his distress signals through 'writ' aid. The Indian human has a constant companion; the Court armed with the Constitution."

Again J. Bhagwati observed "the prisoner or detenu obviously cannot move freely by going outside the prison walls nor can he socialise at his free will with persons outside the jail. But as part of the right to live with human dignity and therefore as a necessary component of the right to life, he would be entitled to have interviews with the members of his family and friends and no prison regulation or procedure laid down by prison regulation regulating the right to have interviews with the members of the family and friends can be upheld as constitutionally valid under Articles 14 and 21, unless it is reasonable, fair and just".

The deep consideration for undertrials was evidenced' where the Court reiterated that right to speedy trial is covered within Article 21 of the

Constitution; the court directed the murder cases to be disposed of within 6 months by nominating Additional Session Judges. It also directed that undertrials who are in jail for more than one year and two years in cases under attempt to murder, cheating, kidnapping if they have been in prison for two years may be released even on their personal bond."

Again deep concern was visible when court recognised that many poor persons languish in jail because of poverty and directed that they be released on personal bond, because as the court said, "If they are poor and helpless, they languish in jails for long periods either because there is no one to bail them out or because there is no one to think of them. The very tendency of criminal proceedings for long periods by itself operates as an engine of oppression In a majority of these cases, whether instituted by police or private complainants, the accused belong to the poorer sections of the society, who are unable to afford competent legal advice .... It appears essential to issue appropriate directions to protect and effectuate the right to life and liberty of the citizens guaranteed by Article 21 of the Constitution. It is also necessary to ensure that these criminal prosecutions do not operate as engines of oppression."

Notwithstanding all this oration, the reality is still very painful. This has been brought out in the incisive report of Ms. Justice Leila Seth, who enquired into the circumstances leading to the death of Rajan Pillai. Thus according to the report the congestion in Tihar Jail is horrible. Against a capacity of 3250 prisoners, average number of prisoners annually is 10,000; out of existing 9500 prisoners, 8200 are undertrials including 80 children.

One of the greatest injustice and violation of Article 2 1, in the can of poor undertrial, who has to remain in jail for his poverty, is the denial of his electoral right and denial of right to vote to elect his representative, which is a basic feature of the Constitution.

In a recent judgement', the Supreme Court unfortunately upheld the denial of law which debars the undertrial to exercise the right to vote, it is respectfully submitted that this judgement runs counter to the long established rights of the undertrial to exercise such rights in all other jurisdictions and under International Covenants. An examination of the recent decision of the Supreme Court upholding the validity of law which debars a slum dweller accused of even a minor offence from voting because he is languishing in jail, being too poor to offer bail bonds while permitting a rich accused facing charges of murder, rape or corruption to be elected as a Member of Parliament or the State Legislature highlights the incongruity and the contradictions in the situation.

A public interest litigation had challenged Section 62(5) of Representation of People Act, *1951 which* denies to undertrials who am in prison or police custody the right to vote while permitting this right to vote to persons accused of heinous offences but outside on bail. The plea that this provision is grossly discriminatory as it favours the rich smugglers, blackmarketeers who could afford bail bonds against poor undertriais failed to persuade the court to hold this provision as unconstitutional.

The Court has upheld this restriction on undertrials by seeking support from the well accepted proposition that criminalisation of politics is the negation of democracy and thus subversive of free and fair election which is a basic feature of the Constitution and that this provision is enacted with that very objective.

A layman however would find absurdity and anomally in a law which at the same time permits a convicted person and sentenced to less than two years to contest election (even from jail) and vote at an election (if out on bail) even though sentenced for 10 years, and wonder as to how this discrimination advances the cause of fair and free elections.

The Court has also justified permitting a person in preventive detention to vote by postal ballot while denying the same right to undertrials in detention by holding that preventive detention is to prevent breach of law while imprisonment on conviction or during investigation is subsequent to the commission of crime and therefore, this classification is reasonable. Now persons under preventive detention are those against whom allegations are of indulging in smuggling and of narcotic offences. But even then such a person can only be kept in preventive detention if the same is held justified on a review by three Judges of the High Court. If in spite of this prima facie strong proof a detenue is permitted to vote at the election, pray what is the logic for denying the right to vote to a poor undertrial in jail, against whom the only allegation of guilt, and that too under a minor offence, say of affray or of a poor mill worker held in jail for allegedly violating a ban on meetings or processions. That too after an investigation by an inspector of police, and whom not even a magistrate has found guilty. This differential attitude against an undertrial would be in conflict with normal criminal jurisprudence and specifically with Article 84 of the Standard Minimum Rules for Treatment of Prisoner adopted by the First United Nations Congress on the Prevention of Crime and the Treatment of Offenders, held at Geneva in 1955, and approved by the Economic and Social Council by its resolutions 663 C (XXIV) of 31st July', 1957 and 2076 (LXII) of 13th May, 1977 to the effect that "unconvicted prisoners are presumed to be innocent and shall be treated as such".

The finding of the Court is also counter to the right guaranteed by Article 25(b) of Human Rights guaranteed under International Bill of Human Rights, namely, International Covenant on Civil and Political Rights, which by Article 25(b) specifically provides that "Every citizen shall have the right and the opportunity, without any of the distinctions mentioned in Article 2 and without unreasonable restrictions: to vote and to be elected at genuine periodic elections which shall be by universal and equal suffrage and shall be held by secret ballot, guaranteeing the free expression of the will of the electors; which specifically recognises a right to vote and to be elected at genuine periodically election".

In U.K. right to vote is denied only if a person is convicted and during the time he is detained in penal institution. In Israel even a convicted person in jail is allowed to vote.

Notwithstanding the international law and conventions the Court felt the classification to be valid by holding that some elbow room must be * available to the legislature in classification. But with due respect, the court has ignored the caution given by the apex Court more than 40 years back that through good faith and knowledge of existing conditions on the part of a legislature has to be presumed, That Is so; yet to carry that presumption to the extent of always holding that them must be some undisclosed intention or reason for subjecting certain individuals to a hostile and discriminatory legislation is to make the protection clause of Article 14 a mere rope of *send*, in no manner restraining state action, The protection afforded by the article is not a mere eye wash but it is a real one.

Another justification mentioned for upholding the, law is that it would mean deploying larger police force for conduct of elections. But it was never pleaded that undertrials should be taken personally to polling booths to cast their votes, all that was claimed was the right to vote by postal ballot just like given to smugglers and others detained under preventive law. This did not require even one extra policeman to be deployed.

But what is of distorting consequence is the reason that as right to vote is subject to the limitations imposed by the statute and therefore, die challenge to any provision of election law cannot be made with reference to a fundamental right in the Constitution.

This finding contrary to Article 13(2) which mandates that any law made by legislature which contravenes any of fundamental *rights in* Part H (e.g. Article 14) shall be void. Thus the election law is no holy cow so as to claim immunity from the sweep and protection of Article 14.

The guarantee of equal protection under Article 14, according to earlier Supreme Court decisions embraces the entire realm of state action, even in the matter of granting privileges and contract. How then can it be said that statute on election law is immune from scrutiny under Article 14.

If the courts finding that Articles 14 and 21 cannot be invoked by a citizen in testing election law, grave consequences will follow. Thus assume that if parliament was to pass a law that only six feet tall and above persons or children of Ministers could alone vote at election could conceivably such a law be upheld and if so what becomes of the courts own dictum that free and fair elections are the basic feature of the Constitution.

Such a law would be completely subversive of our democratic constitution and would have to be held as null and void.

People are always keen observers as to who out of the executive or judiciary appreciates the felt needs of time and acts accordingly. In this judgement of undertrials, unfortunately with all its judicial activism, judiciary has felt helpless because of the wording of statute even though it may have sympathised with the claim of undertrials. May be the executive/legislature in the fiftieth year of independence can come to the rescue of undertrials in prison who are being discriminated only because of their poverty.

Treatment of Prisoners

Preliminary Observations

1. The following rules are not intended to describe in detail a model system of penal institutions. They seek only, on the basis of the general consensus of contemporary thought and the essential elements of the most adequate systems of today, to set out what is generally accepted as being good principle and practice in the treatment of prisoners and the management of institutions.

2. In view of the great variety of legal, social, economic and geographical conditions of the world, it is evident that not all of the rules are capable of application in all places and at all times. They should, however, serve to stimulate a constant endeavour to overcome practical difficulties in the way of their application, in the knowledge that they represent, as a whole, the minimum conditions which are accepted as suitable by the United Nations.

3. On the other hand, the rules cover a field in which thought is constantly developing. They are not intended to preclude experiment and practices, provided these are in harmony with the

principles and seek to further the purposes which derive from the text of the rules as a whole. It will always be justifiable for the central prison administration to authorize departures from the rules in this spirit.

4. (1) Part I of the rules covers the general management of institutions and is applicable to all categories of prisoners, criminal or civil, untried or, convicted, including prisoners subject to "security measures" or corrective measures ordered by the judge.

(2) Part II contains rules applicable only to the special categories dealt with in each section. Nevertheless, the rules under section A, applicable to prisoners under sentence, shall be equally applicable to categories of prisoners dealt with in sections B, C and D, provided they do not conflict with the rules governing those categories and are for their benefit.

5. (1) The rules do not seek to regulate the management of institutions set aside for young persons such as Borstal institutions or correctional schools, but in general part I would be equally applicable in such institutions.

(2) The categories of young prisoners should include at least all young persons who come within the jurisdiction of juvenile courts. As a rule, such young persons should not be sentenced to imprisonment.

Part I: Rules of General Applications

Basic principle

6. (1) The following rules shall be applied

impartially. There shall be no discrimination on grounds of race, colour, sex, language, religion, political or other opinion, national or social origin, property, birth or other status.

(2) On the other hand, it is necessary to respect the religious beliefs and moral precepts of the group to which a prisoner belongs.

Register

7. (1) In every place where persons are imprisoned there shall be kept a bound registration book with numbered pages in which shall be entered in respect of each prisoner received.

(a) Information concerning his identity;

(b) The reasons for his commitment and the authority therefor;

(c) The day and hour of his admission and release.

(2) No person shall be received in an institution without a valid commitment order of which the details shall have been previously entered in the register.

Separation of categories

8. The different categories of prisoners shall be kept in separate institutions or parts of institutions taking account of their sex, age, criminal record, the legal reason for their detention and the necessities of their treatment. Thus,

(a) Men and women shall so far as possible be detained in separate institutions; in an institution which received both men and women the whole of the premises allocated to women shall be entirely separate;

(b) Untried prisoners shall be kept separate from convicted prisoners;

(c) Persons imprisoned for debt and other civil prisoners shall be kept separate from persons imprisoned by reason of a criminal offence;

(d) Young prisoners shall be kept separate from adults.

Accommodation

9. (1) Where sleeping accommodation is in individual cells or rooms each prisoner shall occupy by night a cell or room by himself. If for special reasons, such as temporary overcrowding, it becomes necessary for the central prison administration to make an exception to this rule, it is not desirable to have two prisoners in a cell or room.

(2) Where dormitories are used, they shall be occupied by prisoners carefully selected as being suitable to associate with one another in those conditions. There shall be regular supervisions by night, in keeping with the nature of the institution.

10. All accommodation provided for the use of prisoners and in particular all sleeping accommodation shall meet all requirements of health, due regard being paid to climatic conditions and particularly to cubic content of air, minimum floor space, lighting, heating and ventilation.

11. In all places where prisoners are required to live or work,

(a) The windows shall be large enough to enable the prisoners to read or work by natural light, and shall be so constructed that they can allow the entrance of fresh air whether or not there is artificiel ventilation;

(b) Artifical light shall be provided sufficient for the prisoners to read or work without injury to eyesight.

12. The sanitary installations shall be adequate to enable every prisoner to comply with the needs of nature when necessary and in a clean and decent manner.

13. Adequate bathing and shower installation shall be provided so that every prisoner may be enabled and required to have a bath or shower, at a temperature suitable to the climate, as frequently as necessary for general hygiene according to season and geographical region, but at least once a week in a temperate climate.

14. All parts of an institution regularly used by prisoners shall be properly maintained and kept scrupulously clean at all times.

Personal hygiene

15. Prisoners shall be required to keep their persons clean, an to this end they shall be provided with water and with such toilet articles as are necessary for health and cleanliness.

16. In order that prisoners may maintain a good appearance compatible with their self-respect, facilities shall be provided for the proper care of the hair and beard and men shall be enabled to shave regularly.

Clothing and bedding

17. (1) Every prisoner who is not allowed to wear his own clothing shall be provided with an outfit of clothing suitable for the climate and

adequate to keep him in good health. Such clothing shall in no manner be degrading or humiliating.

(2) All clothing shall be clean and kept in proper condition. Underclothing shall be changed and washed as often as necessary for the maintenance of hygiene.

(3) In exceptional circumstances, whenever a prisoner is removed outside the institution for an authorized purpose, he shall be allowed to wear his own clothing or other inconspicuous clothing.

18. If prisoners are allowed to wear their own clothing, arrangements shall be made on their admission to the institution to ensure that it shall be clean and fit for use.

19. Every prisoner shall in accordance with local or national standards, be provided with a separate bed, and with separate and sufficient bedding which shall be clean when issued, kept in good order and changed often enough to ensure its cleanliness.

Food

20. (1) Every prisoner shall be provided by the administration at the usual hours with food of nutritional value adequate for health and strength, of wholesome quality and well prepared and served.

(2) Drinking water shall be available to every prisoner whenever he needs it.

Exercise and sport

21. (1) Every prisoner who is not employed in outdoor work shall have at least one hour of

suitable exercise in the open air daily if the weather permits.

(2) Young prisoners, and others of suitable age and physique, shall receive physical and recreational training during the period of exercise. To this end space, installations and equipment should be provided.

Medical services

22. (1) At every institution there shall be available the services of at least one qualified medical officer who should have some knowledge of psychiatry. The medical services should be organized in close relationship to the general health administration of the community or nation. They shall include a psychiatric service for the diagnosis and, in proper cases, the treatment of states of mental abnormality.

(2) Sick prisoners who require specialist treatment shall be transferred to specialized institutions or to civil hospitals. Where hospital facilities are provided in an institution, their equipment, furnishings and pharma-ceutical supplies shall be proper for the medical care and treatment of sick prisoners, and there shall be a staff of suitable trained officers.

(3) The services of a qualified dental officer shall be available to every prisoner.

23. (1) In women's institutions there shall be special accommodation for all necessary pre-natal and post-natal care and treatment. Arrangements shall be made wherever practicable for children to be born in a hospital outside the institution. A child is

born in prison, this fact shall not be mentioned in the birth certificate.

(2) Where nursing infants are allowed to remain in the institution with their mothers, provision shall be made for a nursery staffed by qualified person, where the infants shall be placed when they are not in the care of their mothers.

24. The medical officer shall see and examine every prisoner as soon as possible after his admission and thereafter as necessary, with a view particularly to the discovery of physical or mental illness and the taking of all necessary measures; the segregation of prisoners suspected of infectious or contagious conditions; the noting of physical or mental defects which might hamper rehabilitation, and the determination of the physical capacity of every prisoner for work.

25. (1) The medical officer shall have the care of the physical and mental health of the prisoners and should daily see all sick prisoners, all who complain of illness, and any prisoner to whom his attention is specially directed.

(2) The medical officer shall report to the director whenever he considers that a prisoner's physical or mental health has been or will be injuriously affected by continued imprisonment or by any condition of imprisonment.

26. (1) The medical officer shall regularly inspect and advise the director upon:

(a) The quantity, quality, preparation and service of food;

(b) The hygiene and cleanliness of the institution and the prisoners;

(c) The sanitation, heating, lighting and ventilation of the institution;

(d) The suitability and cleanliness of the prisoners' clothing and bedding;

(e) the observance of the rules concerning physical education and sports, in caes where there is no technical personnel in charge of these activities.

(2) The director shall take into consideration the reports and advice that the medical officer submits according to rules 25C2) and 26 and, in case he concurs with the recommendations made, shall take immediate steps to give effect to those recommendations; if they are not within his competence or if he does not concur with them, he shall immediately submit his own report and the advice of the medical officer to higher authority.

Discipline and punishment

27. Discipline and order shall be maintained with firmness, but with no more restriction than is necessary for safe custody and well-ordered community life.

28. (1) No prisoner shall be employed, in the service of the institution, in any disciplinary capacity.

(2) This rule shall not, however, impede the proper functioning of systems based on self-government, under which specified social, educational or sports activities or responsibilities are entrusted, under supervision, to prisoners who are formed into groups for the purpose of treatment.

29. The following shall always be determined by the law or by the regulation of the competent administrative authority:

 (a) Conduct constituting a disciplinary offence;

 (b) The types and duration of punishment which may be inflicted;

 (c) The authority competent to impose such punishment.

30. (1) No prisoner shall be punished except in accordance with the terms of such law or regulation, and never twice for the same offence.

 (2) No prisoner shall be punished unless he has been informed of the offence alleged against him and given a proper opportunity of presenting his defence. The competent authority shall conduct a thorough examination of the case.

 (3) Where necessary and practicable the prisoner shall be allowed to make his defence through an interpreter.

31. Corporal punishment, punishment by placing in a dark cell, and all cruel, inhuman or degrading punishments shall be completely prohibited as punishments for disciplinary offences.

32. (1) Punishment by close confinement or reduction of diet shall never be inflicted unless the medical officer has examined the prisoner and certified in writing that he is fit to sustain it.

 (2) the same shall apply to any other punishment that may be prejudicial to the physical or mental health of a prisoner. In no case may such punishment be contrary

to or depart from the principle stated in rule 31.

(3) The medical officer shall visit daily prisoners undergoing such punishments and shall advise the director if he considers the termination or alteration of the punishment necessary on grounds of physical or mental health.

Instruments of restraint

33. Instruments of restraint, such as handcuffs, chains, irons an straitjackets, shall never be applied as a punishments. Furthermore, chains or irons shall not be used as restraints. Other instruments of restraint shall not be used except in the following circumstances:

(a) As a precaution against escape during a transfer., provided that they shall be removed when the prisoner appears before a judicial or administrative authority;

(b) On medical grounds by direction of the medical officer;

(c) By order of the director, if other methods of control fail, in order to prevent a prisoner from injuring himself or others or from damaging property; in such instances the director shall at once consult the medical officer and report to the higher administrative authority.

34. The patterns and manner of use of instruments of restraint shall be decided by the central prison administration. Such instruments must not be applied for any longer time than is strictly necessary.

Information to and complaints by prisoners

35. (1) Every prisoner on admission shall be provided with written information about the regulations governing the treatment of prisoners of his category, the disciplinary requirements of the institution, the authorized methods of seeking information and making complaints, and all such other matters as are necessary to enable him to understand both his rights and his obligations and to adapt himself to the life of the institution.

(2) If a prisoner is illiterate, the aforesaid information shall be conveyed to him orally.

36. (1) Every prisoner shall have the opportunity each week day of making requests or complaints to the director of the institution or the officer authorized to represent him.

(2) It shall be possible to make requests or complaints to the inspector of prisons during his inspection. The prisoner shall have the opportunity to talk to the inspector or to any other inspecting officer without the director or other members of the staff being present.

(3) Every prisoner shall be allowed to make a request or complaint, without censorship as to substance but in proper form, of the central prison administration, the judicial authority or other proper authorities through approved channels.

(4) Unless it is evidently frivolous or groundless, every request or complaint shall be promptly dealt with and replied to without undue delay.

Contact with the outside world

37. Prisoners shall be allowed under necessary supervision to communicate with their family and reputable friends at regular intervals, both by correspondence and by receiving visits.

38. (1) Prisoners who are foreign nationals shall be allowed reasonable facilities to communicate with the diplomatic and consular representatives of the State to which they belong.

(2) Prisoners who are nationals of States without diplomatic or consular representation in the country and refugees or stateless persons shall be allowed similar facilities to communicate with the diplomatic representative of the State which takes charge of their interests or any national or international authority whose task it is to protect such persons.

39. Prisoners shall be kept informed regularly of the more important items of news by the reading of newspapers, periodicals or special institutional publications, by hearing wireless transmissions, by lectures or by any similar means as authorized or controlled by the administration.

Books

40. Every institution shall have a library for the use of all categories of prisoners, adequately stocked with both recreational and instructional books, and prisoners shall be encouraged to make full use of it.

Religion

41. (1) If the institution contains a sufficient number of prisoners of the same religion, a

qualified representative of that religion shall be appointed or approved. If the number of prisoners justifies it and conditions permit, the arrangement should be on a full-time basis.

(2) A qualified representative appointed or approved under paragraph (1) shall be allowed to hold regular services and to pay pastoral visits in private to prisoners of his religion at proper times.

(3) Access to a qualified representative of any religion shall not be refused to any prisoner. On the other hand, if any prisoner should object to a visit to any religious representative, his attitude shall be fully respected.

42. So far as practicable, every prisoner shall be allowed to satisfy the needs of his religious life by attending the services provided in the institution and having in his possession the books of religious observance and instruction of his denomination.

Retention of prisoners' property

43. (1) All money, valuables, clothing and other effects belonging to a prisoner which under the regulations of the institution he is not allowed to retain shall on his admission to the institution be placed in safe custody. An inventory thereof shall be signed by the prisoner. Steps shall be taken to keep them in good condition.

(2) On the release of the prisoner all such articles and money shall be returned to him except in so far as he has been authorized to spend money or send any such property out

of the institution, or it has been found necessary on hygienic grounds to destroy any article of clothing. The prisoner shall sign a receipt for the articles and money returned to him.

(3) Any money or effects received for a prisoner from outside shall be treated in the same way.

(4) If a prisoner brings in any drugs or medicine, the medical officer shall decide what use shall be made of them.

Notification of death, illness, transfer, etc.

44. (1) Upon the death or serious illness of, or serious injury to a prisoner, or his removal to an institution for the treatment of mental affections, the director shall at once inform the spouse, if the prisoner is married, or the nearest relative and shall in any event inform any other person previously designated by the prisoner.

(2) A prisoner shall be informed at once of the death or serious illness of any near relative. In case of the critical illness of a near relative, the prisoner should be authorized, whenever circumstances allow, to go to his bedside either under escort or alone.

(3) Every prisoner shall have the right to inform at once his family of his imprisonment or his transfer to another institution.

Removal of prisoners

45. (1) When the prisoners are being removed to or from an institution, they shall be exposed to public view as little as possible, and proper safeguards shall be adopted to protect them

from insult, curiosity and publicity in any form.

(2) The transport of prisoners in conveyances with inadequate ventilation or light, or in any way which would subject them to unnecessary physical hardship, shall be prohibited.

(3) The transport of prisoners shall be carried out at the expense of the administration and equal conditions shall obtain for all of them.

Institutional personnel

46. (1) The prison administration, shall provide for the careful selection of every grade of the personnel, since it is on their integrity, humanity, professional capacity and personal suitability for the work that the proper administration of the institution depends.

(2) The prison administration shall constantly seek to awaken and maintain in the minds both of the personnel and of the public the conviction that this work is a social service of great importance, and to this end all appropriate means of informing the public should be used.

(3) To secure the foregoing ends, personnel shall be appointed on a full-time basis as professional prison officers and have civil service status with security of tenure subject only to good conduct, efficiency and physical fitness. Salaries shall be adequate to attract and retain suitable men and women; employment benefits and conditions of services shall be favourable in view of the exacting nature of the work.

47. (1) The personnel shall possess an adequate standard of education and intelligence.

(2) Before entering on duty, the personnel shall be given a course of training in their general and specific duties and be required to pass theoretical and practical tests.

(3) After entering on duty and during their career, the personnel shall maintain and improve their knowledge and professional capacity by attending courses of in-service training to be organized at suitable intervals.

48. All members of the personnel shall at all times so conduct themselves and perform their duties as to influence the prisoners for good by their example and to command their respect.

49. (1) So far as possible, the personnel shall include a sufficient number of specialist such as psychiatrists, psychologists, social workers, teachers and trade instructors.

(2) The services of social workers, teachers and trade instructors shall be secured on a permanent basis, without thereby excluding part-time or voluntary workers.

50. (1) The director of an institution should be adequately qualified for his task by character, administrative ability, suitable training and experience.

(2) He shall devote his entire time to his official duties and shall not be appointed on a part-time basis.

(3) He shall reside on the premises of the institution or in its immediate vicinity.

(4) When two or more institutions are under the authority of one director, he shall visit each

of them at frequent intervals. A responsible resident official shall be in charge of each of these institutions.

51. (1) The director, his deputy, and the majority of the other personnel of the institution shall be able to speak the language of the greatest number of prisoners, or a language understood by the greatest number of them.

(2) Whenever necessary, the services of an interpreter shall be used.

52. (1) In institutions which are large enough to require the services of one or more full-time medical officers, at least one of them shall reside on the premises of the institution or in its immediate vicinity.

(2) In other institutions the medical officer shall visit daily and shall reside near enough to be able to attend without delay in cases of urgency.

53. (1) In an institution for both men and women, the part of the institution set aside for women shall be under the authority of a responsible woman officer who shall have the custody of the keys of all that part of the institution.

(2) No male member of the staff shall enter the part of the institution set aside for women unless accompanied by a woman officer.

(3) Women prisoners shall be attended and supervised only by women officers. This does not, however, preclude male members of the staff, particularly doctors and teachers, from carrying out their professional duties in institutions or parts of institutions set aside for women.

54. (1) Officers of the institutions shall not, in their relations with the prisoners, use force except in self-defence or in cases of attempted escape, or active or passive physical resistance to an order based on law or regulations. Officers who have recourse to force must use no more than is strictly necessary and must report the incident immediately to the director of the institution.

(2) Prison officers shall be given special physical training to enable them to restrain aggressive prisoners.

(3) Except in special circumstances, staff performing duties which bring them into direct contact with prisoners should not be armed. Furthermore, staff should in no circumstances be provided with arms unless they have been trained in their use.

Inspection

55. There shall be a regular inspection of penal institution and services by qualified and experienced inspectors appointed by a competent authority. Their task shall be in particular to ensure that these institutions are administered in accordance with existing laws and regulations and with a view to bringing about the objectives of penal and correctional services.

Part II: Rules Applicable to Special Categories

A. Prisoners Under Sentence

Guiding principles

56. The guiding principles hereafter are intended to show the spirit in which penal institutions should be administered and the purpose at which they

should aim, in accordance with the declaration made under Preliminary Observation 1 of the present text.

57. Imprisonment and other measures which result in cutting off an offender from the outside world are afflictive by the very fact of taking from the person the right of self-determination by depriving him of his liberty. Therefore the prison system shall not, except as incidental to justifiable segregation or the maintenance of discipline, aggravate the suffering inherent in such a situation.

58. The purpose and justification of a sentence of imprisonment or a similar measure deprivative of liberty is ultimately to protect society against crime. This end can only be achieved if the period of imprisonment is used to ensure, so far as possible, that upon his return to society the offender is not only willing but able to lead a law-abiding and self-supporting life.

59. To this end, the institution should utilize all the remedial, educational, moral, spiritual and other forces and forms of assistance which are appropriate and available, and should seek to apply them according to the individual treatment needs of the prisoners.

60. (1) The regime of the institution should seek to minimize any differences between prison life and life at liberty which tend to lessen the responsibility of the prisoners or the respect due to their dignity as human beings.

(2) Before the completion of the sentence, it is desirable that the necessary steps be taken to ensure for the prisoner a gradual return to life in society. This aim may be achieved, depending on the case, by a pre-release

regime organized in the same institution or in another appropriate institution, or by release on trial under some kind of supervision which must not be entrusted to the police but should be combined with effective social aid.

61. The treatment of prisoners should emphasize not their exclusion from the community, but their continuing part in it. Community agencies should, therefore, be enlisted wherever possible to assist the staff of the institution in the task of social rehabilitation of the prisoners. There should be in connection with every institution social workers charged with the duty of maintaining and improving all desirable relations of a prisoner with his family and with valuable social agencies. Steps should be taken to safeguard, to the maximum extent compatible with the law and the sentence, the rights relating to civil interests, social security rights and other social benefits of prisoners.

62. The medical services of the institution shall seek to detect and shall treat any physical or mental illnesses or defects which may hamper a prisoner's rehabilitation. All necessary medical, surgical and psychiatric services shall be provided to that end.

63. (1) The fulfilment of these principles requires individualization of treatment and for this purpose a flexible system of classifying prisoners in groups; it is therefore desirable that such groups should be distributed in separate institutions suitable for the treatment of each group.

(2) These institutions need not provide the same degree of security for every group. It is desirable to provide varying degrees of

security according to the needs of different groups. Open institutions, by the very fact that they provide no physical security against escape but rely on the self-discipline of the inmates, provide the conditions most favourable to rehabilitation for carefully selected prisoners.

(3) It is desirable that the number of prisoners in closed institutions should not be so large that the individualization of treatment is hindered. In some countries it is considered that the population of such institutions should not exceed five hundred. In open institutions the population should be as small as possible.

(4) On the other hand, it is undesirable to maintain prisons which are so small that proper facilities cannot be provided.

64. The duty of society does not end with a prisoner's release. There should, therefore, be governmental or private agencies capable of lending the released prisoner efficient after—care directed towards the lessening of prejudice against him and towards his social rehabilitation.

Treatment

65. The treatment of persons sentenced to imprisonment or a similar measure shall have as its purpose, so far as the length of the sentence permits, to establish in them the will to lead law-abiding and self-supporting lives after their release and to fit them to do so. The treatment shall be such as will encourage their self-respect and develop their sense of responsibility.

66. (1) To these ends, all appropriate means shall be used, including religious care in the

countries where this is possible, education, vocational guidance and training, social casework, employment counselling physical development and strengthening of moral character, in accordance with the individual needs of each prisoner, taking account of his social and criminal history, his physical and mental capacities and aptitudes, his personal temperament, the length of his sentence and his prospects after release.

(2) For every prisoner with a sentence of suitable length, the director shall receive, as soon as possible after his admission, full reports on all the matters referred to in the foregoing paragraph. Such reports shall always include a report by a medical officer, wherever possible qualified in psychiatry, on the physical and mental condition of the prisoner.

(3) The reports and other relevant documents shall be placed in an individual file. This file shall be kept up to date and classified in such a way that it can be consulted by the responsible personnel whenever the need arises.

Classification and individualization

67. The purpose of classification shall be:

(a) To separate from others those prisoners who by reason of their criminal records or bad characters, are likely to exercise a bad influence;

(b) To divide the prisoners into classes in order to facilitate their treatment with a view of their social rehabilitation.

68. So far as possible separate institutions or separate sections of an institution shall be used for the treatment of the different classes of prisoners.

69. As soon as possible after admission and after a study of the personality of each prisoner with a sentence of suitable length, a programme of treatment shall be prepared for him in the light of the knowledge obtained about his individual needs, his capacities and dispositions.

Privileges

70. Systems of privileges appropriate for the different classes of prisoners and the different methods of treatment shall be established at every institution, in order to encourage good conduct, develop a sense of responsibility and secure the interest and co-operation of the prisoners in their treatment.

Work

71. (1) Prison labour must not be of an afflictive nature.

(2) All prisoners under sentence shall be required to work, subject to their physical and mental fitness as determined by the medical officer.

(3) Sufficient work of a useful nature shall be provided to keep prisoners actively employed for a normal working day.

(4) So far as possible the work provided shall be such as will maintain or increase the prisoner's ability to earn an honest living after release.

(5) Vocational training in useful trades shall be

provided for prisoners able to profit thereby and especially for young prisoners.

(6) Within the limits compatible with proper vocational selection and with the requirements of institutional administration and discipline, the prisoners shall be able to choose the type of work they wish to perform.

72. (1) The organization and methods of work in the institutions shall resemble as closely as possible those of similar work outside institution, so as to prepare prisoners for the conditions of normal occupational life.

(2) The interests of the prisoners and of their vocational training, however must not be subordinated to the purpose of making a financial profit from an industry in the institution.

73. (1) Preferably institutional industries and farms should be operated directly by the administration and not by private contractors.

(2) Where prisoners are employed in work not controlled by the administration, they shall always be under the supervision of the institution's personnel. Unless the work is for other departments of the government the full normal wages for such work shall be paid to the administration by the persons to whom the labour is supplied, account being taken to the output of the prisoners.

74. (1) The precautions laid down to protect the safety and health of free workmen shall be equally observed in institutions.

(2) Provision shall be made to indemnify prisoners against industrial injury, including occupational disease, on terms not less favourable than those extended by law to free workmen.

75. (1) The maximum daily and weekly working hours of the prisoners shall be fixed by law or by administrative regulation, taking into account local rules or custom in regard to the employment of free workmen.

(2) The hours so fixed shall leave one last day a week and sufficient time for education and other activities required as part of the treatment and rehabilitation of the prisoners.

76 (1) There shall be a system of equitable remuneration of the work of prisoners.

(2) Under the system prisoners shall be allowed to spend at least a part of their earnings on approved articles for their own use and to send a part of their earnings to their family.

(3) The system should also provide that a part of the earnings should be set aside by the administration so as to constitute a savings fund to be handed over to the prisoner on his release.

Education and recreation

77. (1) Provision shall be made for the further education of all prisoners capable of profiting thereby, including religious instruction in the countries where this is possible. The education of illiterates and young prisoners shall be compulsory and special attention shall be paid to it by the administration.

(2) So far as practicable, the education of

prisoners shall be integrated with the educational system of the country so that after their release they may continue their education without difficulty.

78. Recreational and cultural activities shall be provided in all institutions for the benefit of the mental and physical health of prisoners.

Social relations and after-care

79. Special attention shall be paid to the maintenance and improvement of such relations between a prisoner and his family as are desirable in the best interest of both.

80. From the beginning of a prisoner's sentence consideration shall be given to his future after release and he shall be encouraged and assisted to maintain or establish such relations with persons or agencies outside the institution as may promote the best interest of his family and his own social rehabilitation.

81. (1) Services and agencies, governmental or otherwise, which assist released prisoners to re-establish themselves in society shall ensure, so far as is possible and necessary, that released prisoners by provided with appropriate documents and identification papers, have suitable homes and work to go to, are suitably and adequately clothed having regard to the climate and season, and have sufficient means to reach their destination and maintain themselves in the period immediately following their release.

(2) The approved representatives of such agencies shall have all necessary access to the institution and to prisoners and shall be taken into consultation as to the future of a prisoner from the beginning of his sentence.

(3) It is desirable that the activities of such agencies shall be centralized or co-ordinated as far as possible in order to secure the best use of their efforts.

B. Insane and Mentally Abnormal Prisoners

82. (1) Persons who are found to be insane shall not be detained in prisons and arrangements shall be made to remove them to mental institutions as soon as possible.

(2) Prisoners who suffer from other mental diseases or abnormalities shall be observed and treated in specialized institutions under medical management.

(3) During their stay in a prison, such prisoners shall be placed under the special supervision of a medical officer.

(4) The medical or psychiatric service of the penal institutions shall provide for the psychiatric treatment of all other prisoners who are in need of such treatment.

83. It is desirable that steps should be taken, by arrangement with the appropriate agencies, to ensure if necessary the continuation of psychiatric treatment after release and the provision of social-psychiatric after-care.

C. Prisoners under arrest or awaiting trial

84. (1) persons arrested or imprisoned by reason of a criminal charge against them, who are detained either in police custody or in prison custody jail but have not yet been tried and sentenced, will be referred to as "untried prisoners" hereinafter in these rules.

(2) Unconvicted prisoners are presumed to be innocent and shall be treated as such.

(3) Without prejudice to legal rules for the protection of individual liberty or prescribing the procedure to be observed in respect of untried prisoners, these prisoners shall benefit by a special regime which is described in the following rules in its essential requirements only.

85. (1) Untried prisoners shall be kept separate from convicted prisoners.

(2) Young untried prisoners shall be kept separate from adults and shall in principle be detained in separate institutions.

86. Untried prisoners shall sleep singly in separate rooms, with the reservation of different local custom in respect of the climate.

87. Within the limits compatible with the good order of the institution, untried prisoners may, if they so desire, have their food procured at their own expense from the outside, either through the administration or through their family or friends. Otherwise, the administration shall provide their food.

88. (1) An untried prisoner shall be allowed to wear his own clothing if it is clean and suitable.

(2) If he wears prison dress, it shall be different from that supplied to convicted prisoners.

89. An untried prisoner shall always be offered opportunity to work, but shall not be required to work. If he chooses to work, he shall be paid for it.

90. An untried prisoner shall be allowed to procure at his own expense or at the expense of a third

party such books, newspapers, writing materials and other means of occupation as are compatible with the interests of the administration of justice and the security and good order of the institution.

91. An untried prisoner shall be allowed to be visited and treated by his own doctor or dentist if there is reasonable ground for his application and he is able to pay any expenses incurred.

92. An untried prisoner shall be allowed to inform immediately his family of his detention and shall be given all reasonable facilities for communicating with his family and friends, and for receiving visits from them, subject only to restrictions and supervision as are necessary in the interests of the administration of justice and of the security and good order of the institution.

93. For the purposes of his defence, an untried prisoner shall be allowed to apply for from legal aid where such aid is available, and to receive visits free his legal adviser with a view to his defence and to prepare and hand to him confidential instructions. For these purposes, he shall if he so desires be supplied with writing material. Interviews between the prisoner and his legal adviser may be within sight but not within the hearing of a police or institution official.

D. Civil Prisoners

94. In countries where the law permits imprisonment for debt, or by order of a court under any other non-criminal process, persons so imprisoned shall not be subjected to any greater restriction or severity than is necessary to ensure safe custody and good order. Their treatment shall be not less favourable than that of untried

prisoners, with that reservation, however, that they may possibly be required to work.

E. Persons arrested or detained without charge

95. Without prejudice to the provisions of article 9 of the International Government on Civil and Political Rights, persons arrested or imprisoned without charge shall be accorded the same protection as that accorded under part I and part II, section C. Relevant provisions of part II, section A, shall likewise be applicable where their application may be conducive to the benefit of this special group of persons in custody, provided that no measures shall be been taken implying that re-education or rehabilitation is in any way appropriate to persons not convicted of any criminal offence.

7

Torture and Custodial Violence

The Constitution of India and the International Instruments on Human Rights attach great importance to the protection of life and personal liberty of an individual and emphasise the respect for human dignity. Our Basic Law and the substantive and procedural laws stress the need to observe human rights in the administration of criminal justice.

Arrest involves the deprivation of the liberty of an individual by legal authorities. From the time a person is arrested, if not released on bail, he or she is under custody. Any use of force, threat, psychological pressure etc., against the person in custody by the authorities is termed as custodial violence. We have seen the basic legal philosophy of the Constitution, the international instruments and the procedural law, which presume the innocence of the accused till the contrary is proved in a court of law. Keeping this in view, the legal procedures are weighted in favour of the accused and his innocence. Custodial violence takes place due to social, psychological, professional and administrative factors. Sometimes it also takes place due to, psychological aberrations of the custodian: sadism, sexual weaknesses, social hatreds etc.

Social factors: in our country, we are accustomed to think in terms of "an eye for an eye and a tooth for a tooth". Therefore, society tacitly expects and approves of the use, of violence on suspects to get at the truth. Complainants themselves, particularly in property offences, incite the police to use force or violence to "break" a suspect. Therefore, in a society where the public is indifferent to the use of force, on fellow human beings, policemen get, as it were, social support for these illegal acts. Frequently, reports appearing in the press about lynching and stoning to death of alleged thieves, child lifters, sorcerers etc., reflect the state of mind of Indian society on this issue. Thus, there is no social stigma attached to the use of custodial violence by the police.

Psychological Factors: Stories of brutalities indulged in by the police, in all their unsavoury details, circulate widely among the public, including members of the underworld. Though many of these stories may be the product of fertile imagination, the fact remains that the general public believe them to be true. Therefore, when a suspect is picked up for interrogation by the police, he anticipates "full police treatment" and is apprehensive of his physical safety, Any use of force or even a threat to use force breaks him down completely and he Is prepared to come clean. Due to this fear psychosis, petty criminals, on many occasions, are known to admit their complicity in heinous crimes in which they had no part at all. Unscrupulous police officials tend to play on this fear psychosis and freely use violence to obtain confessions.

Professional and Administrative Factors

(a) In normal police work, law and order takes

priority and the prevention and detection of crime gets only secondary attention. To be a successful detective, a Police Station House Officer should have a thorough knowledge of his jurisdiction; the incidence and pattern of crimes; the modus operandi and other details of the criminals residing in his area; full details of harbourers and receivers of stolen property; and complete knowledge of undesirable and antisocial elements of the area. To acquire this knowledge, the officer should have sufficient time and leisure at his disposal. Unfortunately, with his preoccupation with law and order duties, he is not able to concentrate on this important aspect of his work. Thus, his approach to crime work tends to be unsystematic and unscientific.

(b) Interrogation of a suspect is a battle of wits. It presupposes superior knowledge and wisdom on the part of the interrogator. He needs, in addition to full possession of facts and figures, enough time at his disposal. Under the law of our country, a suspect has to be produced in court within 24 hours. Courts are reluctant to grant 'police remand. Thus, the interrogator is forced to work against time. He is prepared to adopt any short-cut method to gain time. In sensational cases, subordinate police officers are subjected to tremendous pressure from their departmental superiors, the press and the public to produce quick results. In the absence of professional expertise and lack of time, custodial violence presents itself as a panacea for the interrogator and the investigating officer to obtain quick results.

(c) Legal hurdles like the inability to keep a suspect for longer than a day, the Evidence Act being weighed against the police etc., are factors which

> induce the police to keep Suspects in unofficial custody. Once a Suspect is in unofficial Custody, he ceases as such to exist on record, for the purposes of law. What is done to him is known only to police officials within the precincts of a police station. This helps and encourages the police to indulge in custodial violence with impunity.

While custodial violence is common in the sphere of crime investigation to extract information/confession about crime and to recover property etc., it also occurs in maintenance of order situations particularly while dealing with political violence like terrorism, extremism etc. Unable to face the pressure from political extremists and in the absence of legal remedies to neutralise them, the police often indulge in elimination of adversaries through illegal methods.

The law has prohibited the use of custodial violence in unmistakable terms. The Indian Penal Code makes it an offence to voluntarily cause hurt to extort confession or to compel rest oration of property. The. Constitution of India gives the fundamental right to the citizen not to be compelled to be a witness against himself. The Criminal Procedure Code prohibits offering of threats, promises or inducements to extract information, The. Indian Evidence Act prohibits the use of confession made before a Police Officer and the one obtained through inducement, threat or promise, in criminal trials. The Indian Penal Code makes it an offence to wrongfully confine a person to extract confession or compel restoration of property. The Indian Police Act, under which the entire police organisation in India derives its legitimacy and the policeman his powers to function, prohibits unwarranted personal violence by police officers to any person in police custody, The Indian Penal Code lays down minimum punishment for rapes occurring in police custody. There are punitive procedures both administrative and judicial, in case of complaints of custodial violence against police officers.

Thus, it is clear that custodial, violence is illegal and policemen who are to uphold the law cannot indulge in illegal acts. Custodial 'Violence undermines human dignity, brutalises the police system, forfeits the trust of the people and the judiciary and also affects the image of police organisation as a whole. Finally, It also exposes the police officer to the risk of criminal liability and punishment.

In spite of these clear legal prohibitions and negative aspects, the police indulge in custodial violence due to the erroneous belief that it is a short Cut to Success, Studies prove that custodial violence is counter-productive and does not add in any significant way to the achievement of the goals and objectives of the police organisation. Further, investigation of crime is a battle of wits with the criminal and calls for sustained and prolonged efforts on the part of police. As pressure of work mounts, custodial violence is resorted to, to achieve crime control objectives. While crime does not pay, neither do custodial violence.

In situations of political violence, elimination of adversaries through "fake encounters" only strengthens the cause of the adversaries. The public gets alienated from the State and their non-cooperation with the authorities strengthens the cause of the rebels. The root cause of political violence is political in nature a and the cures should also be political in nature. The police should confine themselves to fighting the criminality involved in the actions of the rebels and, through better tactical and professional skills and methods, attempt to neutralise them. To fight the rebels one needs information and cooperation from the public. Custodial violence takes the people away from the police and weakens their efforts to get information.

The Supreme Court of India and various State High Courts have condemned custodial violence and spoken strongly against it. They have proposed stringent punishment for custodial violence. The Supreme Court has observed: "The Police, with their wide powers are apt to overstep their zeal to detect crimes and are tempted to use the strong arm against those who happen to fall under their secluded jurisdiction. That tendency and that temptation must, in the larger interest of justice, be nipped in the bud."

Human Rights Awareness

A sustained publicity campaign should be undertaken to educate the public and the police about the sanctity *of* human rights. This should be a positive campaign and not a negative one to denigrate the police. Instead of concentrating on custodial violence only, this campaign should speak in terms of the rights of women, children, the schedule castes, the scheduled tribes and others and protection from unlawful custody and violence while under custody should be brought in as part of the general picture. This is to ensure that the police do not feel that they have been singled out for denigration in public. In all police publications, an advertisement regarding human rights should be carried. The electronic media should be used extensively, Such a campaign is necessary as the police force, with a strength of about ten lakhs, is spread out in small groups all over the country and it is not easy to reach them to sensitise them on this issue.

Custodial violence is anathema in any civilized society. Law enforcement agencies, particularly the police, should make a conscious effort to banish this evil practice from their organisations. Till this is done, the police will not earn the respect and co-operation of the public and find a honourable place for themselves in society.

Torture is 'severe pain or suffering, whether physical or mental, inflicted by, or at the instigation of, a public official on a person, for such purposes as obtaining from him, or a third person, information or confession, punishing him for an act he has committed or is suspected of having committed or intimidating him or other persons for the same purpose. Torture has been in practice for centuries and has debased human conduct. It degrades and affects the dignity of person. All international instruments on human rights prohibit torture.

The Universal, Declaration of Human Rights in Article 5 states: No one shall be Subjected to torture, or to Cruel, inhuman or degrading punishment.

The International Covenant on Civil and Political Rights in Article 7 states: No' one shall be Subjected to torture or to cruel, inhuman or degrading treatment or punishment. In particular, no one shall be subjected, without his free consent, to medical or scientific experimentation.

The Constitution of India has no special provisions on the subject. However, the Supreme Court has drawn this protection against torture, cruel and unusual punishment from a combined reading of Articles 14, 19 and 26.

The Indian Penal Code, in Section 348, punishes wrongful confinement of a person to extort confession or compel restoration of property. Similarly, Section 330 regards the act of voluntarily causing hurt to extort confession or compel restoration of property as a punishable offence. In Section 362(2)(a), minimum punishment has been laid down for rape occurring in police custody.

To preserve human dignity, to ensure that the basic freedoms proclaimed in the Charter of United Nations are available and to promote universal respect for and the observance of human rights and fundamental freedoms, a Convention against Torture and Other Cruel or Inhuman or Degrading Treatment or Punishment was adopted by UN General Assembly on December 10, 1984.

Universal Declaration of Rights

Article 10 reads: Everyone is entitled to full equality to a fair and public hearing by an independent and impartial tribunal, in the determination of the rights and obligation% and of any criminal charge against him".

International Covenant on Civil and Political Rights

Article 14(3) says: In the determination of any criminal charges against him, every one shall be entitled to the following minimum guarantees, in full equality:

(a) To be informed promptly and in detail in a language which he understands, of the nature and cause of his charge against him;

(b) To have adequate time and facilities for the preparation of his defence and to communicate with counsel of his own choosing;

(c) To be tried without undue delay;

(d) To be tried in his presence, and to defend himself in person or through legal assistance of his own choosing : to be informed, if he does not have legal assistance, of this right, and to have legal assistance assigned to him, in any case where the interests of justice so require, and without payment by him in any such case, if he does not have sufficient means to pay for it;

(e) To examine, or have examined, the witnesses against him and to obtain the attendance and examination of witnesses on his behalf under the same conditions as witnesses against him;

(f) To have the free assistance of an interpreter if he cannot understand or speak the language used in court; and

(g) Not to be compelled to testify against himself or to confess guilt.

Constitution of India in Article 21 says: No person shall be deprived of his life or personal liberty except according to procedures established by law.

Procedures established by law or the due process as applied in India, requires that the trial Should:

(a) Give notice of hearing to the accused;

(b) Give accused an opportunity to be heard in defence;

(c) The hearing should be by an impartial tribunal; and

(d) 'Reasonable' restrictions can be placed on enjoyment of the rights of procedures.

The Supreme Court of India, through many decisions, has now made a compact set of rights accessible to an accused. They are:

(1) Fair Hearing: This right starts as soon as the magistrate takes the Charge on his file and invokes the provisions of section 202 Cr.P.C.

(2) Notices: The accused is entitled to have a notice of the hearing under section 204 Cr.P.C,

(3) Open Trial: Under section 327 Cr.P.C., the trial should be open and public. However, in cases of rape and sensitive national security matters, the court has a right to bar access to public.

(4) Speedy Trial: This right has been given as an extension of the concept of fairness enunciated in Article 21, The Supreme Court has extended this to pre-trial processes including investigation.

The accused can get relief through the medium of 'writs'. The right to a speedy trial is embodied in Section 309 of the Code of Criminal Procedure.

(5) Right to an Interpreter

This duty is cast on the court to ensure that the accused understands the proceedings and if necessary, the court can arrange for an interpreter. This is provided for in Section 279 of the Criminal Procedure Code, As a further safeguard, Section 318 of the Cr.P.C. stipulates where it appears that the accused has not understood the proceedings and the case ends in conviction, the matter should be placed before the High Court for orders.

(6) Right to proper defence

Constitution of India in Article 22(1) says - 'No person who is arrested shall be detained in custody without being informed, as soon as may be, of the grounds for such arrest nor shall he be denied the right to consult, and to be defended by a legal practitioner of his choice.

This right commences from the moment of arrest and extend throughout the trial, even if released on bail. If the accused is poor, he is entitled to legal assistance at State' cost. This is provided for by Article 39(A) of the Constitution of India, Section 304(1) of the Code of Criminal Procedure and Legal Services Authorities Act of 1987.

(7) Right to the opportunity to make a proper and full defence

The accused has the right to get free copies of Police. Report, FIR, Confession, Statements of witnesses tinder Section 207, 208 and 238 of Criminal

Procedure Code. In all appealable cases, he should get a free certified copy of the judgement under Section 363 of the Cr.P.C.

All the witnesses against him—the prosecution witnesses are to be examined in his presence and he can cross-examine them. He can also get all the witnesses to speak on his behalf summoned by the Court and examined. The court however has a right not to summon all, as per Cr.P.C. 233(2) and 243(2), it it is of the opinion that they are not relevant and are being summoned as a dilatory tactics while the accused can not be examined to prove the guilt against him, he can offer himself as a witness to produce his defence. But any thing said in the nature of confession can not be admitted against him. Please see 315 Cr.P.C. Fie can only be called as a witness, when he makes a request for it.

(8) Final opportunity: After hearing both the sides and before pronouncing an order of punishment, the court has to give an opportunity to the accused to make a representation against the same.

(9) Right to Appeal: The accused has a right to appeal against his conviction at higher judicial forums. All assistance and help should be given to him if he is a prisoner (please see Chapter 20 on rights of prisoners).

It will be seen that the Indian judicial and legal systems are very progressive in this area, and all the international standards were present in operation in spirit long before they came into vogue through covenants.

While it is the duty of the court to ensure that all these rights are available to the accused, the magistrate often needs the assistance of the police to provide copies of the statements of prosecution witnesses, serve summons, produce witnesses for examination etc. Police should willingly and readily co-operate with the courts to ensure that the accused get all their basic rights.

The main reason why torture continues to be practised on such a wide scale throughout India is that the police feel themselves to be immune - they are fully aware that they will not be held accountable, even if they kill the victim and even if the truth is revealed. Institutional factors which contribute to the persistence of torture include: the negative public image and bad working conditions of the police, the inadequate training and facilities available to them, the high degree of political involvement in directing their activities and the failure of the government to accept responsibility for ensuring that the police operate within the limits of the law.

The police in India enjoy only a low level of public confidence and respect. In a comment that epitomizes public perceptions, The Statesman in September 19,89 observed that "...irrespective of the ruling party's professed Ideology, the police remains, in the words of an Allahabad High Court judge, the most organized group of criminals In India". Indeed, some police officers have expressed similar concerns themselves. A Haryana head constable complained in October *1991:* "we are shunned by the public we are supposed to protect"

Recommendations for police reforms, such as those proposed by the National Police Commission since *1979,* have been consistently ignored by successive central and state governments. Upendra Baxi, Vice-Chancellor of Delhi University and a noted analyst of police behaviour, states that the police remain an "exploited, neglected and despised minority" who are denied the most basic minimum working conditions and who are "subservient to the rulers rather than responsive to the people". The police are poorly paid, suffer difficult working conditions, lack adequate housing and have little job security. The police have no rights of association tinder the Police Forces (Restriction of Rights) Act 1966.

These conditions led to a police revolt in Haryana state in mid-1991. A leader of the unofficial Haryana Police Association said "We ate the lowest paid among the government employees, misused by politicians and officials alike, run around for twenty-four hours and earn finally not two square meals but a bad name from the public"64. After conducting a series of interviews of senior police officials in June 1988, *The* Statesman reported: "Undoubtedly many of the excesses committed by the police an due to a tremendous degree of frustration in the lower rungs of the force".

Central to the demands of the Haryana police was freedom from improper political influence and interference, which is alleged to be present in all aspects of police operations from recruitment to methods of investigation. "We are pawns in the hands of the powerful politicians and clever officers the leader of the Haryana police said. Earlier, a senior police officer was quoted as saying that "... out of nearly 8,000 station house officers In India, practically two-thirds are political appointees whose main job is to make money and give part of it to their political patrons to keep them happy"65. The NPC also confirmed this practice: "It is common knowledge now that postings of officers at this level are rarely left to the district Superintendent of Police but are regulated by instructions, mostly oral and sometimes written, from the Government. The Andhra Pradesh Police Association, in a resolution adopted at its annual meeting in October 1986, specifically attributed deaths in custody to such political interference, as did two opposition members of the Maharashtra legislative assembly during a July 1991 debate on custodial deaths.

This problem has long been recognized. The NPC concluded that such prevalent political interference often resulted in "discretionary enforcement of the law while dealing with public order situations, with emphasis on severity and ruthlessness in regard to persons opposed to the ruling party". In September 1988 a former Director of the National Police Academy in Hyderabad wrote: "it now seems to be taken for granted that...the police, would be available to the ruling party to protect its supporters, to harass its opponents, and to further its political interests.... In many places the politicians, the police and lumpen elements have developed a vested interest. For the policeman who joins this combine it is both a means of enrichment and an insurance against punishment if exposed "

The National Police Commission has analysed how, in post independence India, political interference over the police Was fostered by the long sustained rule of one political party, the Congress Party: "Prolonged one-party rule at the Centre and in the States for over 30 years coupled with the natural desire of ruling partymen to remain in positions of power resulted in the development of [a] symbiotic relationship between politicians on [the] one hand and the civil services on the other. Vested Interests grew on both sides. What started as a normal interaction between the politicians and the services for the avowed objective of better administration... soon degenerated into different forms of inter cession, intervention and with malafide objectives unconnected with public Interest".

Police organization is still structured on the 1861 Police Act, Section 23 of which requires as police officer "promptly to obey and execute all orders and warrants lawfully issued to him by any competent authority".

This allows civil and political executives authority to control the police. As Upendra Baxi concluded in a study of the India legal system: "No wonder 'third degree' methods prevail... since the order to use them on suspects in police custody comes from such 'competent' authority *(including not* infrequently from the Superintendent of Police...)." At its 1986 annual meeting, the Andhra Pradesh police said that most custodial deaths were due to pressure on police to detect crime from senior officers and the local ruling party.

In May 1991, the former inspector general of police in Tamil Nadu gave the following explanation: 'When the police are pressurised to deliver results when they don't have adequate time or manpower to devote to crime investigations they take short cuts to achieve their ends. In this process violations of fundamental rights do occur'.

Concern that inadequate police training contributes to custodial violence is also long-standing, but again recommended improvements have not been implemented. Officials have similarly complained that a total lack of modern investigative techniques contributes to police excesses. In 1988 S.N. Roy, then Director General of the Bihar police, said he totally disapproved of torture but pointed out that the police were not encouraged to use other methods, and that they lacked training in modern, scientific techniques of interrogation.

Article 246 of the Constitution assigns responsibility for the police to the state governments. Through their superiors - headed by the director general of police—the police report to the state home minister. At the same time, central government also has important constitutional responsibilities for the police and wide powers to influence their performance and behaviour. These include the recruitment and management of the most senior police officers *belonging to* the Indian Police Service UPS), the promotion of police research and the development of professional training institutions. Police agencies such as the Central Bureau of Investigation (CBI), the Central Reserve Police Force (CRPF) and the Border Security Force (BSF) report directly to the central government Ministry of Home Affairs. Article 355 of the Constitution requires the central government to protect states against both external aggression and internal disturbance. This provision has also been used in non-emergency situations to deploy paramilitary forces, such as the BSF and the CRPF, to assist the police in areas affected by armed opposition. Most importantly, although the funding of the police is a state expenditure, the central government has powers to ensure that adequate resources are allocated to policing and to provide additional financial support.

The central government bears a large measure of responsibility for the misbehaviour of the police because of its long-standing failure to ensure that adequate resources are allocated to their training and operation. Between 1979 and 1981 the NPC made a series of well thought-out and detailed recommendations relating to the selection of police officers, their training, supervision, working conditions and pay, and proposed an effective machinery to investigate human rights violations by the police. It also recommended that a special unit should be created in the Home Ministry to examine and implement these recommendations. However, the central government has so far failed to implement the NPCs recommendations or take any other effective steps to halt torture, rape and other forms of custodial violence. Instead, It has simply denied to the International community that these violations occur, and insisted that effective remedies exist for anyone who wishes to complain about it.

UN Support to Victims of Torture

Torture continues to occur on a worldwide basis, despite enhanced efforts by Governments and organizations in keeping with provisions contained in domestic law and international human rights conventions whose objective is its total eradication.

The practice of torture was first prohibited in 1948 by the Universal Declaration of Human Rights and by the International Convention on the Prevention and Punishment of the Crime of Genocide; the concept was reaffirmed in 1966 by the International Covenant on Civil and Political Rights; and more recently, in 1984, by the Convention against Torture and Other Cruel, Inhuman or Degrading Treatment or Punishment.

The effects of torture should not be under-estimated. Physical and mental consequences of torture can endure for several years and may be irreversible, often affecting not only thousands of victims themselves, but also their relatives. One of the means of mitigating the subsequent effects of torture on victims and their families is to provide them with medical, psychological, social, legal and economic aid. With this in mind, the General Assembly' created the United Nations Voluntary Fund for Victims of Torture in 1982. The purpose of the Fund is to receive voluntary contributions and distribute them to non-governmental organizations and treatment centres for assisting victims of torture and their relatives whose human rights have been severely violated as a result of torture, as well as for the funding of projects for training health care professionals specialized in the treatment of victims of torture.

The Fund is administered by the United Nations Secretary-General with a Board of Trustees acting in an advisory capacity and comprising five members with wide experience in the field of human rights. The members serve in their personal capacity and are appointed by the Secretary-General for a renewable three-year term of office on the basis of equitable geographical distribution. Currently, members of the Board of Trustees are Jaap Walkate, Chairman, from The Netherlands; Ribot Hatano from Japan; Elizabeth Odio-Benito from Costa Rica; Ivan Tosevsky from the Former Yugoslav Republic of Macedonia; and Amos Wako from Kenya.

The inadequacy of available resources is a limiting factor in the field of assistance to victims; as a consequence, programmes of assistance are subjected to interruptions. For some 100 organisations the support of the United Nations Voluntary Fund remains essential.

During its sixtieth session, held in May 1997, the Board of Trustees examined 143 proposals for projects from 70 countries to be funded. The Board recommended that US$ 3,036,854 be allocated. The High Commissioner fir Human Rights approved the recommendations of the Board on behalf of the Secretary-General. 20 new projects were launched and 104 projects were financed worldwide: 14 in North America, 21 in Central and South America, 30 in Western Europe, 10 in Eastern Europe, 14 in Africa, 15 in Asia, Oceania and the Middle East.

It is important to note that the grants allocated to organizations based in North America and Western Europe are used for the treatment of as asylum-seekers and refugees victims of Torture coming from other regions of the world. It is a known fact that at least 50% of asylum-seekers and refugees who have been detained in their country of origin have been subjected to one or more forms of torture.

The Fund receives projects which focus on providing medical, psychological, economic, social and legal assistance to victims of torture and to members of their families. A few projects also share the objective of organizing training seminars for health professionals specialized in the treatment of torture victims.

Each May, the Board of Trustees makes recommendations on grants to the High Commissioner for Human Rights. Subsequently, in the following month, on the basis of those recommendations, the High Commissioner takes decisions on behalf of the Secretary-General. As a final step, grants are made available at the end of July.

From 1983 to July 1997, the Fund has financed 255 projects for direct assistance to torture victims. From US$ 2.5 to US$ 3 million of voluntary contributions received from about 30 Governments and a few individuals are disbursed every year to projects in some 60 countries representative of all the regions of the world. Further information on the activities of the Voluntary Fund can be found in the latest annual reports of the Secretary-General to the General Assembly (UN document A/52/387) and to the Commission on Human Rights (UN documents E/CN.4/1998/37 and Add. 1).

Torture involves not only physical but also psychological forms, sometimes with long-term sequelae: in this regard, the Fund is supporting a project whose objective is to provide global assistance to formerly disappeared children of victims of torture in Latin America. The organization identifies disappeared children as those born in detention, abducted by security forces and illegally adopted. Once located by the organization, the children may be returned to their biological families. The best interests of the child have to be taken into consideration. This project consists of two main parts: investigation - some 1,030 interviews were carried out in the past year in conjunction with blood tests and analyses of genetic data - and psychological support provided to some 43 1 persons during 1996. Most of these persons suffer from sequelae of post-traumatic stress disorder including anxiety, nightmares, depression, as well as affective and intellectual inhibitions and benefit from individual psychotherapy. The number of youths seeking assistance remains high while many children have yet to be found: to date, 172 children still need to be located and 6 who were found have yet to be returned to their biological families.

8

Rights of Disabled Persons

Everyone cherishes good health and long life. Health and human happiness go together. That is why, Perhaps, right to health is regarded as one of the basic human rights. But on the other hand, human life, sometimes, is marred by the ravages of natural disaster, birth and accidents, causing disability of one kind or the other so many people. No doubt, the incidence of disability is the most catastrophic situation inflicted by the forces of nature on human beings, yet it does not, in any way, take away the inalienable rights of deprived people. The movement for the rights of disabled persons has grown out of the realization that they are firstly human beings. Any discrimination between the disabled and the able-bodied tentamounts to the naked violation of the human rights of the disabled persons.

The dimensions of the incidence of disability at the global are managingly glaring at the future of making. Though, several steps have been taken in this regard, yet their outcome has shown little change in the situation. In this paper, an attempt is made to focus on the prevalence of the incidence of disability ~and the impact of the world-wide campaign for the prevention of disability and rehabilitation of the disabled on the rights of the disabled. The disabled, like others, are social beings. They have similar hopes, aspirations and lights as their fellowmen. Yet man focuses his attention on their disabilities rather than potentialities. Consequently, the disabled have been socially and economically marginalized and denied opportunities to seek self-development. The problems arising out of disability are varied and complex, but most of the problems encountered by the disabled stem from prejudices and ignorance on the part of the so-called able-bodied persons.

The concept of disability is directly linked with the societal attitudes towards disabled persons. Since the societal attitude towards the disabled has undergone change through different stages of social evolution, the concept of disability has also changed accordingly. The traditional societal attitude towards the disabled was one of pity, sympathy and charity. The disabled were considered as incapable of leading independent and productive lives.

Accordingly, the persons with a physical defect of Some kind or the other were, for centuries, termed as 'crippled'. The world 'crippled' and its synonyms imply some sort of social stigma. It also refers to a state of helplessness, Under the traditional perception of disability, an important element of the welfare of the disabled-recognition and respect of human dignity and self-esteem of the disabled person-was completely missing.

A marked shift in the societal attitude towards the disabled was noticed in the second quarter of the twentieth century. As a result of several scientific and social advancements, an entirely new concept of welfare with regard to the disabled has emerged which is responsible, on the one hand, for the gradual awakening of the society towards the rights of the disabled and on the other hand, for the creation of a new consciousness among the disabled themselves towards their rights and obligations. The new approach for the welfare of the disabled in directed at the socio-economic integration of the disabled in the mainstream of active social life. Therefore, the use of such words as 'disabled' and 'handicapped' is advocated, because they seem to take an objective view of disability.

Very often, the terms like 'disabled', 'physically handicapped', 'impaired' and 'crippled' are used almost synonymously. It is necessary to make distinction between these different terms. The term 'disabled' or 'disability' refers to a solution wherein the functional capabilities are either lost or reduced considerably due to impairment. Contrary to this, 'handicap' is a value judgement passed by others about an impaired, disabled person. It is not necessary that disability may become handicap under all circumstances. It becomes handicap, only when it causes interference with the individual's expectations, job performance or relationship with others. The term 'impairment' refers to any deviation from the normal which leads to defective structure, function, organization, or development of the whole of any part of individual's faculties. Thus, the term 'disabled' appears mere appropriate with its broad based meaning.

Besides these terminological problems, the concept of disability faces another kind of problem, i.e. the lack of any well-conceived definition of 'disability'. This problem is due to the fact that different countries follow different criteria to define disability. So much so that the scholars and international bodies have also adopted various approaches to the study of the disability. These approaches may be categorized as, medical approach, psychological approach, economic-vocational approach and socio-political approach.

The medical approach emphasizes on the physical functioning and its whole orientation is individual centred. The World Health Organization (WHO) is its best representative example. The second approach lays stress on the psychological aspect of disability. It aims at making the disabled self-reliant, The economic-vocational approach is concerned with the vocational limitations of the disabled and it is directed towards the vocational rehabilitation of the disabled. The International Labour Organization (hereafter ILO) is the most ardent proponent of this approach. The socio-political approach regards disability as a by-product of interaction between individual and environment. Contrary to the medical approach, it holds the failure of structured social environment responsible for disability instead of personal disorders or deficiencies.'

It, therefore, emphasizes on the need for strengthened laws to combat discrimination against the disabled. All the above approaches take a narrow view of disability and confine themselves to only one aspect of disability. From the holistic viewpoint, the definition of the term 'disability' as given by the United Nations, seems to be quite exhaustive in its meaning. There are different types of disability, namely, (i) visually disabled; (ii) hearing disability (deafness), (iii) speech disability (dumbness); (iv) mental retardness, and (v) orthopaedic disability. All these types of disabled are covered in the definition of the term 'disabled' as given by the United Nations.'

Another perplexing dimension of the problem of disability is the colossal magnitude of the problem. Though, at the global level, it is difficult to provide accurate data on the incidence of disability, however, the never growing population of the disabled in the world is a matter of grave concern to all. According to one UN estimate," more than 500 million people in the world are physically or mentally disabled. The population of the disabled increases every year by some 15 million as a result of war, accident, malnutrition and diseases,' which means a country like Afghanistan is added to the disabled population every year. If this trend continues, then the figure may surpass 700 million mark by 2000 A.D.' Out of the total disabled population, women account for above one-third of it, but if female disabled children are included in this calculation, then the total female population with disability would be around 250 million which comes to about 5% of the world population.'

The overall plight of disabled persons in both the developing and developed countries presents a gloomy picture. While in developing societies, disability is basically caused by poverty and malnutrition, on the other hand, in developed societies, it is linked with aging and accidents. That is why, In developing countries, mostly children are victims of disability, whereas elder persons and industrial workers, for the most part, affected by disability in the developed countries. The situation of disabled women is more distressing. They are subjected to dual discrimination-firstly, due to their feminine gender and secondly, due to disability. Thus the dimensions of disability are enormous and it needs to be fought on all fronts with concerted, persistent and bold efforts.

Until the first quarter of the twentieth century, disability was regarded as life long dependence and despondency, misery and squalor. Consequently, hardly any efforts for its prevention were initiated at that time. However, international concern for the improvement of public health and prevention of diseases was manifested in various health related provisions of the League of Nations.'

The first international initiative with regard to the rehabilitation of the disabled came from the ILO which came into being in 1919 as an autonomous body associated with the League of Nations. As back as 192 for the first time, the ILO turned its attention towards the employment problems of the disabled persons. Since then, the rights of the disabled lie at the very heart of its mission. A major part of the ILO activities for the rehabilitation of the disabled consists of the adoption of international labour standards in the form of various recommendations, conventions and resolutions.' The most recent among them include Vocational Rehabilitation and Employment (Disabled Persons) Convention, 1983 (No. 159) and Recommendation, 1983 (no. 168). These instruments are very significant in the sense that they contain useful guidelines on methods and measures for widening the employment opportunities for the disabled. Thus, the ILO has played an instrumental role in the field of vocational rehabilitation of the disabled.

With the inception of the United Nations (UN), the campaign for disability prevention and rehabilitation gained world wide currency. The incorporation of the human rights provisions in the Charter of the United Nations and the adoption of the Universal Declaration of Human Rights, followed by the two covenants," manifest the resolve of the international community to right the menance of disability. The United Nations together with other specialized agencies have been working towards the goals set in different instruments. The United Nations, through its various resolutions and declarations," had laid down international norms, standards and guidelines concerning the rights of the disabled persons. A number of specialised agencies, such as, the International Labour Organization (11.0); the United Nations Educational, Scientific. Cultural Organization (UNESCO), The World Health Organization (WHO), the United National International Children Emergency Fund (UNICEF), have oriented their activities towards the disability prevention and rehabilitation programme within the scope of their organizations. In addition, other international bodies associated with the rehabilitation programmes for the disabled Include: the United Nations Development Programme (UNDP), the Food Agricultural Organization (FAO), the United Nations Industrial Development Organization (UNIDO) and the Office of the United Nations High Commission for Refugees (UNCHR), etc. Besides these, there are many other non-governmental bodies engaged in the rehabilitation task.

As of now, no international body is specifically assigned with the responsibility of implementation of the United Nations' recommendations and various other instruments. The most important reason behind it is that the global concern for the integration of the disabled has yet not been articulated in the legally binding conventions. The United Nations' activities in this regard have been, so far, confined to the adoption of resolutions and declarations. However, the Sub-Commission on the Prevention of Discrimination and Protection of Minorities is the most important body dealing with the violation of the rights of the disabled persons.

In brief, it may be said that the international bodies may only provide guidelines and set norms for the promotion of the rights of the disabled persons, but the main task of integrating and rehabilitating them rests with the member states. Unless the disabled are assigned the status of equality in these societies, the promotion of their rights shall remain a mere myth.

Rehabilitation is the most strategic weapon to combat the menance of disability. There are two perceptions of rehabilitations. One is medical perception which views rehabilitation as assisting all those medical measures which expedite recovery in the physical sense, whereas according to the other view, rehabilitation means the restoration of the disabled to the fullest physical, mental, social, vocational and economic usefulness of which lie/she is capable. In other words, rehahilitation is a goal oriented programme which alms at enabling an Impaired person to reach an Optimum mental, physical or social functional level.

The rehabilitation process, thus, involves basically three aspects. These aspects are: physical rehabilitation, vocational rehabilitation and psycho-social integration. All three aspects am interlined:

Physical Rehabilitation

It is the first and most important aspect of the whole process of rehabilitation. It is directed towards the improvement of the functional loss caused by disability. Physical rehabilitation involves two phases, namely, prevention of disability and restoration of the disabled.

Prevention of Disability

Prevention is better than cure. Most of the disabilities are preventable if adequate precautionary and educative measures are taken against its outbreak. There are numerous ways of disability prevention. Some of these attack the cause of disease directly (for instance, vaccination and inoculation); while the others deal with it indirectly, such as, community education, early detection, genetic counselling etc. The whole scheme of disability prevention comprises following steps.

Immunization is one of the most powerful and effective means of disability prevention. The diseases like polio, measles, tetanus, whooping cough, diptheria, neo-natal and tuberculosis are responsible for the growing incidence of disability, especially in the developing countries. Immunization against these diseases, though, a challenging task, but the promise held is even greater. The World Health Organization (WHO), as a part of its global efforts, launched the Expanded Programme on Immunization (EPI) in 1974. As a result of this programme, two-thirds of the children in the developing world have been covered by vaccines and approximately two million lives are being saved each year. The Rotary International, a non-governmental organization, is also busy with its polio-immunization programme. In fact, the elimination of all these diseases constitutes a major contribution to the prevention of in fact and childhood disability.

Certain types of disability are linked with malnutrition. There arc primarily four nutritional disorders in the developing countries which lead to widespread impairment, and disability. These am: (1) protein-energy malnutrition (PEM), (ii) endemic goitre, (III) xerophthalmia leading to blindness, and (iv) nutritional anaemia. There is a paucity of precise data on the people affected by malnutrition, but most of them are centred in the underdeveloped countries and the developing countries.

Pre-natal, peri-natal and post-natal care as well as obstetric practices used at the time of child birth are also related to the disability causes, especially in the developing countries where it is found that inappropriate obstetric practices and improper neo-natal care lead to neurological impairments. Lack of Immunization of pregnant mothers render the new borns more susceptible to all communicable diseases resulting in various conditions. All this can be successfully prevented by taking recourse to the immunization of pregnant mothers and observance of elementary hygiene.

Accidents and Hereditary Defects are two causes of disability are the least controllable factors. Accidents am usually of two kinds—industrial and traffic. Industrial accidents are more common In the developed countries, whereas the developing countries sire mainly in the grip of traffic accidents. There are other causes of accidents also as, fall, slip, explosion, animal and insect bites, etc. In the case of hereditary defects, endogamous marriages are responsible for genetic disorders. The hereditary defects may be prevented only if the disorder is a dominant one, but not if the disorder is necessible.

Restoration of the Disabled means that every medical, surgical and auxiliary services should be used to reduce the impact of disability. There is a co-relation between restoration and the vocational rehabilitation. Restoration, eventually, helps in the vocational rehabilitation of the disabled. The process of physical rehabilitation involves adequate training, evaluation of the working capacity of the individual and remedial gymnastics and prosthetics.

Vocational rehabilitation may he defined as a service necessary to render a disabled person fit to engage in remunerative occupation. The end product of vocational rehabilitation is resettlement of the disabled into gainful economic life. Work or employment has a psychological, social and economic value for the disabled and it instills a feeling of self-confidence in them. But, in actual practice, the successful placement of the disabled is affected by several factors, such as, attitude of the community, the attitude of the disabled towards disability and job-availability for them.

If a community accepts the potentialities of the disabled, the placement of the disabled becomes easy. But employers usually rationalize their feelings on economic grounds. They argue that disability reduces productivity and so, an economic liability or that the disabled are prone to accidents and if injured at work, the employers become liable to employ them.

— The vocational rehabilitation of the disabled is co-terminus with his own self-perception. In any community where the disabled have been over protected by their families, or have been given a negative role by the community, it may he quite difficult to convince him of the benefits of vocational rehabilitation.

— Severe unemployment or underemployment creates the greatest obstacle to the placement of the disabled. In such a situation, it is necessary to concentrate on a few selected groups for vocational rehabilitation. The agriculture based community may offer good prospects of their placement in industrial enterprises, provided they are properly skilled in the job. Much can be accomplished by educating the public about the capabilities of the disabled.

Psycho-Social Integration of the Disabled is the most crucial stage in the process of rehabilitation. The physical and vocational rehabilitation cannot achieve the desired results, unless the disabled may feel themselves Psychologically integrated and the society is willing to accept them as productive members.

Disability brings in its wake so many adjustment problems, the disabled has to bear a double burden of handicaps—'social handicap' in addition to his 'specific handicap'. Rehabilitation encompasses the whole process of adjustment and readjustment of the disabled in various spheres of life. The disabled faces quite many adjustment problems of different nature which may be categorized thus.

The disabled faces a great deal of uncertainty in his life due to permanent structural and functional disorders of his body. He needs to assure himself whether he would be able to move around in the outside world. According to psychologists, the self-concept is a determining factor in the personality development of the disabled individual. It determines not only his own perception, but also of others towards his disability. Therefore, it is imperative that the self concept should be reconciled.

The feeling of insecurity, both physical and emotional, is greater in a disabled person than in any other able-bodied person. The perpetuation of false notions about sex and disability in the minds of common men deprives the disabled person of his right to lead a married life. This causes a deep mental agony in him. Besides, some other factors such as, physical discomfort, aversion ridicule and scorn of the able-bodied, escalate emotional problems in him Love and affection give them emotional satisfaction and helps in his psycho-social integration.

Family is the most important agent of socialization of the disabled. The impact of-disability is Closely interlinked which the is the most important agent of socialization of the disabled. The impact of disability is closely interlinked with *the* adequacy or inadequacy of the parental attitude. If the parents view the disability of their child as calamity, the disabled child also thinks likewise. Therefore, the parents and family members should objectively accept the limitations potentials of their disabled child.

In spite of the wise scope of rehabilitation strategy to combat the incidence of disability, it has failed to deliver the desired goods. The reason is that due to the cumulative effect of several factors, the pace of rehabilitation process is hampered. These factors are: poverty, ignorance and illiteracy, neglect of public health, lack of commitment on the part of planners and statesmen, lack of political and administrative will and social barriers. Besides these, the manpower problem and problems concerning technology need sonic elaboration.

The Problem of manpower is a great stumbling block in the way of the proper placement of the disabled. The functioning of rehabilitation institutions in the developing countries affords a good example of it. In most of these countries, the last few decades have witnessed high specialization of rehabilitation manpower which has culminated in the creation of too many new professional groups and sub-groups. This is because more than one experts are generally involved In the treatment of one disabled individual. Needless to say that 'the team work' is a .must In the rehabilitation process. But experience shown that it has very often led to the decline in the efficiency of utilisation of the viable manpower. In fact, the need for rehabilitation is so great that it cannot be Properly met by Specialists alone, Unless each country introduces basic task concerning rehabilitation in the training curricular of doctors, nurses, social workers, teachers and others, any solution of such manpower problem cannot be Imagined.'?

In recent Years, there has been a rapid development of rehabilitation technology. Much more Is known today regarding 1343" exercise and other active forms of training for the disabled. But the development of technical aids and devices cannot yield the desired results, unless the disabled are adequately trained in their use.

The problem arising out of the incidence of disability are varied and complex. It is gratifying to note that as of now, the question of disability prevention and rehabilitation is receiving *due* consideration at different levels. Yet, several measures initiated by national and international agencies for the disability Prevention have resulted In limited success. The fact that the *world* or organisation is merely a voluntary association of sovereign states father than a supra-national body, is the most obstructive limitation in this regard.

While considering some constructive steps for the promotion of the rights of disabled persons and their rehabilitation as well as integration into the mainstream of socio-economic life, this fact must be taken into account that the problem of disability is a mere syndrome; the root causes are inherent In mass poverty, social segregation and illiteracy. Therefore, the only permanent solution of disability problem could be their psycho-social and economic integration and proper placement which would enable them stand on their own with dignity and decency. With this objective in mind, following suggestions are offered:

(1) Education can go a long way in creating an awareness among the people about the basic causes of disability, its prevention prospects and rehabilitation. It may also prove an effective weapon in eradicating the dogmatic fears attached to disability.

(2) The development of community based rehabilitation services is another step necessary to expedite the integration of the disabled. It also entails the balanced development of community based services in both urban and rural areas. It should be based on an appraisal of the most appropriate forms of service delivery so assist the disabled in accommodating to the life of their social milieu.

(3) The development of technical aids and devices may be another significant step in the physical rehabilitation of the disabled. Steps should be initiated in each country to allow the disabled to have financial and physical access to technical aids and devices.

(4) Rehabilitation technique should be simplified and made more economical.

(5) Disability prevention and rehabilitation should be incorporated as an integral and high priority component of national socio-economic policies and development plans. Action in these fields should be recognized as legitimate targets for development assistance.

(6) Allocation of financial resources for rehabilitation of the disabled should be enhanced by all countries to give boost to existing educational, medical, social and vocational systems.

(7) Society should realize that the disabled are not second class citizens. Disability does not deprive them of their liberty and equality of opportunity. Social structure should be revamped in such a way so as to facilitate their full participation in the socio-economic and political life.

(8) Man power should be mobilized with efficient and dedicated rehabilitation experts and sincere and committed government officials to hasten the pace of rehabilitation.

(9) Public opinion should be educated to protest against any discriminatory policy adopted by the government. The people must be vigilant against any violation of human rights. If any such violation takes place, this should be forthwith brought to the notice of local authorities.

(10) In order to prevent any atrocity and violation of the rights of the disabled, special cells and courts should he set up to monitor such Incidents.

(11) Non-governmental organizations and voluntary agencies have a significant role to play in this field. Legislative measures and efforts at official level along cannot be effective In solving this challenging problem.

(12) The last but not the least important thing is that a general consciousness should be created at grass-root level against the incidence of disability.

To conclude, it may be said that the global problems of disability are of such a colossal magnitude that as of now, any worthwhile effort to meet the challenge does not seem to be in sight. However, there is enough scope for optimism and let us hope for the day when, with all necessary changes in social perceptions and with greater opportunities for the development available, the disabled would feel that they are no longer disabled.

9

Apartheid

Apartheid, as a State-imposed system of institutionalized racial discrimination and segregation, has been practised by South Africa as an official policy since 1948. Under apartheid, black South Africans-the overwhelming majority of the people of the country-are denied fundamental rights and liberties. They are not allowed to participate in the political life of the country and are subject to hundreds of repressive laws and regulations. Both the General Assembly and the Security Council have declared apartheid incompatible with the Charter of the United Nations. The Assembly has condemned apartheid as a crime against humanity, and the Security Council, which has considered the question since 1960, has termed apartheid a crime against the conscience and dignity of mankind.

The racial policies of South Africa have been under discussion by the United Nations since 1946, when India complained that South Africa had enacted legislation against South Africans of Indian origin. Beginning in 1952, the wider question of the policies of apartheid of the South African Government was included in the General Assembly's agenda.

During the 1950s, the General Assembly made repeated appeals to the South African Government to abandon its apartheid policies in the light of the principles of the Charter. South Africa, however, consistently refused to heed the appeals and resolutions of the General Assembly and the Security Council, viewing the United Nations decisions as illegal and unacceptable and as violating the principle of non-interference in its internal affairs.

The principal United Nations decisions and actions with regard to the question of apartheid in South Africa since 1960 are summarized below.

1960

The Security Council met at the request of 29 African and Asian Member States to consider "the situation arising out of the large-scale killings of unarmed and peaceful demonstrators against racial discrimination and segregation" in South Africa. This followed an incident at Sharpeville on 21 March in which South African police fired on peaceful demonstrators protesting the requirement that all Africans carry "reference books"; 69 persons were killed and 180 wounded. The Council stated that the situation in South Africa had led to international friction and, if continued, might endanger international peace and security. It called on the South African Government to abandon its policy of apartheid.

1962

The General Assembly, deploring the failure of South Africa to comply with its repeated requests and demands and those of the Security Council, asked Member States to break off diplomatic relations with South Africa, boycott South African goods, and refrain from all exports to South Africa, including armaments.

The Assembly established a special body, known since 1974 as the Special Committee against Apartheid, to keep South Africa's racial policies under review, reporting to the Assembly and/or the Security Council. The 19-member intergovernmental Committee was later given a wider mandate to review all aspects of South Africa's apartheid policies and their international repercussions.

The Committee conducts hearings, sends missions of consultation, organizes conferences and seminars, and implements United Nations resolutions, particularly by promoting sports, cultural, consumer and other boycotts. With the Centre against Apartheid, it co-operates with Governments, organizations, trade unions, religious leaders, youth movements and anti-apartheid groups in mobilizing international public opinion in support of United Nations resolutions against apartheid.

1963

The Security Council instituted a voluntary arms embargo against South Africa, calling on all States to stop the sale and shipment of arms, ammunition of all types and military vehicles to that country. Both the Council and the Assembly asked South Africa to grant unconditional release to all persons imprisoned for having opposed apartheid.

1965

The Assembly established the United Nations Trust Fund for South Africa. The Fund is based on voluntary contributions from which grants are made to organizations for legal aid to persons persecuted under South Africa's repressive and discriminatory laws, relief to such persons and their dependants, and relief for refugees from South Africa.

1966

In commemoration of the 1960 Sharpeville incident, the Assembly proclaimed 21 March as International Day for the Elimination of Racial Discrimination, to be observed annually.

1967

The General Assembly established the United Nations Educational and Training Programme for Southern Africa, which grants scholarships to students from South Africa and Namibia for study and training abroad.

1970

The Security Council condemned violations of the arms embargo and called on all States: to strengthen and implement it unconditionally; not to supply vehicles, equipment and spare parts for use by South African military forces and paramilitary groups; to revoke all licences and patents granted for South African manufacture of arms, aircraft or military vehicles; prohibit investment or technical assistance for arms manufacture; and cease all military co-operation with South Africa.

The Assembly urged States to terminate official relations and co-operation with South Africa, and condemned the establishment of and forcible removal of 3 million Africans to the so-called "homelands" (bantustans) as a violation of their inalienable rights.

1972

The Security Council, meeting in Addis Ababa, recognized the legitimacy of the anti-apartheid struggle and requested all States to adhere strictly to the arms embargo.

1973

The Assembly adopted the International Convention on the Suppression and Punishment of the Crime of Apartheid. It also established the Trust Fund for Publicity against Apartheid. The Fund, which became operational in 19175, is used in particular for the wider dissemination of United Nations publicity material on apartheid and for the production of audio-visual material on apartheid.

1974

The Assembly invited representatives of the South African liberation movements recognized by the Organization of African Unity (OAU)-the African National Congress of South Africa and the Pan Africanist Congress of Azania-to participate as observers in the debates on the question of apartheid in the Assembly's Special Political Committee. It later recognized the two organizations as "the authentic representatives of the overwhelming majority of the South African people" and invited them to participate as observers in the debates on the question in the Assembly's plenary meetings.

The Assembly rejected South Africa's credentials and recommended that South Africa be totally excluded from participation in all international organizations and conferences held under United Nations auspices so long as it continued its policies of apartheid. Since then, South Africa has not participated in the proceedings of the General Assembly.

1975

The Assembly proclaimed that the United Nations and the international community had a special responsibility towards the oppressed people of South Africa and their liberation movements and towards those imprisoned, restricted or exiled for their struggle against apartheid".

1976

The Security Council strongly condemned South Africa's aggression against Angola in March and its attack against Zambia in July as flagrant violations of the sovereignty and territorial integrity of those countries. In both cases, and in a number of other cases since then, the Council demanded that South Africa desist from using the international Territory of Namibia as a base for launching armed attacks against neighbouring African countries and called for international assistance to States bordering South Africa that have suffered economic hardship as a result of their support of United Nations efforts to isolate South Africa.

In June, following the shooting of demonstrators in Soweto, the Security Council strongly condemned South Africa for its resort to massive violence against and killing of Africans, including schoolchildren. The General Assembly proclaimed 16 June, the day of the uprising, as International Day of Solidarity with the Struggling People of South Africa. Later in 1976, it proclaimed 11 October as the Day of Solidarity with South African Political Prisoners. Both Days are observed annually.

In October, the General Assembly rejected South Africa's declaration of "independence" of the Transkei "homeland" called on all States not to recognize the

Transkei and requested them to prohibit all individuals, corporations and institutions under their jurisdiction from any dealings with any bantustan. Subsequently, the Assembly rejected other "homelands" established as "independent States" by South Africa.

1977

On 4 November, the Security Council made the arms embargo against South Africa mandatory, the first time that such action had been taken against a Member State under Chapter VII of the Charter, which provides for enforcement action in cases such as threats to international peace and security. The Council also decided that States should refrain from any cooperation with that country in the manufacture and development of nuclear weapons. In December, the Council established a committee to examine implementation by States of the mandatory arms embargo.

The World Conference for Action against Apartheid, organized by the Special Committee against Apartheid in co-operation with OAU, was held at Lagos in August. In December, the Assembly adopted the International Declaration against Apartheid in Sports, which calls on States to take all appropriate action to cease sporting contacts with any country practising apartheid and towards the exclusion or expulsion of any such country from international and regional sports bodies. The Assembly also asked the Security Council to consider mandatory economic sanctons against South Africa.

1978

International Anti-Apartheid Year, proclaimed by the

General Assembly, began on 21 March, International Day for the Elimination of Racial Discrimination.

1979

In January, the General Assembly asked the Security Council to consider imposing a mandatory embargo on oil and oil products to South Africa under the United Nations Charter.

1981

The International Conference on Sanctions against South Africa (Paris, May) called for further international action to isolate South Africa, including the imposition of sanctions, under Chapter VII of the Charter. The Assembly also decided that 9 August, the anniversary of the 1956 march of women to the government offices in Pretoria in protest over the extension of pass laws to African women, should be observed annually as the International Day of Solidarity with the Struggle of Women in South Africa and Namibia.

1982

Proclaimed as International Year of Mobilization for Sanctions against South Africa by the Assembly in 1981, the Year aimed at mobilizing world public opinion in support of comprehensive and mandatory sanctions against South Africa and of encouraging action by States, individually and collectively. To achieve those objectives, a number of conferences and seminars were held in different parts of the world, including the Asian Regional Conference for Action against Apartheid, which Adopted the Manila Declaration for Action against Apartheid. On the Day of Solidarity with South African Political Prisoners, the

Special Committee against Apartheid launched a world-wide campaign for the release of South African political prisoners.

1983

Conferences to promote further international action against apartheid included the Latin American Regional Conference for Action against Apartheid, which adopted the Caracas Declaration on Action against Apartheid; the International Conference on Sanctions against Apartheid in Sports held at London; and the International Conference on the Alliance between South Africa and Israel, held at Vienna.

The General Assembly rejected "constitutional proposals" endorsed in 1983 by South Africa and all manceuvres to entrench white minority rule and apartheid". It declared "that only the total eradication of apartheid and the establishment of a non racial democratic society based on majority rule, through the full and free exercise of adult suffrage by all the people in a united and non-fragmented South Africa, can lead to a just and lasting solution of the explosive situation in South Africa"

1984

In June, the Special Committee against Apartheid held, in New York, the North American Conference for Action against Apartheid, and, in August, in Tunis, the Conference of Arab Solidarity with the Struggle for Liberation in Southern Africa, among others.

The General Assembly rejected the South African Constitution that created a racially segregated tricameral Parliament, including Asians and Coloureds but excluding Africans.

1985

In March, the Security Council condemned the Pretoria regime for the killing of defenceless African people protesting against their forced removal, as well as arbitrary arrests of members of organizations opposed to apartheid.

The International Conference on Women under Apartheid, held in Arusha, United Republic of Tanzania, in May, promoted further material and moral assistance to women and children and the struggle for national liberation.

The International Conference on Apartheid in Sports (Paris, May) adopted a declaration strengthening the sports boycott against South Africa. The boycott was further strengthened in December by the General Assembly, which adopted the International Convention against Apartheid in Sports. The treaty obliges States parties not to permit sports contacts with countries practising apartheid.

The Security Council has condemned several attacks by South African forces on neighbouring States, and has demanded the immediate and unconditional cessation of such acts of aggression and the withdrawal from the territory of independent States. It asked the Secretary-General to send a mission to Botswana in July and August to assess damage there, and in September it appointed a three-member Commission of Investigation for a similar purpose in Angola. It called for compensation to those countries for the damage done. In accordance with a December resolution of the Council, the Secretary-General appointed a Representative in Lesotho to keep him informed of developments affecting that country's territorial integrity.

In July, the Council condemned the establishment of a state of emergency imposed that month in 36 South African districts, and demanded that it be lifted. It urged Member States to adopt such measures as suspending all new investment in South Africa, prohibiting the sale of coins minted there, restricting sports and cultural relations, suspending guaranteed export loans, prohibiting all new nuclear contracts, and prohibiting sales of computer equipment that could be used by the army or police.

1986

The World Conference on Sanctions against Racist South Africa (June, Paris) reviewed developments since the 1981 Paris Conference on sanctions, and called for comprehensive and mandatory sanctions against South Africa aimed at bringing an end to that country's apartheid system, to its illegal occupation of Namibia and to its attacks on neighbouring States.

Also in June, the Council issued a statement condemning the imposition of the nation-wide state of emergency in South Africa and called for it to be lifted immediately. Efforts in the Council in July to make mandatory such "selective economic and other sanctions" as those it had urged States to adopt a year earlier-and several subsequent efforts as well-were not successful. However, to close loopholes and reinforce and make the arms embargo more comprehensive, the Council in November urged States to ensure that components of and spare parts for embargoed items did not reach the South African military or police forces through third countries, and asked States to investigate violations of and prevent circumventions of the arms embargo.

In November also, the General Assembly urged the United Kingdom and the United States and others opposed to applying comprehensive and mandatory sanctions to reassess their position. It also set up an Intergovernmental Group to Monitor the Supply and Shipping of Oil and Petroleum Products to South Africa.

1987

In April, the Security Council expressed deep concern about a South African decree of 10 April prohibiting nearly all forms of protest against detentions without trial or support for detainees, and called on South Africa to revoke it.

Pending comprehensive mandatory sanctions, the General Assembly urged Member States in November to adopt coordinated legislative measures against South Africa, to strictly monitor them, and to impose penalties on individuals and enterprises that violated them.

The Assembly spelled out measures that the South African Government should introduce to create the appropriate conditions for "free consultations among all the people of South Africa with a view to negotiating a just and lasting solution to the conflict in that country". It demanded in particular: the lifting of the state of emergency and the ban on political parties and other organizations; the immediate and unconditional release of all political prisoners; the return of political exiles; and an end to the policy of bantustanization and forced removals, and to military and paramilitary activities in neighbouring countries.

1988

The Security Council expressed grave concern at South Africa's renewal of the state of emergency, at the imposition of new severe restrictions on anti-apartheid and labour organizations and individuals committed to peaceful opposition against apartheid, and at the harassment and detention of church leaders. The Council also condemned Pretoria's decision to execute the Sharpeville Six, referring in particular to their conviction on the grounds of "common purpose". It called on South African authorities to commute the death sentences and it urged all States and organizations to use their influence to save the lives of these six persons.

On 4 April 1988, the International Convention against Apartheid in Sports entered into force. The States parties (currently 41 States) to the Convention elected on 23 March 1989 the members of the Commission against Apartheid in Sports.

In December 1988, the General Assembly criticized some States for continuing their economic relations with South Africa, and others who exploited the opportunities created by sanctions imposed by other States. It called on those States which had increased their trade with South Africa to sever all trade relations.

1989

On 12 and 13 April 1989, the Intergovernmental Group to Monitor the Supply and Shipping of Oil and Petroleum Products to South Africa, and the Special Committee against Apartheid, held hearings at United Nations Headquarters in New York on the oil embargo against South Africa. The panel for the hearings recommended that the Security Council impose a mandatory oil embargo, and that pending this, all oil-producing, shipping and handling States should enact legislation to stop the flow of oil to South Africa.

10

Freedom of Speech and Expression

Universal human right of thought and expression

Article 1 of the Universal Declaration of Human Right runs a under:

> Everyone has the right to freedom of opinion and expression; this right includes freedom to hold opinions without interference and to seek, receive and impart information and ideas through any media and regardless of frontiers.

Article 18(1) of the second Covenant runs as under:

> Everyone shall have the right to freedom of thought, conscience and religion. This right shall include freedom to have or to adopt a religion or belief of his choice, and freedom either individually or in community with others and in public or private, to manifest his religion or belief in worship, observance, practice and teaching.

In this regard Article 19 of the Covenant on the Civil and Political Rights is, also important. Article 19(1) lays down that everyone shall have the right to hold any opinion with interference. Article 19(2) lays down that every one shall have the right to freedom of expression. This right shall include freedom to seek, receive and impart information and ideas of all kinds regardless of frontiers, either orally, in writing, in print, in the form of art or through any other media of his choice.

Freedom of Speech and Expression under Indian Constitution

"The destiny of private thought is to gain power and effect through shaping public behaviour or public enactment. Nothing could more describe a human failure than a man physically prolific whose ideas should count nothing to his group or his time. A suppression of speech, in its most painful consequences would be mental sterilization of the community."' In the words of K.K. Mathew. "As expression of thought and ideas is an integral part of die development of personality of a human being, suppression of the same is an affront to the dignity of that personality. The purpose of the State and the society is to make the individual lead a good life. An individual owes a debt to the society and he repays it by making his individual contribution to the reservoir of thought and ideas". Mathew, it is submitted rightly, considers the freedom of speech and expression from two aspects:

(a) Freedom of expression concerning public affairs, and

(b) Freedom of expression as a private right.

Since participation of' the governed, he says, in the governing process is the essence of the responsible government, it presupposes and absolutely requires free expression of the will of several segments of the body politic. As the freedom of expression concerning public affairs is indispensable to the operation of the democratic system. It is a necessary implication from the provisions of the Constitution establishing it. On the other hand, freedom of expression as a private right of the individual is mainly for self-fulfilment in all spheres of life and not only in the matters of governing importance in a democracy. In order that the governed may form a wise and intelligent judgment and create an enlightened public opinion, it is necessary that the people must be informed of all the aspects of a question and therefore, public discussion assumes the nature of public duty. In a democracy the right to free expression is not intended to define an individual fight but rather a right of the community to hear and be informed. Freedom of speech and expression concerning public matters exists independently of the individual right of freedom of speech and expression guaranteed under Article 19(1)(a). It is a necessary implication of the Constitution. Mathew. J.. observed:

The crucial point is not that the freedom of expression is politically useful bill that it is indispensable to the operation of a democratic system. In a democracy the basic premise is that the people are both governors and the governed. In order that governed may form intelligent and wise judgment, it is necessary that they must be appraised of all the aspects of a question on which a decision has to be taken so that they might arrive at the truth.

This means that even if the fundamental fight to freedom of speech under Article 19(1)(a) is expunged from the Constitution, the freedom of speech concerning public affairs will remain, since it is necessary implication of the democratic form of government which the Constitution establishes. In short, it is one of the basic postulates of Constitution.

Freedom of Speech and Expression: Article 19(1)(a)

Article 19(0)(a) of the Constitution guarantees the freedom of speech and expression in both its aspects. In the words or Mathew. J.: "Though freedom of expression is essential to a democratic society, it is not the sole aim of good society. As a private right of the individual, freedom of expression might be an end in itself ... But it is not the only end of man as an individual. In its social and political aspects, freedom of expression is primarily a process or method for reaching other goals, h is a basic element in the democratic way of life and as a vital process, it shapes and determines ends of the democratic society. But it is not through this process alone that a democracy will attain its ultimate end. Any theory of freedom or expression must therefore take into account other values such as public order, Justice and equality and the progress of the society as a whole and the need for substantive measure desired to promote those ideals. Hence there arises the problem of reconciling freedom of expression with other values and objective sought by a good society."' Article 19(1)(a). does not guarantee freedom of speech in absolute terms. Article 19(2) permits the State to impose reasonable restriction on the rights "in the interests of sovereignty and integrity of India, the security of the State, friendly relations with foreign States, public order, decency or morality, or in relation to contempt of court, defamation or incitement to an offence."

In some cases the Supreme Court has observed that the Freedom of Speech under the Indian Constitution has been based on the First Amendment of the US Constitution which lays down 'Congress shall make no law ... abridging the freedom of speech or of the press." It is submitted that in substance it is not so. The freedom of speech in the First US. Amendment is in absolute terms and the limitations on it have been evolved by the courts, while freedom of speech under the Indian Constitution is subject to limitations laid down in Article 19(2). The task before the Indian court is not to evolve limitation but to rind out whether a law imposing limitations falls within the framework of Article 19(2).7 The fact of the matter is that our Constitution has tried to resolve the dilemma between the absoluteness of freedom of speech and the curtailment of the freedom in the interest of social security. "The choice is not between order and liberty. It is between liberty with order and anarchy without either."

Ramesh Thapar v. State of Madras, and in *Brij Bhusan v, Stole of Delhi*, the Supreme Court (by majority) held that freedom of speech and expression under Article 19(1)(a). was so wide as not to render a person culpable even if he advocated murder and other crimes of violence. Fazl Ali, J., in his dissenting judgment, took the view that if freedom of speech affected "public order" it could be legitimately curtailed. The First Amendment amended the Constitution retrospectively by incorporating Fazl Ali, J's view by adding, *inter alia*, the words "public order" in Article 19(2).

In a series of cases the Supreme Court has enunciated the scope of freedom of speech and laid down how far reasonable restrictions can be imposed on it. In *Kedar Nath Singh v. State of Bihar*, the Supreme Court held that sedition as laid down in Section 124-A, Indian Penal Code, if a rightly construed, did not violate Article 19(1)(a). The right construction of section 124-A, (in the opinion of the Supreme Court) is that only those acts amount to sedition which involve an intention or a tendency to create disorder or disturbance of law and order or incitement to violence. Similarly, section 144 Cr.P.C. (old Code) was held not violative of Article 190)(a) as it imposed reasonable restriction on the right of freedom of speech since power was exercised in extraordinary circumstances by a Magistrate and was hedged with adequate protections. The Kerala Security Prisoners Orders, 1971 empowered the Government to direct that security prisoners could be denied access to books, periodicals, etc., which it considered not permissible. In *K. Narayanan v. State*, this restriction was held valid. The court observed that though under Article 19(1)(a). freedom to acquire knowledge by reading books and periodicals or any other literature was included, it would be reasonable restriction of this right if security prisoners were denied access to literature which incited them to violence and endangered the security of the State,

Freedom of Press and Right to Listen

Article 19(2) of the Covenant on the Civil and Political Rights is the backbone of the right to listen and tight to know. Right to freedom of expression includes freedom to seek, receive and impart information and ideas of all kinds, regardless of frontiers, either orally, in writing or in print, in the form of art, or through any other media of his choice.

The US Constitution guarantees freedom of press specifically. But the Indian Constitution does not expressly mention about the freedom of press. However, it has never been doubted that freedom of expression guaranteed by Article 19(1)(a) includes the freedom of press. In democracies the press has come to be regarded as the fourth estate, an effective check on all organs of the Governments. In our contemporary world the freedom of press includes not merely the freedom of expression of the press but the right to listen and to know listeners also. "With the right of editors and publishers to express themselves, there must be associated a right of the public to be served with substantial and honest basis of facts for its judgment of public affairs. Of these two it is the latter which today (ends to take precedence and importance. The freedom of the press has to change its point of focus from the editor to the citizen."

The Indian Constitution regards freedom of press as part of the citizen's fundamental right of freedom of speech and expression and does not place it on any higher pedestal, Article 19(2) also permits the State to regulate the freedom of press. The question is: how far our courts have been able to strike a balance between the freedom of the press and the right to listen? With this is tagged the State's right to control the press in public interest.

The freedom of press obviously implies freedom of circulation, and therefore banning a paper from entering a State is violative of freedom of press. 19 The same is true of the imposition of precensorship on a newspaper or prohibiting it from publishing the view of its editor and correspondents on current topics. 20 In Sakai Paper v. Union of India, the interesting question relating to price-page schedule regulations came for consideration, Newspaper (Price Page) Act, 19% empowered the Union Government to regulate the prices of the newspapers in relations to their pages and sizes and to regulate the allocation of the space for advertising matter. The Daily Newspapers (Prices and Page) Order, 1960 made under the Act fixed the minimum number of pages to be published by a newspaper according to prices charged. It also prescribed the number of supplements that could be published. The Act and the Order were held void. The court observed that since regulation of pages in accordance with the price was bound to affect the circulation of the newspapers by making their price unattractively high and since reduction in the area for advertisement would affect the finances of the newspapers with a consequent risk of their closure., the Act and the Order impinged upon the freedom of not merely what one might circulate but also to whom it might be circulated. The Union Government sought to justify the regulation on the ground that it was merely regulating the commercial activities of the newspapers. The Supreme Court observed that citizen's right to carry on trade or business could not he so regulated as to affect the freedom of speech and expression, One freedom cannot be curtailed on the pretext of imposing reasonable restrictions on another freedom.

Bennet Coleman and Co. v. Union of India illustrates that in India freedom of press has adequate protection. The Union Government issued News Print Control Order, 1902 under section 3, Essential Commodities Act, 1955 laying down that no consumer of newsprint should, in any licensing period, consume or use newsprint in excess of quantity authorized by the Controller. The 1973-newsprint policy laid down a system of newsprint quota for newspapers. The year 1970-71 or 1971-72 was taken to be the base year on the basis of which actual consumption of a newspaper was determined. Under the policy, an increase up to 10 per cent for dailies having a circulation upto 100.000 and an increase upto 3 per cent for dailies with a larger circulation on the basis entitlement was allowed. It was further laid down that newspapers with less than 10 pages daily could increase the number of papers by 20 per cent but subject to ceiling of 10 pages. It appears to be evident that the idea behind newsprint policy was to curtail the growth of monopoly press. The Supreme Court, by majority, declared the policy unconstitutional. The majority observed that though the Government had the power to evolve a policy of distribution of newsprint, on a fair and equitable basis, keeping the interest of small medium as well as big newspapers in view, it could not under the pretext of regulating the distribution of newsprint, control the growth and circulation of newspapers. Thus, it would appear, the Supreme Court missed the opportunity of considering the question from the point of view of the right to listen. Should the monopoly press have the right to dictate to the people as to what they have to read or listen and the State could not interfere on behalf of citizens'? It was this aspect of the matter which led Mathew, J. to dissent. He held the view that in the interest of listeners, regulations could be imposed even outside Article 19(2). The learned judge observed:

> Protection against Government is not enough to guarantee that a man who has something to say will have a chance to say it. The owners and the managers of the press determine which persons, which facts, which version of facts, which ideas shall reach the public. Through concentration of ownership, the variety of sources of news and opinion has become limited . . . A realistic view of our freedom of expression requires the recognition that right of expression is some what thin if it can be exercised only on the sufferance of the managers of the leading newspapers. The freedom of speech, if it has to fulfil its historic mission, namely, the spreading of political truth and the widest dissemination of news, it must be freedom for all citizens in the country ... what is, therefore, required is an interpretation of Article 19(1)(a) which focuses on the idea that restraining the hand of the Government is quite useless in assuring free speech, if a restraint on access is effectively secured by private groups. A constitutional prohibition against Government restriction on the expression is effective only if Constitution ensures an adequate opportunity for discussion.

In the result the learned judge was of the view that any scheme of distribution of newsprint which would make the freedom of speech a reality by making possible the dissemination of ideas and view with as many different facts and colours as possible would not be violative of the fundamental right of the freedom of press.

In a series of cases the Supreme Court has upheld social legislation in respect of the press. In Express Newspapers v. Union of India, the law regulating the conditions of service of employees of" newspapers was challenged on the ground that financial position of the marginally situated newspapers might he so adversely affected that they might be forced to close down or curtail their circulation and this would obviously be violative of Article 19(1) (a), The court observed that the objective of law was the amelioration of the conditions of the employees in the employment of the newspaper industry and therefore the law was held valid. Moreover, the court observed in India the press has no immunity from general laws such as tax or social legislation. Similarly, a law providing for an enquiry into the financial position of newspapers. or requiring that on publication of every newspaper and book the name of printer, publisher and editor, and place of publication etc., should be printed (the intention being' to provide information to the people about these) is not violative of Article 19(1)(a).

Under the Press Council Act 1969, the Press Council was established with a fairly wide jurisdiction so much so that it was empowered to take cognizance of any violation of the freedom of press by the State, or any department or agency of the State, public authority, companies, individuals or by any person. It was empowered to take action against any newspaper which offended against the standards journalistic ethics or public tests or if in editor or journalist committed professional misconduct. It was required to comply with the requirements of the natural justice, Conceived as any agency of self-regulation and consisting of working journalists, managers and owners of newspapers, with an objective of safeguarding the freedom of press, the Press Council was also entrusted with the responsibility of maintenance and improvement of the standard of newspapers.

In Indian Express Newspapers (Bombay) Private Lid. v. Union of India. The Supreme Court reiterated its earlier view that freedom of press is included in Article 19(1)(a). and observed that in today's world freedom of press in the heart of social and political intercourses, though in the interest of general public reasonable restrictions can be imposed. But newspapers have two aspects: (i) they exercise freedom of press and (ii) they engage in business. Thus as regulars to the latter aspect it cannot be said that they are immune from taxation, but the taxing power should not he so exercised as to destroy freedom of press.

The question again came before the Supreme Court in another context in Express Newspapers Pvt. Ltd. v. Union of India. The Express Newspapers Pvt. Ltd.. constructed express building at 9 and 10 Bahadurshah Zafar Marg, Delhi with the sanction of the Union of India. The Express Newspapers were given a notice for the demolition of the buildings on the assertion that the buildings were constructed in breach of regulations. The Supreme Court took the view that "where the impugned notices of re-entry upon forfeiture of lease and of the threatened demolition of the Express Buildings are intended and meant to silence the voice of the Indian Express, it must logically follow that the impugned notices constitutes a direct and immediate threat to the freedom of press and are thus violative of Article 19(1)(a) read with Article 14 of the Constitution."

Freedom of Speech and integrity and sovereignty of India

The Preamble of India makes it abundantly clear that the Constitution has created an indestructible union and no state has a right to secession. To make this position unimpairable, the 16th Amendment introduced an amendment to Article 19(2) which empowers the State to impose restrictions on the freedom of speech in "the interest of the sovereignty and integrity of India." Thus Paramount can validly make a law which prevents any individual from propagating secession of a state from the Indian Union. However; the new clause permits restriction with respect to the territorial integrity of India and not of any State: Article 3 of the Constitution stipulates for the change of boundaries of the State and for reorganisation of the State territories and in that process it is possible that a state may lose its existence.

11

Life, Physical Integrity and Liberty

Human Rights aim at promoting and protecting the dignity and integrity of every individual human being. If there are any rights more fundamental than others for achieving that aim, surely they are the rights to life, to physical integrity, and liberty. On these, all other rights depend; without these, other rights have little or no meaning.

The Right to Life

Article 6 of the Covenant on Civil and Political Rights proclaims that ever human being has the inherent right to life. The right to life is incontestably the most important of all human rights. Civilized society cannot exist without legal protection of human life. The inviolability or sanctity of life is, perhaps, the most basic value of modern civilization. In the final analysis, if there were no right to life, there would be no point in the other human rights. Describing the right to life as "inherent" may be questioned on the ground that legal rights never actually inhere in nature; they are always created within the framework of a legal system.

Still, the framers of the Covenant apparently regarded human rights as preexisting in a moral order and perhaps even in an immaculate jus naturale. Whether they were right or wrong is immaterial; what matters is that the right to life is validated in the Covenant as a legal right. That only this night is characterized by the Covenant as inherent may attest to its primacy and emphasize that it derives from the very fact of a human being's existence. But whether or not one accepts human rights as based on natural law or an antecedent morality, any rights and duties created by the Covenant are legal rights under international law and must be considered as binding in the international legal system.

The term "inherent" may indicate also that the framers of the Covenant felt that the human right to life is entrenched in customary international law, so that Article 6 is merely declaratory in nature and does not create new international law. Indeed, the right is also recognized in Article 3 of the Universal Declaration of Human Rights, Article 2 of the European Convention for the Protection of Human Rights and fundamental Freedoms, and Article 4 of the American Convention on Human Rights, If the right to life is guaranteed under general international law (and it is submitted that such is the case), obviously the right is guaranteed vis-a-vis all states (including those which are not parties to the Covenant). If the right is protected apart from the Covenant, its inclusion in the Covenant is important not only to reaffirm the right but to articulate its content and implications.

Article 6 requires that the right to life be protected by law. That is to say, each state party is oblige within its internal legal system a law protecting the right to life. The term "law" is-broad: in general, it denotes all strata of the legal order, not only statutes (and constitutions) but also unwritten law and administrative regulations. The inviolability of life is so important, however, that a strict interpretation of "law" is here called for. The international obligation requires that the right to life be protected by higher forms in the legislative, hierarchy, by statute or constitutional provision.

What is the ambit of the protection that must be given to the right to life? Unfortunately, Article 6 is not specific. Basically, what it tells us, by way of guidance, is that no one shall be arbitrarily deprived of his life. The emphasis must be both on "deprive" and "arbitrarily." First, deprivation of life means homicide. The right to life is not freedom to live as one wishes. It is not a right to an appropriate standard of living. Of course, a human being needs certain essentials-particularly food, clothing, housing, and medical care-in order to remain alive. These are aspects of the social rights to an adequate standard of living and to health which are recognized in Articles 11 and 12 of the International Covenant on Economic, Social, and Cultural Rights. The human right to life per se, however, is a civil right, and it "does not guarantee any person against death from famine or cold or lack of medical attention."

The right of life, in effect, is the right to be safeguarded against (arbitrary) killing. To be sure, homicide may be carried out through a variety of means, including starving someone, exposing a person to extreme temperatures or contamination with disease. But, for example, the mere toleration of malnutrition by a state will not be regarded as a violation of the human right to life, whereas purposeful denial of access to food, e.g., to a prisoner, is a different matter. Failure to reduce infant mortality is not within Article 6, while practicing or tolerating infanticide would violate the Article.

Some members of the Human Rights Committee have expressed the view that Article 6 requires the state to take positive measures to ensure the right to life, including steps to reduce the infant mortality rate, prevent industrial accidents, and protect the environment.

Not all deprivation of life constitutes an infringement of the right to life; only a deprivation of life that is "arbitrary. The cardinal question, therefore, is when a deprivation of life may be labelled as arbitrary. The term "arbitrary" (which appears also in Article 9 and elsewhere in the Covenant) is not easy to define. Its use in Article 6 was, indeed, criticized at the time of drafting as "ambiguous and open to several interpretations." There is a conceptual question-to which we shall return-whether any action sanctioned by statute may qualify as arbitrary. There are a number of practical issues regarding deprivation of life.

Physical Integrity

Freedom from Torture and Degradation

Article 7 of the Covenant forbids (a) torture; (b) cruel, inhuman, or degrading treatment or punishment; and (c) medical or scientific experimentation without free consent. The fundamental freedom from torture and degradation is also enshrined in Article 5 of the Universal Declaration of Human Rights, Article 3 of the European Convention, and Article 5 of the American Convention, The Covenant alone includes in this freedom the right not to be subjected to medical or scientific experimentation without free consent.

The prohibition of torture may be regarded as an integral part of customary international law, and it may even have acquired the lineament of a peremptory norm of general international law, i.e., jus cogens. There is no definition of the term "torture"' in Article 7 or in other instruments. Such a definition (which, while not legally binding, is entitled to great weight) appears in Article 1 of the Declaration on the Protection of All Persons from Being Subjected to Torture and Other Cruel, Inhuman, or Degrading Treatment or Punishment, adopted by the General Assembly in 1975. The article reads:

1. For the purpose of this Declaration, torture means any act by which severe pain or suffering, whether physical or mental, is intentionally inflicted by or at the instigation of a public official on a person for such purposes as obtaining from him or a third person information or confession, punishing him for an act he has committed or is suspected of having committed, or intimidating him or other persons. It does not include pain or suffering arising only from, inherent in or incidental to, lawful sanctions to the extent consistent with the Standard Minimum Rules for the Treatment of Prisoners.

2. Torture constitutes an aggravated and deliberate form of cruel, inhuman or degrading treatment or punishment.

The key elements of this definition are beyond dispute. First, torture may be either a mode of punishment (for instance, drawing and quartering) or a form of treatment having other purposes. Second, the reason motivating torture-inducing confessions, eliciting information, instilling fear (in the victim or another person) or even sheer sadism-is immaterial. Third, torture may be either physical or mental. What is less clear is whether the term "torture" has a subjective element as applied to the individual, i.e., whether the victim's particular tolerance to pain may be a determining factor in establishing whether a specific act amounts to torture.

Whatever the constituent elements of torture are, the term must be distinguished from cruel, inhuman or degrading treatment and punishment. As the European Court of Human Rights ruled in the Northern Ireland case: "This distinction derives principally from a difference in the intensity of the suffering inflicted. " That is, the expression torture attaches a "a special stigma to deliberate inhuman treatment causing very serious and cruel suffering." On that basis the Court reached the conclusion that certain techniques for interrogation in depth (sometimes called "disorientation" or "sensory deprivation") used by the British security forces in Northern Ireland in 197163 amounted to inhuman and degrading treatment but not to torture.

Liberty

Freedom from Slavery and Forced Labour

Article 8 of the Covenant proclaims the fundamental freedom from slavery and forced labour. This human right is also enunciated in Article 4 of the Universal Declaration of Human Rights, Article 4 of the European Convention, and Article 6 of the American Convention. There is also a series of conventions dealing with the subject: the 1926 Slavery Convention, the 1930 ILO Convention (No. 29) concerning Forced or Compulsory Labour, the 1956 Supplementary Convention on the Abolition of Slavery, the Slave Trade, and Institutions and Practices Similar to Slavery; and the 1957 ILO Convention (No. 105) concerning the Abolition of Forced Labour,

Article 8 prohibits slavery, the slave trade, servitude, and forced or compulsory labour. None of these expressions is defined in the article. The common denominator of slavery, slave trade, and servitude-as distinct from forced or compulsory labour-is that they are forbidden irrespective of the consent of the person concerned. A proposal to insert the adjective "involuntary" before the word "servitude" was opposed for this very reason: servitude (like slavery and slave trade) is prohibited in any form, whether involuntary or not, and no person may "contract himself into bondage." The term "slavery" is technical and limited in scope, inasmuch as it implies ownership as chattel by another person and "the destruction of the juridical personality." "Slave trade" is also an expression that should be strictly construed. A proposal to substitute for it "trade in human beings" (a phrase covering traffic in women for sexual exploitation as well as slaves) was not accepted. "Servitude" is a broader term "covering indirect and concealed forms of slavery. It seems to include, though it is not limited to, peonage and serfdom.

The expression "forced or compulsory labour" is defined in Article 2 of the 1930 ILO Convention in the following terms (subject to five exceptions enumerated in the Article): "all work or service which is exacted from any person under the menace of any penalty and for which the said person has not offered himself voluntarily." Yet this definition was not considered by the framers of the Article as "entirely satisfactory for inclusion in the covenant.

Article 8 expressly states that the prohibition of forced or compulsory labour does not preclude (a) the performance of hard labour as a punishment concomitant with imprisonment pursuant to a sentence by a competent court; (b) any other work or service normally required of a person who is under detention in consequence of a lawful order of a court (or during conditional release from such detention); (c) any service of a military character (as well as national service required by law of conscientious objectors); (d) any service exacted in cases of emergency or calamity threatening the life or well-being of the community; (e) any work or service which forms part of normal civil obligations.

The difference between hard labour as a punishment (a) and service normally required of a person under detention (b) is that the former pertains to a specific punishment of "hard labour" to which a competent court expressly sentences a convicted person, whereas the latter covers ordinary prison work which all persons under detention may be required to perform. Even when hard labour is imposed by a court of law, however, the hardship entailed must be within reason. As for service normally required of a person under detention, the adverb "normally" is used with a view to providing "a safeguard against arbitrary decisions by prison authorities." Regarding service of a military character, as well as national service required by law of conscientious objectors (c), the question arises whether conscientious objectors are entitled to be compensated with pay equal to that received by soldiers. Proposals to deal with the subject in Article 8 failed. Services exacted in times of emergency (d) do not present a problem. But what is meant by "normal civil obligations" (e)? It is noteworthy that in the case of Iverson v. Nonvay, the European Commission of Human Rights refused to view the obligatory public service of a Norwegian dentist assigned (by law) for one year to a remote area in the northlands as unlawful forced labour.

Right to Liberty and Security

Article 9 of the Covenant sets forth the right to liberty

and security of the person. This right is confirmed in Article 3 of the Universal Declaration of Human Rights (together with the right to life), Article 5 of the European Convention, and Article 7 of the American Convention,

The term "right to liberty' which may be paraphrased as the "freedom of freedom"-sounds like an abstract slogan. But it implies physical freedom and encompasses the very concrete and specific freedom from arbitrary arrest and detention, a right which is as critical as any, and too commonly dishonoured in our time.

Every society uses criminal law and institutions to maintain order and justice, as well as to protect the rights of others. The procedures and sanctions of the criminal process, however, impinge on the freedom of the individual charged with and convicted of crime (and in extreme cases take his life). Such invasions of freedom are justified because they are necessary to protect society, but they are justified only if and to the extent that they are indeed necessary. The criminal process, however, is subject to failures and abuses, which are among the greatest threats to human rights, particularly to the rights to life and liberty.

Protection against inadequacies of the criminal process is a principal concern of international human rights. It is the subject of several articles in the Covenant and of a separate essay in this volume. In this essay, the emphasis is on one crucial aspect of that protection: the protection against arbitrary arrest and detention. Too often, in too many societies, individuals are arrested and detained without proper cause, not as part of the criminal process but in situations where the criminal law has no legitimate place.

Article 9 of the Universal Declaration "I deals

with freedom from arbitrary arrest, detention, or exile as an independent human right, separate from the right to liberty in Article 3. Article 9 of the Covenant, however, brings the freedom from arbitrary arrest or detention (though not the freedom from arbitrary exile) within the bounds of the right to liberty, as do Article 5 of the European Convention and Article 7 of the American Convention. Article 9 of the Covenant spells out this freedom as follows: "(1) No one shall be deprived of his liberty except on' such grounds and in accordance with such procedure as are established by law."

Once more we encounter a reference in the Covenant (an international legal instrument) to the national legal system. The generic term "law" in its ordinary use embraces not only statutory enactments but also subordinate legislation and even unwritten ("common") law. The European Court of Human Rights held in the Golder case, that such subordinate forms of legislation may fulfill the condition "in accordance with the law," which appears in the European Convention in a different context. In yet another frame of reference, the Court observed in the Sunday Times case that the word "law" in the expression "prescribed by law" covers "not only statute but also unwritten law." The Court added that any other interpretation would strike at the very roots of the legal system of a common-law state. Still, the Court ruled that a law must be (a) adequately accessible to all citizens; and (b) formulated with sufficient precision to enable the citizen to regulate his conduct. The citizen, in the Court's words, "must be able-if need be with appropriate advice-to foresee to a degree that is reasonable in the circumstances, the consequences which a given action may entail. The principle governing restrictions of human rights, according to this judgment, is "the principle of legal certainty," though the Court stressed that absolute certainty is unattainable and, indeed, that excessive rigidity is undesirable.

Generally speaking, the requirement that both the grounds for detention and the procedure leading to it must be "established by law" emphasizes the need to promulgate ground rules and to circumscribe the freedom of action of public officials. Not every policeman (or other state functionary) is entitled to decide at his discretion, and on his own responsibility, who can be arrested, why and how. The Permanent Court of International justice pointed out in its Advisory Opinion in the Danzig Decrees case that "the principle that fundamental rights may not be restricted except by law" does not necessarily exclude the use of discretion in applying the law. But the Court went on to say that there are some cases in which the discretionary powers left to a public authority are so wide that they exceed acceptable limits. That statement has important implications for Article 9 of the Covenant, too.

A major question is whether the requirement that grounds and procedures of detention be established by law exhausts the injunction against arbitrary arrest and detention. This brings to the fore the meaning of the pivotal term "arbitrary." Several opinions were expressed on this issue in the process of drafting Article 9. According to one school of thought, "arbitrary" is synonymous with "illegal" or "contrary to the national legislation." In other words, an arrest is arbitrary only if it is not sanctioned by law: any detention carried out under the imprimatur of law is by definition non-arbitrary and therefore permissible. On the other hand, it was argued that "arbitrary" means "unjust" and that all legislation must "conform to the principle of justice." This was the position of the American Delegation in the Third

Committee of the General Assembly: "Arbitrary arrest or detention implied an arrest or detention which was incompatible with the principles of justice or with the dignity of the human person irrespective of whether it had been carried out in conformity with the law."

The allusion to "justice" in this context may have referred to the principle in traditional international law that a state is responsible for a "denial of justice" to a national of another state. In essence, the question is whether there exists an objective international minimum standard so that a law incompatible with it may be declared in contravention of human rights. The prevailing and better view is that Article 9 imports such an international minimum standard, although proposals listing the possible grounds on which deprivation of liberty may be justified were rejected by the framers of the article. As the European Court of Human Rights held in the Winterwerp case: "In a democratic society subscribing to the rule of law . . . no detention that is arbitrary can ever be regarded as 'lawful.' It is manifestly the purpose of the Covenant to protect individuals from despotic legislation and to establish that deprivations of liberty, such as occurred under the Nazi regime, are not consistent with human rights merely because they were prescribed by national law. The duties corresponding to international human rights are incurred by states. If states are free to determine the scope of their own obligations, international human rights are liable to become empty shells. Only an international minimum standard which operates independently of the vagaries of national legal systems can effectively protect human rights. The idea that no one can be subjected to arbitrary arrest or detention was imported into Article 9 of the Covenant from Article 9 of the Universal Declaration. A study of the drafting of the earlier document supports the conclusion that the intent of the framers of the original clause was to bring national legislation into line with an international minimum standard.

The rights to life, physical liberty, and integrity are all (in the taxonomy of the Covenant) civil rights. As such, their roots are derived from time-honoured traditions of modem civilization. Some have become generally accepted norms of customary international law, at least in their broad outlines.

12

Socialism and Education

Socialism basically means public ownership of the means of production. It seeks to abolish the capitalist system and conflicting classes in the society. It aims at establishing classless society, free from exploitation, oppression and disparity and based on mutual cooperation and fellow-feeling. On the contrary, capitalism sustains on competition and satisfaction of self-interests. Human beings fulfil and realise themselves individually as well as socially.

Socialism is therefore called a way of life, a special culture and a design for collective living. It is not merely an 'ism', a mere doctrine or a principle. It anticipates certain virtues and values of citizens who would constitute a socialistic order. Social justice and equality are the cardinal principles of socialism. A socialist activity participates in the production processes of the society. He must have necessary skills, and favourable attitude towards work. He is essentially social, rational and just.

India after Independence has given herself a Constitution which adumbrates socialism, democracy and secularism as its trinity. During the first two decades of free India "Socialistic Pattern" in lieu of "Socialism" was very popular and during the first three Five Year Plans the spirit of socialism gained ground without much extrinsic expression.

Nationalisation is not socialism, but this is taken as the first step in the direction of social transformation from capitalism to socialism. Various agrarian and industrial legislation promoted the Socialistic trend and paved the way for socialism. "Land to the Tiller" and sharing of the Labour force in the management of factories opened new pages in the history of socialism. In 1973, Sri V.V. Giri in his speech opening the budget session of Parliament said:

> "After the attainment of Freedom, Pandit Nehru espoused the cause of socialism and mixed economy. He expressed robust faith in the public sector which was felt suitable in the then prevailing global environment. But the public sector proved to be a white elephant, and started incurring heavy losses. This happened due to high percentage of inefficiency and maladministration. Bureaucratic bottlenecks prevailed more in public sector than in private one, thus resulting in huge losses and wastages."

In the past the Government in the UK resorted to denationalisation and privatisation. Ultimately, the economy there turned from bearish to bullish. Similarly, China's market economy contrary to socialism has been vibrant and reforms were far more successful than those of India. Such approach proved that nation has either to privatise or to perish.

In view of the world scenario and the universal experience of privatisation, India had to change her socialistic strategy and the Union Government initiated economic reforms in 1991 which were surprising to many at home and abroad. The reform package was far away from the traditional socialistic approach. The new economic policy has contained delicencing, deregulation and liberalisation. Consequently, there has been satisfactory improvement in the India's economic condition and tremendous progress in her industrial and commercial scenario. It has been rightly observed by a London-based economist, "India is like a caged tiger. If it is unshackled, it would become an economic giant in Asia". Given proper scope and freedom, she could work miracles in economic front and bring about prosperity unprecedented in the history.

"Ultimately, production and the quality of service to the people in all these fields depend on the dedication and workers. In the changed context, both managers and workers have to give up the traditional concept of their attitudes and look upon workmen as participants in the service of the people. Workers should not allow trade union rivalry to prevent them from fulfilling their historic role of being in the vanguard of socialist transformation by making our public enterprises successful and models of service to the people. On its part, Government recognises the central role of the workers on the economic process and will do every thing in its power to ensure that his legitimate rights are protected.

Socialism was reflected in different aspect of the modem Indian life and affected the education, polities, industry, trade and commerce. In a sense, socialism and its gradual development in all the countries of the world was inevitable. Particularly in the developed countries where majority of people live below the poverty line, and suffer from miserable wants of all kinds, infusion and spread of socialism could not be checked. Even in some countries revolutions for socialism raised their ugly heads and blood and tears stained the soil. But in India such revolutions were not successful on account of its liberal, spiritual and tolerant culture, its vastness, its heterogeneity and diversity. Moreover, its political leaders, social workers, writers and religious savants, tried to effect socialism without violence and bloodshed.

Socialism, had thus an inevitable impact on various aspects of the Indian life. The Constitution of India laid down the Directives for provision of free elementary education throughout the country for all its children upto the age of 14 irrespective of class, creed, sex and economic condition. It was to be achieved again within ten years of the implementation of the Constitution. But it has not yet been possible due to many social and economic constraints.

The various Committees and Commissions have also suggested socialistic measures for widespread education. The Kothari Commission have observed, "One of the important social objectives of education is to equalise opportunity, enabling the backward or underprivileged classes and individuals to use education as a lever for the improvement of their condition. Every society that values social justice and is anxious to improve the lot of common man and cultivate all available talent, must ensure progressive equality of opportunity to all sections of population. This is the only guarantee for the building up of an egalitarian and human society in which the exploitation of the weak will be minimised".

Equality of educational opportunity is a prerequisite for a socialistic society. Inequalities of educational opportunities are however rampant in the Indian society. They have arisen in various ways, for example, in places where no primary, secondary or collegiate institutions exist, children do not have the same opportunities as those who have these facilities in the neighbourhood. Attempts are therefore being made for wide dispersal of educational institutions consistent with economy and efficiency, for instituting adequate number of scholarships at various stages, for providing needed hostel facilities and for making suitable transport arrangements. Regional imbalances in the development of education are going to be reduced to the minimum.

An important cause of such inequality of educational opportunity is the dire poverty of a large section of population and the great affluence of a small minority. Even in the same neighbourhood of an educational institution, children from poor families do not have the same opportunity as those who come from richer ones. With a view to overcoming this obstacle steps are being taken for abolition of fees progressively, for provision of free textbooks, reading and writing materials, etc. Besides, the expanded programme of scholars would help alleviating this difficulty.

Since differences in the standards of educational institutions create inequality in such opportunity, more existence of educational institutions can not help much. When admission into higher institutions and selection for service are made on the basis of marks obtained at public examinations, such inequality becomes very evident. For instance, the works provides a common yardstick for a student from a rural area who attends in ill-equipped school and a student from an urban area who attends a well-equipped school. Similarly, wide differences in home-environment cause inequalities in education. A child from a rural family with illiterate parents cannot have the same opportunity which a child from an urban family with highly educated parents has. So remedial teaching or boarding houses are provided for under-privileged children. Another category of educational inequalities is due to disparities existing between boys and girls as well as SC/ST and high class students. The Kothari Commission have rightly remarked, "On grounds of social justice as well as for the furtherance of democracy it is essential to make special efforts to equalise educational opportunities between these groups."

The wide differences in the management of school and vast disparities as existing in the service conditions of teachers and physical facilities in different schools pose a stumbling block in equalising educational opportunities. Attempts are being made to bring all schools under the same management or public control. All teachers would be or deemed to be government servants and be recruited by the same body.

As an impact of socialism on education all textbooks at the school stage have been nationalised, so that their writing, printing, publication and distribution are now state controlled. In this process not only quality and content of textbooks are oriented and regulated according to the National Policy and natural ethos, the price-range is made appropriate to the economic conditions and requirements of children. Like other socialistic states and as found necessary from the psychological as well as pedagogical points of view, Indian languages are being used as media of instruction not only at the school stage but also at the college level. Besides, English has been maintained as the medium of instruction at the University and higher/advanced learning centres. It is still being used as the language of international communication and language of the library.

At present various research studies being conducted at the national laboratories, Universities and educational organisations; are mostly related to production processes and national/regional needs. Utmost attempts are being made to raise the equality and quantity of production and distribution.

In order to introduce a similar pattern of education throughout the country, conspicuous steps have been taken at the national level. This new pattern of education has also been made socially more relevant, sociologically more dynamic and psychologically more suitable to children of a socialistic country.

In order to set up an integrated and egalitarian society, the educational institutions should try to brine different social classes and groups together. But in India the educational system has increased social segregation and disparities. The so-called Public schools provide better education to the children of rich families, whereas rural schools impart substandard education to poor children. So instead of providing good education to all children or to all able children from every stratum of society, it is available to a microscopic minority of rich children. This is one of the major defects of the existing educational system. So the Kothari Commission suggested the system of common school throughout the country which will be open to all children irrespective of caste, creed, community, religion, economic conditions or social status. In this context, the example of the then USSR educational system was worth emulating. Even in the capitalist countries the important documents like the Plowden Report in the UK and Robins Report in the USA have provided ample guidelines for socialising education.

It is the responsibility of the educational institutions to bring about adequate awareness regarding socialism among the teachers and students. All of them should be oriented towards salient features and significant principles of socialism. Children as future citizens of the country should know their rights and responsibilities in a socialistic state. Besides theoretical knowledge, practical skill and experiences should be provided about a socialistic state or organisation. Proper attitudes and interests in socialism are to be developed through actual participation in various socialistic programmes like industrial concerns, agricultural cooperatives and so on.

India has enunciated democratic socialism in her Constitution. She has accepted that socialism is to be achieved through democratic methods like many Western States. But democratic methods are slow processes and it is naturally difficult to get anything done by one's consent.

To bring about changes in One's way of life, traditional attitudes and values through democratic methods are therefore not only time consuming, but also difficult. Such changes are however permanent in nature and do not involve any anti or adverse reactions from any body.

Mass media are being engaged at present to form public opinion and change attitudes and values in the desired direction.

There is no set model of socialism which is internationally acceptable or a fool-proof copy of perfection. Even two protagonist socialist countries former USSR and China for a period, belonged to two opposite to ideological camps. USA and UK are also not following the same model of Capitalism. It has been amply proved that the traditional form of socialism and capitalism will not survive. They have to be modified is according to circumstances and national needs.

In future, it is more plausible as well as feasible that the best elements and features of capitalism and socialism must come together and present a hybrid variety of democratic socialism. In India, Gandhian model of socialism would be more acceptable as well as successful as it is based on Human Rights, democratic values and cultural heritage. Education should be reoriented and reconstructed accordingly to achieve socialism suiting to the Indian needs and conditions and facilitating promotion of human rights in the country.

Index